INTERNATIONAL AWARD–WINNING AUTHOR JENNIFER SCHELL

THE BUTCHER, THE BAKER, THE WINE & CHEESE MAKER
BY THE SEA

RECIPES & FORK-LORE FROM THE FARMERS, ARTISANS,
FISHERS, FORAGERS & CHEFS OF THE WEST COAST

TouchWood
Editions

HAIDA
GWAII

COVER CAST

TOP ROW (left to right): Jay Gildenhuys (restaurant maker), Andrew Shepherd (sea salt maker), John Bishop (chef), Vikram Vij (chef), Naty King (farmer), Jennifer Schell, Bailey Williamson (wine maker), Aaron Jonckheere (beer maker), Jonathan Chovancek (chef), Iain Hill (beer maker)

BOTTOM ROW (left to right): Justin Henry (sea farmer), Peter Jenney (butcher), Julia Smith (farmer) with Lucy the urban hen, Melissa Cartwright (urban bee farmer), Cory Spencer (cheese maker), Lauren Mote, (cocktail maker / bitters maker), Jackie Kai Ellis (baker)

THE WEST COAST
OF BRITISH COLUMBIA

PACIFIC
OCEAN

LILLOOET

PEMBERTON

WHISTLER

READ
ISLAND

CORTES
ISLAND

CAMPBELL RIVER

BLACK CREEK

QUADRA
ISLAND

KAMLOOPS

COMOX

COURTENAY

TOFINO

SUNSHINE COAST

BOWEN ISLAND

LAKE COUNTRY

VANCOUVER

BURNABY

PITT MEADOWS

KELOWNA

NANOOSE BAY

NEW
WESTMINSTER

KENT

NANAIMO

SURREY

CHILLIWACK

NARAMATA
PENTICTON

YARROW

DUNCAN

SALT SPRING ISLAND

LANGLEY

OLIVER

COBBLE HILL

PENDER ISLAND

CANADA

ALDERGROVE

OSOYOOS

MILL BAY

ABBOTSFORD

SAANICHTON

SAANICH

USA

VICTORIA

BIRCH BAY

N
W E
S

All photos by Jennifer Schell unless otherwise noted. For a full list of photo credits see page 208.
Designer: Kate Hill of K(re)ATE STUDIOS

Printed in Canada

LIBRARY AND ARCHIVES CANADA CATALOGUING IN PUBLICATION
Schell, Jennifer, 1968–, author
The butcher, the baker, the wine & cheese maker by the sea / Jennifer Schell.

Issued in print and electronic formats.
ISBN 978-1-77151-150-6

1. Cooking, Canadian—British Columbia style. 2. Food—British
Columbia—Pacific Coast. 3. Cookbooks. I. Title.

TX715.6.S2695 2015   641.59711   C2015-904905-9

Canadian   Patrimoine
Heritage   canadien

The publisher acknowledges the financial support of the
Government of Canada through the Canada Book Fund (CBF) and the
Province of British Columbia through the Book Publishing Tax Credit.

15 16 17 18 19   5 4 3 2 1

This book was produced using FSC®-certified, acid-free papers,
processed chlorine free, and printed with vegetable-based inks.

To our beautiful, generous Pacific Ocean.
May we keep you well.

CONTENTS

FOREWORD ⚓ JOHN BISHOP

There is an incredible cast of people featured in this book—chefs, farmers, foragers, and fishers. This is a community I have deeply depended on, and have become very close to.

My personal local-seasonal journey began far away from here (in the UK) whilst helping with my family's backyard garden. My father was an avid gardener and angler. He was able to grow an amazing array of organic fruits and vegetables, as well as beautiful flowers, on a small plot. The garden was partially weeded by a flock of Rhode Island Red hens that we kept for eggs. It was inspiring to me as a kid.

The next part of my journey found me living and working in a fishing village by the sea in the south of Ireland. I stayed for almost ten years in the small town of Kinsale. A friend who I had met whilst attending hotel school in Wales had recently moved there and opened a restaurant called the Man Friday, and he had asked me to become the chef. Our menu was composed of all locally sourced ingredients, such as daily caught seafood purchased directly from the fisherman. There was lobster, turbot, and black sole that would hang over the edge of the plate, as they were so large and meaty. There was grass-fed Irish beef, freshly baked bread (still warm from the oven) served with hand-churned butter, and of course there were Irish potatoes. And there were always wonderful artisanal cheeses to finish up a meal. These products were all caught, raised, or produced just steps from the restaurant. We lived a village life—shopping daily and meeting the shopkeepers, fishers, and farmers as we went.

Fast forward to 1973. When I arrived in Vancouver, the west coast food scene was very different than it is today. Local farmers were scarce back then, and the menus in the fine dining restaurants where I began cooking were composed almost entirely of ingredients imported from elsewhere. Occasionally local families would venture out to places like Richmond or Fort Langley in the summer to pick strawberries or blackberries for home use. These berries did not appear on menus. In fact there was very little, if any, local content. That's where California and Mexico came into the picture for fruits and vegetables. New Zealand or Australian lamb was preferred to locally raised lamb, which was more expensive and at that time difficult to source. It is quite shocking to think back. Frozen Icelandic scampi was used—not fresh spot prawns—and Dover sole—not local petrale sole. Also, there were very few, if any, locally produced wines offered on the wine lists.

In 1985 I opened Bishop's Restaurant and was determined to serve all locally grown food with the help of farmers Naty and Gary King. There were lots of ingredients to work with, and the menu changed with the rhythm of the seasons. Today we can say that west coast cooking truly has arrived, and is coming into full bloom. There is a growing army of impassioned chefs, fishers, and farmers in all parts of the province who are leading the charge. Locals and visitors alike attend farmers' markets, or go right down to the dock and meet the fishers with their daily catch. This is such an exciting time for Pacific Northwest cooks. Enjoy!

—John Bishop
Vancouver, BC

....

"We lived a village life—shopping daily
and meeting the shopkeepers, fishers,
and farmers."—John Bishop

....

AN ODE TO THE SEA → THE OYSTER MAN

Who can deny that we need more love on this planet? Or that we need a healthier relationship with the natural world, including our oceans? And a healthier relationship with the fish and seafood that was once a plentiful source of sustenance, nutrition, and even national identity, but that is now becoming scarce? And even with the cast of characters who live and work on the water?

British Columbia has a very long, rich, and varied seaside history. Canneries once dotted the entire coastline. Fish and shellfish, along with fishing boats, were so plentiful that one can only describe the abundance as otherworldly. But we've taken our natural resources for granted and we've practically fished our oceans and rivers to the point of depletion. If it weren't for the modern practice of farming the oceans, seafood would no longer be readily featured on restaurant menus or sold in public markets.

The way Canadians eat and dine has changed radically over the past few decades and Canadian cuisine has been refined and redefined. This land is no longer a "meat and potatoes" kind of country (thank god!). But our new tastes have led to over-harvesting fish and seafood from our oceans and rivers. We desperately need to learn from this mistake. Life from the sea deserves to be respected before it can be truly enjoyed.

If we wish to seek to forge a sea-ethic love affair, each and every time we sit down to dine—whether it is in a nice restaurant or in the comfort of our homes—can we all try a little harder to educate ourselves on where the seafood originates? Can we commit to eating lower on the food chain and dealing with smaller portion sizes? Can we seek to appreciate just how and when the seafood was harvested and experience firsthand, whenever possible, the power and joy of being connected to that process?

To care about your seafood is much more than simply discovering a new recipe or taking guilt-free comfort in recognizing logos of seafood certification organizations. It might mean that we learn to shuck our own oysters or steam our own clams, which we dug during a weekend of camping on Salt Spring Island. It might mean that we reach deeper into our wallets to pay a fair premium price for locally harvested wild fish. It might mean adjusting our assumption that it is our inalienable right to continue buying inexpensive seafood. Duh.

The next time you purchase cheap-as-peanuts, previously frozen prawns from Asia, think about who pays the full cost. Lush mangrove forests are being destroyed in the name of feeding the world's insatiable demand for shrimp. Is it not a travesty that much of the world's "bycatch" is disrespectfully wasted just so that a few species of seafood can adorn the tables and whet the appetites of the world?

The people and stories in this book are, simply stated, inspirational. Maybe, just maybe, we will all recognize the secret ingredient (hint: it's in the sea-ethic love affair). If we all recognize the ocean's importance to the continued existence of life on this planet and to the future of humans, we might be able to make the world everybody's oyster! And then eat it, too!

—Brent Petkau
(aka the Oyster Man)
Cortes Island, BC

INTRODUCTION 🐚 JENNIFER SCHELL

I am proud to come from a long line of farmers. I grew up on a beautiful apple orchard in the Okanagan Valley of British Columbia, and my parents, grandparents, and great grandparents all made their living from the good earth. I had a magical childhood with lots of freedom to explore fields and forests and plenty of time to swim and fish in pristine creeks and lakes. I couldn't have asked for more. Until I met the sea.

From the moment I laid eyes on the blue Pacific Ocean, inhaled its intoxicating aromas, and heard the lullaby of its waves, I was utterly captivated. And so our love affair began. I will never forget our first family trip to Campbell River. Not fussed at all by the misty rain, I simply donned a yellow slicker and rubber boots and, for hours, I became lost in an exciting search: seashells, purple starfish, kelp balls, sand dollars . . . oh, what a treasure hunt! One of those pretty purple starfish actually made its way back home with me in the backseat of our station wagon (bad idea).

I was a child with a vivid imagination and so the seaside offered me a portal to another world, much like C.S. Lewis's wardrobe. After that trip, I drew endless mermaids and fanciful seascapes, and even tried to learn how to breathe underwater by training myself slowly through wet towels as demonstrated on the TV show *Man from Atlantis*. My brother Jonathan and I were both young and avid fans of fishing, as you can see from the photo opposite.

The annual "boys trip" that has been a longstanding part of the Schell family tradition took a turn one year when my brothers finally gave in to my pouting and invited me along. As we flew out of Bella Bella and into a floating camp at Milbanke Sound, my heart soared. We were up before dawn, into our gear, and in the boat with enough time to see the sunrise. It was heaven. I think I shocked and amazed them all with my stamina and glee while I was fighting my first big fish. It was a moment of utter elation. Drifting with the currents of the wild ocean, no civilization in sight, eagles soaring overhead, whales drifting by—I was at peace.

Part of my motivation to create this book was to help educate people about the importance of nurturing these enchanted, supernatural waters. And this is not just a labour of love for the sake of its beauty; it is necessary for its very survival. Luckily we have many advocates and heroes of both the sea and land, and you will meet many in this book. Former Chief Moses Martin, who led his community to save Meares Island from being logged, told me that his brother referred to the sea as his "best friend." Moses says, "We are all one."

And so in this book I pay tribute to the fishers, farmers, the ranchers, the foragers, and the food artisans who have adopted that mentality. Trust them. Thank them. They have a bond with Mother Nature, and they work side by side with her so that the rest of the village can thrive and sustain itself.

I also pay tribute to the people who support these integral stewards of our land, and that includes you. Thankfully, a renaissance of sorts has occurred: we are once again looking to sustainable producers to provide us with healthy food. They are being celebrated once again for the essential role they play—just as it has been since the beginning of time. They are the heroes on this planet and will save us all.

In these pages I will take you to some of the most beautiful places on the planet: from the laid-back surfing village of Tofino on Vancouver Island, through the urban hustle of Vancouver, up the Sea to Sky Highway, through the majestic mountains of Whistler, and down into the lush farming regions of the Pemberton Valley and the Fraser Valley. And this is only a small, but delicious, taste of our amazing local food and drink culture.

To all of you—the butchers, the bakers, the wine and cheese makers, the farmers and sea farmers, fishers and foragers, and the chefs by the sea: I thank you with my whole heart for your labour of love.

(Please note that each recipe has been written in the style and measurement choice that the chef prefers, and we have not standardized them in the interest of keeping their individual styles intact.)

Bon appétit!

—Jennifer Schell

BRUNCHIE-LUNCHIE

★ THE FARMER
Seann J Dory
Vancouver, BC

♙ THE PASTRY MAKER
Jackie Kai Ellis
Vancouver, BC

♙ THE WINE MAKER
Harper's Trail Winery
Kamloops, BC

······· FEATURED INGREDIENT ·······
Sole Food Farms carrots

TART SHELL

50 g (about 3 Tbsp) half and half cream
10 g (approx ½ a yolk) egg yolks
7 g salt
15 g (about a heaping Tbsp) granulated sugar
250 g (about scant 2 cups) all-purpose flour
200 g (1.75 sticks) butter, cold and cubed

FROMAGE FRAIS FILLING

1 lb Fromage Frais (Jackie used Little
    Qualicum Cheeseworks)
½ tsp sea salt
¼ tsp freshly cracked black pepper,
    medium grind
½ cup half and half cream
¼ cup fresh Italian parsley, finely chopped

CUMIN CARROTS

680 g peeled carrots, cut into 1" diagonals
90 g (approx ¼ cup) shallots, cut into ¼" slices
4 cloves of garlic
1 tsp freshly grated ginger
1.5 tsp whole cumin seeds
4 strips of orange zest, approx 1" x 3"
3 Tbsp orange juice, freshly squeezed
3 sprigs of thyme
⅓ cup honey
1 tsp Maldon sea salt
¼ tsp freshly cracked black pepper, coarse
1 Tbsp lemon juice

GARNISH

thyme, Maldon salt, cracked black pepper

CARROT & CUMIN TART

This tart is gorgeous and exotic, just like its creator. It is a celebration of locally sourced ingredients featuring Sole Food Farms carrots and Little Qualicum Cheeseworks cheese; the flavours will dance on your palate.

TART SHELL In a medium container with a spout, like a liquid measuring cup, combine the cream, yolks, salt, and sugar and whisk lightly with a fork until combined. Place flour in the large bowl of a mixer. Slowly add the cubed butter to the flour while mixing on low speed until the flour begins to look like rough, wet sand. Slowly add the egg mixture in a stream to the flour while mixing on low. Keep mixing until the dough just comes together. You will see bits of butter in the dough—don't over mix. Wrap the dough in plastic wrap and refrigerate overnight or for a minimum of 4 hours. You can reserve this dough in the fridge for up to 2 days. When ready to bake the shells, preheat oven to 325°F and butter your tart mould(s). Place the mould(s) on a sheet tray. Roll the dough on a floured board to about ¼" in thickness. Work fast, keep flouring the surface if it sticks and keep the dough cold. Line your tart and rest at room temperature for 1 hour. Place the lined tarts in the freezer for 1 hour. Line the inside of the dough with parchment and fill with pie weights. Bake for 35–45 minutes until golden, remove pie weights and the tart shell from the mould, place back into the oven, lower temperature to 250°F, and bake for an additional 10 minutes until medium-dark golden brown. Allow to cool completely on a rack and reserve for filling.

FILLING While the shell is baking, mix all the ingredients together in a large bowl and reserve in the fridge for later use. Can be made up to 2 days in advance.

CUMIN CARROTS Preheat the oven to 475°F. Combine all the ingredients in a large bowl and toss. Prepare a large sheet pan or two half sheet pans and fill with the carrot mixture, making sure the carrots are in one layer. Roast the carrots for 15–20 minutes. Once the carrots are fork tender but not mushy, remove. Edges should be well caramelized and the liquid should be mostly evaporated. Let cool to room temperature.

ASSEMBLY Using a small palette knife, fill the bottom of the tart shell with fromage frais filling, about ¾ of the way up the sides. Arrange the roasted carrot mixture on the tart shell, leaving out the thyme and orange peel. Garnish with fresh thyme sprigs, Maldon salt, and cracked black pepper. Serve at room temperature and within 1 hour.

···· DRINK PAIRING ···

2012 Harper's Trail Chardonnay
This Chardonnay is surprisingly bright and refreshing on the palate considering the full, complex aromas of lime, peach, caramel, and smoke. The finish is medium and carries through citrus, making it enjoyable with salmon, pasta with cream sauce, or white meats. Very versatile.

SEANN J DORY ✳ THE FARMER

MAGICALLY TRANSFORMS EMPTY LOTS INTO FARMS. GROWS FOOD, COMMUNITY, AND GOOD WILL.

Seann J Dory is the co-director of Sole Food Farms and a founding member of the Young Agrarians—an initiative to recruit, promote, and support young farmers in Canada. Steeped in a passion for farming and community social issues, Seann has been a revolutionary for the future of innovation and agriculture as well as social conscience and community. Seann envisioned an innovative urban farm project that would also employ people in need from the east side community–a big issue in the urban Vancouver scene.

In 2008 he hooked up with Michael Ableman, an organic farmer and author, and together they dreamed up a plan to build an urban production that would also seek to train and employ individuals suffering from addiction, poverty, or mental illness. It began in the empty lot on the former Expo lands on the north side of False Creek, which became a very visible two-acre urban, organic farm using raised, movable planter beds and high-density planting methods. The plan continues by leasing abandoned spaces like parking lots and former gas stations and transforming them into viable urban farming sites. Sole Food offers a Community Supported Agriculture (CSA) program for locals to participate in.

"Our mission is to empower individuals with limited resources by providing jobs, agricultural training, and inclusion in a supportive community of farmers and food lovers."

CSA is an innovative program that connects the consumer and grower, each making a commitment to the other in a mutually beneficial relationship. Members purchase a "share" in the farm early in the season, which assists the farm with the purchasing of seeds and farm materials at a time of year when financial resources are limited. In exchange, the farm commits to providing a weekly share of the harvest to each member. As a member you will receive a weekly email with a list of the produce in the share, a recipe to complement the items, and an update about activities on the farm and in the wider urban farming community.

FARM Sole Foods Farms LOCATION Granville Island, Vancouver, BC
WEB Solefoodfarms.com FB SoleFoodFarms TWITTER @SoleFoodFarms

JACKIE KAI ELLIS 🐙 THE PASTRY MAKER

GLAMOUROUS MAKER OF DELICIOUS THINGS. MAKES LIFE BEAUTIFUL.

Jackie Kai Ellis is the quintessence of great style—it manifests through her beautiful food, and her brand radiates an effortless elegance with meticulous attention to detail. She uses only the best ingredients in her array of delicious offerings at her local café/pâtisserie, Beaucoup Bakery and Café, and it has become a cozy local hub for those with a penchant for the delicate art of French pastry. As celebrated on the chalkboard inside Beaucoup, Jackie works with as many local farmers and artisans as possible. For her recipe, she has chosen to work with an ingredient from Sole Food Farms, a stellar choice for both its high-quality local farm produce as well as a philosophy that reflects Jackie's big heart.

Jackie jokes about growing up in an Asian "non-baking" household where the oven was used as extra storage space. Regardless, she followed her passion and found a way to bake. She eventually began selling her sweet treats, such as cookies and bars, under the name Yummy Baked Goods at the local farmers' market. After years of operating a successful design company, she again focused on her first love: baking. She studied at Paris's École Gastronomique Bellouet Conseil before returning back to Vancouver to open Beaucoup. Since her business opened in 2012, Jackie has continued her relationship with Paris through her intimate group trips to the very best Parisian pâtisseries and chocolate shops through the "Paris Tours" portion of her business.

BAKERY Beaucoup Bakery & Cafe   LOCATION 2150 Fir St., Vancouver, BC
WEB beaucoupbakery.com   FB beaucoupbakery   TWITTER @JackieKaiEllis

HARPER'S TRAIL WINERY 🍷 THE WINE MAKER

WRANGLING GRAPES IN PIONEER NORTH WINE COUNTRY.

Harper's Trail: Taste the untamed land. The first winery in the Kamloops region (yes, they are growing grapes and making wine up north!) to make its wine 100% from grapes grown in the area, it is definitely in the pioneer category. Jackie has chosen its Chardonnay to pair with her Carrot & Cumin Tart, describing the wine as "unique and wonderful." The winery and vineyard property does sound amazing–and the land holds a major historical significance. Named for the cattle drive trail of pioneer rancher Thaddeus Harper, Ed and Vicki Collett's vineyard is nestled on the banks of the South Thompson River. Described as "rolling hills of sage and grass, home to bighorn sheep, bears, and myriad birds," its intrigue grows further. The wine maker at Harper's Trail is Michael Bartier.

WINERY Harper's Trail Winery   LOCATION 2761 Shuswap Road, Kamloops, BC   FB HarpersTrail   TWITTER @HarpersTrail   WEB harperstrail.com

✦ **THE FARMER**
Aubin van Berckel
Bowen Island, BC

⚓ **THE CHEF**
Christophe Langlois
Bowen Island, BC

🍶 **THE CIDER MAKER**
Merridale Estate Cidery
Cobble Hill, BC

···· FEATURED INGREDIENT ·····················
Organic Bowen Island apples

1 litre canola oil for deep frying

250 mL water

150 g butter

750 g flour

150 g sugar

10 g salt

10 g milk powder

75 g fresh yeast

3 large eggs, whisked together

BAKED APPLE SAUCE FILLING

16–24 apples, depending on size

2 cups sugar

vanilla bean, cut in half and
    sliced down the centre

BEIGNET WITH BAKED BOWEN APPLES

These beignets (pronounced ben-YAY)—a French and more poetic name for a donut or fritter—are to die for. These delectable delights are only available on certain days at Artisan Eats, and they sell out lightening fast. A to-go coffee and a warm beignet are the perfect antidote to waiting in line for the morning ferry on Bowen Island.

Preheat oven to 350°F (190°C). Toss the apples with the sugar and place in an ovenproof baking dish. Insert the two pieces of vanilla into the apples. Bake until apples are tender, approximately 30–40 minutes. Let cool. Put the water and butter in a saucepot and heat just until butter melts entirely. In a separate bowl, mix the remaining ingredients. Add the melted butter and water and stir to a smooth paste. Let the dough rest at room temperature for 40 minutes, then knead a few times, and let rest for a further 30 minutes. Portion the dough into 80 g pieces and leave in a warm spot until they have doubled in size. If you don't have a warm corner, you can rest the dough balls in your oven at 100°F. Heat the oil to 300°F (150°C). Carefully drop the dough balls into the hot oil. They should not be touching each other and should have enough room to move around a bit. When golden brown, flip the dough balls over so the other side cooks to golden brown. Repeat until all of the beignets are cooked.

Using kitchen scissors, insert the closed blades into one end of the beignet about ¾ of the way through. Without further puncturing the beignet, open the scissors to create a whole for filling it. Use a teaspoon to fill the holes in the centre of each beignet with the applesauce.

Try not to eat the entire batch—*mon Dieu!*

···· DRINK PAIRING ·································

Merridale House Craft Cider
This pub draft cider is a lighter, sweeter version of our Traditional cider, but still very dry. You'll find house cider on tap in Vancouver Island's finest pubs and restaurants.

LEFT TO RIGHT: Aubin, Christophe, and Julie

AUBIN VAN BERCKEL ✳ THE FARMER

WASSAILING AWAY ON BOWEN ISLAND.

Aubin and David van Berckel live on a lush farm wonderland in the middle of Bowen Island. Complete with a tiny island on a pond, their land is populated with various and sundry plants ranging from blueberries and goji berries, to quince and fig trees, all growing in harmony with multitudes of indigenous flowers and glorious organic vegetables. In the middle of all of this incredible earthy chaos, lies a small orchard of twisty heritage apple trees planted on a slope—adding to that feeling that one just might have slipped through a rabbit hole.

Aubin herself sparkles with magic. Besides selling her fruits, vegetables, and various preserves at the farmers' market and from their farm gate, she is also a beloved local storyteller and volunteers her time to provide animated tales for the children at the local library. Aubin was not born into the art of farming nor was she well versed in gardening and plant life; however, through the tutelage and guidance of their good friend Richard Redding (now passed), their utopian farm flourished. David purchased it in 1994, and wanted to build a garden with an "edible landscape" where everything planted was to have a use. One could refer to its prior state as an empty canvas *per se*—quite apropos since the

van Berckels own the OPUS art stores located in various locations around the Lower Mainland, Victoria, and Kelowna.

"It was a communal effort." Aubin explains. "There were so many people involved in the farm and garden's creation. Over the years, we hosted big work parties with 50 or 60 of our friends who came to help landscape and plant followed by a big feast to celebrate their hard work. Because of that, people here share a certain ownership in the garden."

They also make a batch of apple cider and juice every year and have a winter solstice party to celebrate the farm and apple trees. "We have a wassail in the orchard! We dance around with a few local musicians called The Black Sheep and fling cinnamon toast at the apple trees!" The custom of wassailing dates back to pagan times but has enjoyed a minor resurgence in recent years as apple cider has regained popularity among drinkers. This ancient act of wassailing refers to a traditional ceremony that involves singing and drinking the health of trees on the Twelfth Night in the hopes that they might better thrive.

FARM 609 Cates Hill Road, Bowen Island

CHRISTOPHE LANGLOIS AND JULIE CREE ✱ THE CHEF

THE CHEF AND HIS LOVER.

Julie Cree and Chef Christophe Langlois together have a long and delicious history on the Vancouver food scene. She, a local with a resume that includes time at the iconic Raincity Grill back in its heyday, he a chef from Paris who also spent time at Le Crocodile and also Raincity Grill . . . coincidence? Nope—this is where they first laid eyes on each other and fell in love. Their relationship didn't begin until later, when their paths crossed again while both working at C Restaurant in the early 2000s where it blissfully ended in marriage and plans to open their own eatery one day.

A restaurant romance eventually led the couple to Bowen Island to breathe new life into a restaurant called Tuscany Pizza. "Christophe took over the kitchen and I the front of house. We expanded and grew that business for almost 9 years," says Julie. "In 2009, we started Artisan Eats Cafe. After a number of failed businesses in this location, we opened with a vision of a casual cafe/restaurant, the kind of place where one could come for just a latte or a complete lunch of duck confit, house-made burger, or Malaysian curry bowl, to name a few. The stunning room with mountain, ocean, and forest views was just begging to service the community and tourists alike." Chef Michael Lecourt eventually joined their partnership. Trained in pastry, bread, and vienoisserie he enhanced their menu with a beautiful variety of croissants and other specialties.

"Life on Bowen Island has been a remarkable experience." Julie reflects. "We also have a yearly Apple Festival on Bowen–it's a real treat. We bake TONS of stuff with apples—apple breads, turnovers, beignets, candied apples, apple croissants . . ." (Keep your ears open! These two islanders may be returning to the mainland sometime soon . . . .)

CAFE Artisan Eats Cafe & Bakery   LOCATION 539 Artisan Lane, Bowen Island, BC
FB Artisan-Eats-Cafe-Bakery   TWITTER @ArtisanEatsCafe   WEB www.artisaneats.ca

*Each Fall, The Bowen Island Heritage Preservation Association organizes the Bowen Island Apple Fest to celebrating the island's farm community and the history of its fruit industry. The Association is also working on resurrecting an ancient orchard (first settlers–1890s) by collecting cuttings and graftings taken from all the ancient trees on the island and replanting them where the original settler had his orchard," says president Judy Gedye. www.bowenheritage.org

Here's to thee, old apple tree,
That blooms well, bears well.
Hats full, caps full,
Three bushel bags full,
An' all under one tree.
Hurrah! Hurrah!
—wassailing song

MERRIDALE ESTATE CIDERY 🍶 THE CIDER MAKER

THEY HOST LEPRECHAUN HUNTS IN THE ORCHARD.

The iconic BC apple is getting its shine back on during this age of apple cider mania. We can thank jolly old England for this re-trend, as their love for this appleicious libation has never left the spotlight. Merridale Cider has been referred to as "the best English-style cider in Canada," with owners/operators Janet Docherty and husband Rick Pipes making seven unique cider varieties. In addition to creating high-quality cider from their orchards, the Merridale team now also makes three fortified dessert wines and a range of brandies and spirits to round out their portfolio.

Janet Docherty

CIDERMAKERS Janet Docherty and Rick Pipes et al LOCATION 1230 Merridale Rd, Cobble Hill, BC
FB merridalecider   TWITTER @merridalecider   WEB merridalecider.com

THE FARMER
UBC Farm
University of British Columbia
Vancouver, BC

THE CHEF
Jonathan Chovancek
Vancouver, BC

THE BITTERS MAKER
Lauren Mote
Vancouver, BC

····· **FEATURED INGREDIENT** ·················
UBC Farm festival squash

2 festival or acorn squash from UBC Farm

2–3 Tbsp vegetable oil

salt and pepper to taste

2 rashers double smoked bacon

½ cup Swiss chard, chopped

2 small potatoes, cut in half and roasted

¼ tsp fennel seeds, toasted

¼ tsp coriander seeds, toasted

6 whole eggs

½ cup heavy cream

1 Tbsp Manchego cheese, grated

FESTIVAL SQUASH FRITTATA
WITH BACON & SWISS CHARD

Festival squash is the fun guy of the squash world. It is similar to acorn squash, but this variety is much more flamboyant. With bright orange and green skin and covered in stripes and dots, it is perfect to use as a serving bowl. Party on!

Preheat the oven to 350°F.

Cut the squash in half and remove the seeds. Season with vegetable oil, salt and pepper, and roast in the oven at 350°F until the squash is tender.

Use the deepest half of the roasted squash as a bowl to hold the frittata.

Dice bacon and render over medium high heat until crispy and set aside to drain. Keep the fat in the pan, and sauté the other half of the squash, diced, along with the Swiss chard and potatoes until tender. Add the toasted fennel and coriander seeds and stir to combine and then distribute evenly between the squash bowls.

Use a blender to combine the eggs and cream. Strain and then pour the egg mixture into the squash bowls.

Sprinkle with cheese and bake on a sheet pan in the oven at 300°F until set.

Serve with a side of lightly dressed arugula—on the beach with a cocktail if possible!

····· **DRINK PAIRING** ···································

Bittered Sling Clingstone Peach Bitters
This one's a peach, alright! Widely known as the juiciest, sweetest, and most succulent of all peaches, the clingstone's flesh grips the pit for dear life, but you won't have to pry to savour the bold and robust flavours of this peachy-keen extract and its uplifting, spicy back-notes.

THE ORACLE

1.00 oz Okanagan Spirits Aquavitus
0.50 oz Okanagan Spirits Poire Williams
0.50 oz Fidencio Mezcal
0.75 oz Cocchi Americano
1 bar spoon peach-quinine syrup
2 dashes Bittered Sling Clingstone
    Peach Bitters

This fruity cocktail will add the most delicious sparkle to your Sunday brunch. Or lunch, or dinner, or, well heck, it pairs well with life any old time!

Stir ingredients with ice and serve neat in a chilled cocktail glass. Garnish with an orange peel.

JONATHAN CHOVANCEK ✴ THE CHEF

JONATHAN + LAUREN.

Romantic, and shall we say stirring, the pairing of Vancouver chef Jonathan Chovancek, of the wildly successful Café Medina, and Lauren Mote, of UVA Wine & Cocktail Bar fame, have together shaken up the Vancouver cocktail scene through their brainchild, Bittered Sling.

"I'd been reading about these flavour combinations that she was putting together. I came in and not only was I blown away by what we were tasting and drinking, but she was stunning—a six-foot goddess—and I knew that one day she would be mine. The next day we had brunch at Café Medina, where I'm now the executive chef," Jonathan recalls.

The couple shares a long list of accolades in their respective food and cocktail worlds—both becoming well-loved members of their community and main players in the urban culture on the coast.

Jonathan was born and raised on Vancouver Island, so his ties to the west coast run deep. Lauren comes to us from the east coast—ominously arriving in 2007 on the heels of a massive windstorm that wreaked havoc on Stanley Park: "Treacherous winds, rain, and swells bashed the shores, only to reveal a perfect, blue-skied sunny day afterwards, as well as fragrant gardens, picturesque mountains and ocean, and year-round local markets. That was my first day. I arrived after the storm, and fell in love with the environment, the mood, the smell, and the lifestyle, and I never looked back."

Jonathan recalls his first time in Vancouver. "I remember the smell of the air and the shimmering ocean as the sun set over English Bay. I was 19 at the time and knew I had to live here one day—and now I find myself living in this exact location some 20 years later. My equilibrium in life is when I'm near the water, so this is exactly where I need to be."

The duo feels strongly about sourcing local and supporting the local farming industry. Jonathan chose UBC Farm to partner with because of their strong values and source for education. Lauren sources many herbs, fruits, and berries from the Okanagan to create the bitters formulas for Bittered Sling.

RESTAURANT Café Medina   LOCATION Vancouver, BC   FB cafemedina
TWITTER @cafemedina   WEB medinacafe.com

⚓

LAUREN MOTE 🍸 THE BITTERS MAKER

A LOVE STORY BY THE SEA.

In line with the resurgence of the glamourous age of cocktails, Lauren and Jonathan created their award-winning line of artisanal bitters in 2012. Sourcing the best local ingredients, they make a unique, personal brand of the product.

With 15 flavours now out, Bittered Sling has garnered local and international acclaim with several gold medal wins at the Beverage Testing Institute's 2014 International Review of Spirits (America's Oldest and Most Influential Spirits Competition). The bitters are not only used for cocktail making—they are, as demonstrated by Jonathan, used in creating delicious food (check out their website for recipes).

The irony here is that Bittered Sling's lineup of flavours "underscores a singular and delicious irony that while all of their bitters are extracts, not all of their extracts are bitter."

Lauren explains,"We chose the name for our first company, Kale and Nori, the parent company of Bittered Sling Extracts, because it's a combination of both land and sea. I'm an earth sign and Jonathan is a water sign, and we incorporate land and sea into every dish we cook, and concept we conceive. Both Jonathan and I have a strong emotional connection to our environment and respect for our ingredients. We find that living near the ocean gives us plentiful options, and is also incredibly inspiring creatively."

Lauren wears another fabulous hat as one of the city's hottest mixologists and manages UVA Wine and Cocktail Bar and she is also a sommelier. The two love to be in the kitchen together at home. Jonathan says, "We love role reversal when Lauren cooks and I make cocktails. Our favourite meal together, quite honestly, is a giant bag of cherries, bottled cocktails on ice, and the sun and sand of Third Beach in August. Pure bliss."

COMPANY Bittered Sling   LOCATION Vancouver, BC
FB BitteredSling   TWITTER @bittered_sling   WEB bitteredsling.com

"We have access to incredible farmers, fishers, and foragers here in BC. In general, we're also a very new group of agrarians compared to Quebec and Ontario, so the scene here is full of youthful optimism and fresh ideas. Working with a farm like UBC is great for a multitude of social and environmental reasons, but quite frankly their soil is incredible and their produce tastes delicious. They grow 12 different varieties of squash and pumpkins alone, and the flavour, sweetness, and texture they achieve is awesome."—Jonathan

UBC FARM ✳ THE FARMER

U OF FARM.

Located on 24 beautiful hectares, the UBC Farm is in a 90-year-old coastal hemlock forest that includes cultivated annual crop fields, perennial hedgerows and orchards, pasture, teaching gardens, and forest stands. The UBC Farm grows over 200 varieties of fruits, vegetables, and herbs as well as being a home to beehives and free-range chickens for honey and egg production. The education mandate for the farm also extends into the community, offering great programs for kids with summer camps called FarmWonders.

"A farm of some description has been a part of UBC's Vancouver campus since the establishment of the university site on Point Grey. However, the farm's size, location, purpose, and operations have all seen many changes since the first clearing for agriculture began in 1915," explains Shannon Lambie, communications coordinator.

The UBC Farm grows and sells its produce through different venues including weekly farmers' markets operating from early June through mid-October. It offers a CSA (Community Supported Agriculture—see page 6 for further description) program and offers wholesale produce to restaurants and other businesses like Café Medina.

The Centre for Sustainable Food Systems (CSFS), located at the UBC Farm, is a unique research centre that aims to drive local and global food systems toward a more sustainable, food secure future. The program models itself as a "living laboratory," working to develop systems that are key to operating sustainable communities.

Here are some important facts that the CSFS is concentrating on, which we should all be conscious of:

*Currently only 2.6 million of the 4.7 million hectares of Agricultural Land Reserve in British Columbia is actively farmed.

*The average age for farmers in British Columbia is 56 years of age.

*Nearly 82% of prospective local farmers were not from a farming background, and therefore had no access to succession or inherited land. Respondents identified the high cost of agricultural land as the biggest barrier to entering farming.

FARM UBC Farm—Faculty of Land & Food Systems   FB UBC.Farm   WEB ubcfarm.ubc.ca
LOCATION The University of British Columbia 3461 Ross Drive, Vancouver, BC

THE FARMER
Naty King
South Surrey, BC

THE CHEF
Eric Pateman
Granville Island, BC

THE BEER MAKER
Driftwood Brewery
Victoria, BC

····· FEATURED INGREDIENT ··············
Hazelmere organic veggies

7 oz potatoes, diced large

1¾ oz celeriac, diced large

1¾ oz carrots, diced large

¼ cup extra virgin olive oil

1⅖ oz boar bacon, diced large

1¾ oz red onion, diced large

3½ oz Brussels sprouts, trimmed
    and cut in half

grapeseed oil for deep frying

1⅖ oz kale, roughly torn

2 farm fresh eggs

HAZELMERE HASH

This recipe is a true celebration of Naty's beautiful farm, where most of these ingredients come from when in season. It is named for her farm and is a favourite brunch item on the menu at Edible Canada. Serves one—so spoil yourself! Or, invite others and double the recipe accordingly.

Fill a medium-sized pot with water and bring to the boil. Season the water generously with kosher salt.

Add potatoes and simmer until fork tender then cool and set aside.

Heat oven to 350°F, toss celeriac and carrots in a little extra virgin olive oil and roast until tender.

Heat a frying pan on medium to medium-high heat, add the boar bacon and render (cook until the fat releases) then add onions and sauté until translucent, about 5 minutes.

Add Brussels sprouts and sauté for 5 minutes and then add the carrots and celeriac to the pan. Taste and season if necessary.

Deep fry boiled potatoes in a deep fryer at 350°F until crispy and add to the pan. Add torn kale and toss well to combine all the ingredients and flavours.

Soft poach two eggs and present atop the heavenly hash. Bibbity bop!

DRINK PAIRING ·······························

Driftwood Brewing Farmhand Saison
"Farmhand Saison is our 'foodie' beer! It has a unique savoury profile to it that is typical of a lot of Belgian styles. We actually sour the mash with a little lactic acid, then we add cracked peppercorns at the end of the wort boil. The Belgian yeast strain also creates phenolic notes of clove, so there is a distinct herb and spice profile throughout the taste of the beer and that would resonate with the hash dish!"—Gary Lindsay

DRIFTWOOD BREWERY ⚬ THE BEER MAKER

THE WIZARD OF WORT, THE COMMANDING OFFICER OF GETTIN 'R DONE, AND THE PURVEYOR OF PRECIOUS LIQUIDS—BY THE SEA.

There is something about Victoria and beer. Must be the salt in the air, but those island folks do so love a cold brew. Even back in 2008, when Jason Meyer (Wizard of Wort) and Kevin Hearsum (Commanding Officer of Gettin 'r Done) were gearing up an old industrial space in Rock Bay to kickstart their brewery, Victoria was already known as a top beer destination in Canada. "Driftwood has always been about beer first and foremost as the inspiration for the brewery came from Jason Meyer and Kevin Hearsum as they wanted to create and brew the beers they love," says Gary Lindsay (Purveyor of Precious Liquids), who joined the partnership in August of that year bringing with him years of craft beer promotion experience to the table.

FROM TOP LEFT TO RIGHT: Brendon, Julie, Travis, Brendan Cook, Paul, Tim

LOCATION 102–450 Hillside Ave, Victoria, BC   FB driftwoodbeer   TWITTER @driftwoodbeer   WEB Driftwoodbeer.com

ERIC PATEMAN ✴ THE CHEF

KING OF LOCAL.

Eric Pateman is a fourth generation Vancouverite and a pioneer in local culinary tourism. Starting out as a one-man-band culinary concierge, his concept quickly grew into a retail store, a restaurant, a touring company plus events, then into Edible Canada. It grew indeed, and made Profit Magazine's Fastest Growing Companies in Canada list twice in the past few years! Edible Canada started as Edible Vancouver in 2005 and morphed into Edible BC in 2006. The shop features all things created locally and the restaurant does the same, featuring local wines and drinks as well. It's one big ol' local love fest!

Obviously Pateman's philosophy includes sourcing local ingredients and products to sell in his store, serve in his restaurant and promote through tours and events. Naty King, Pateman's choice of a farmer partner for this book, is also a favourite for many local chefs.

"I met Naty through her late husband, Gary King, who was introduced to me by John Bishop—the long term leader in Vancouver's local food movement. We did a trip up to the Similkameen Valley where I got to learn and cook with Gary and John which began what has been over a decade long relationship. The first ingredients that got me hooked on Hazelmere Farm were Gary's kale tips from the spring buds of the kale plant—the most tasty sign of spring!"

What makes our West Coast cuisine so special? "It is the local ingredients that make our style of cooking so unique and top ranked . . . that is what makes Vancouver so unique—the authenticity and quality of the ethnically influenced foods, using local delicacies such as seafood, meats and produce," says Eric.

RESTAURANT Edible Canada   FB ediblecanada   TWITTER @ediblecanada
LOCATION Granville Island Public Market, Vancouver, BC   WEB ediblecanada.com

⚓

NATY KING ✴ THE FARMER

LIVE GRACEFULLY, GIVE GENEROUSLY.

Naty King and her late husband Gary of Hazelmere Organic Farm were two of the first farmers to forge direct relationships with local chefs. She is a favourite choice, not only for her high standards in farm ethics and lovely organic produce, but because she is just such a beautiful spirit and someone who is so very connected to the earth.

Naty has a glorious grove of sunchokes on her farm. A relative of the sunflower, the tubers are the edible portion—the rest is just a wonderful bonus. What is so remarkable is that the stalks and beautiful yellow flowers grow over 10 feet tall and make for quite a show of colour. "My sunchokes, or as others call them, Jerusalem artichokes, are so versatile, so refreshing in the winter time. You can eat them raw in salads or make a beautiful velouté—they are also a great substitute for water chestnuts," says Naty.

Naty's sustainable, organic farm is meticulously kept. Row upon row, her near-perfect vegetables are proof that organic farming works using only natural products and methods like companion planting to keep pests at bay. A couple of years ago she introduced bee hives to the farm, calling their inclusion "responsible stewardship." "It was so rewarding to see the increase in the harvest of my fruits and vegetables."

"I try to share what I know about living a holistic life rather than educate," says Naty. "I hope that through our example, our lifestyle, we can show others that we can co-exist with Mother Nature and still live in the present. That our present is not only caring for ourselves but also the community we live in, be it our neighbourhood or the world community. We are in the world to help one another. The future of farming is dependent on how we look at the purpose of food. If it is to sustain life—the future is good. If it is only a vehicle to accumulate wealth (big agriculture companies), then we will have a challenge for the next generation."

FARM Hazelmere Organic Farm   LOCATION 1859 184th St Surrey, BC V3S 9V2
PHONE 604-538-3018

····· **FEATURED INGREDIENT** ·······················
Nextjen Sprouted Buckwheat
Pancake and Waffle Mix

8 chicken thighs, boneless with skin on

BRINE

4 cups water

1 tsp salt

2 cloves garlic crushed (optional)

BUTTERMILK MARINADE

2 cups buttermilk

⅛–¼ tsp cayenne pepper (adjust depending
    on how hot you like it)

¼ tsp sweet paprika

1 clove crushed garlic

FOR DREDGING

1½ cups Nextjen Fried Chicken Mix,
    enough to coat

CHILI HONEY GLAZE

½ cup of your favourite local honey

1 tsp chili flakes

2 Tbsp sherry vinegar or apple cider vinegar

1 tsp fresh grated horseradish or Dijon mustard

salt and pepper to taste

WAFFLE BATTER

3 egg yolks

3 egg whites

1 cup Nextjen Sprouted Buckwheat
    Pancake and Waffle Mix

½ cup milk

3 Tbsp melted butter

CHICKEN & WAFFLES

If you have not had the pleasure of sinking your teeth into this old Southern combo, you are in for a treat. Relatively new on our west coast eat beat, its history goes way back, way down South and now has become a fast favourite in our local comfort food category. Great news for the gluten intolerant, Nextjen Gluten-Free's awesome flour blends allows you to jump back into the naughty world of deep-fried foods and delicious baked goods, like waffles. Bring it on. **SERVES 4**

Brine chicken in brine liquid overnight (12 hours) in the refrigerator.

    Then drain and place in buttermilk marinade below.

    Marinate for 6–8 hours in the refrigerator, the longer the better. Do not drain.

    Dredge in Nextjen Fried Chicken Mix and for a really thick coating, dip in buttermilk marinade and dredge again.

    Heat a large pot with fresh frying oil no more than ⅓ full (room for the hot oil to bubble to 350°F and carefully lower 4 chicken thighs into pot and fry for 6–8 minutes or until golden brown and internal temp 165°F (75°C) then repeat with the rest of the chicken.

    Stir together the glaze and taste—mmmm.

    Separate eggs into yolks and whites. Whisk together pancake mix, egg yolks, milk, vanilla, melted butter. Whip the egg whites until they are at soft peaks. Fold into batter. Scoop onto preheated, lightly oiled waffle iron, and cook until golden brown.

    Drizzle with delicious Chili Honey Glaze and get your mojo on.

····· **DRINK PAIRING** ·······································

Sea Cider Rumrunner
The secret to Rumrunner lies in the barrel. Rich, full-bodied, and intriguing, Newfoundland Screech barrels were the inspiration for this semi-dry cider, which opens up to reveal complex notes of molasses, apples, and rum. Raise a glass of Sea Cider and let your apples out of the barrel!

JENNIFER PETERS 🐟 THE FLOUR MAKER

WRITES FLOURY POETRY.

Jennifer Peters began her career as protégé of Chef Bruno Marti, the beloved godfather of fine dining cuisine in Canada. She went on to work and train at Michelin starred restaurants in England and was executive chef at the Raincity Grill, one of Vancouver's most legendary culinary establishments and one that focused on eating and sourcing local, sustainable cuisine. She was one of the pioneer chefs in executing the extra measures needed to source, recycle, and connect with the local farm and fishing community.

Nextjen's traditional stone mill is from Germany and it produces the finest flour possible. The buckwheat used to make the flour is created by scratch, Old World style. She actually sprouts the buckwheat in house! The end result is a baking flour blend that is GMO-free, corn-free, preservative-free, dairy-free, and sulphite-free. So now, Jen and Hamid say, "all you have to do is bake." These blends are not just for the gluten intolerant! They are for everyone and make the perfect choice for crispy-coated fish or fried chicken.

COMPANY Nextjen Gluten-Free   TWITTER nextjenglutenfree
FB @nextjenGF   WEB nextjen.ca

THE TALE OF NEXTJEN GLUTEN-FREE

I studied and I read,
I turned ideas over in my head!
I tried and tried to bake some bread,
It kept me awake even in my bed!
I thought about it long and hard . . .
Many recipes I did discard.
Then, finally, one sunny day
There was no more dismay.
Now I bake to heart's content
All the recipes to you I've sent.
Making it quite hassle free,
The way that baking ought to be!
           —Jen Peters, GF baker and
                poetess extraordinaire!

LEFT TO RIGHT: Hamid and Jennifer

HAMID SALIMIAN ☀ THE CHEF

THE CHEF, THE BAKER,
THE GLUTEN-FREE YUM MAKERS.

Two incredibly talented and acclaimed chefs fall in love; one finds out she is gluten intolerant and so they decide to make gluten-free flour. The story is much more poetically described in Jen's poem (left) on the creation of their new joint venture Nextjen Gluten-Free. Get it? Her name is Jen and this is her new gig, so Jen also stands for "gen" as in generation—as in the gluten-free generation that she makes with her partner in crime and love, Hamid Salimian.

Chef Hamid is known for his warm disposition and passion for his craft and his peers adore him. Hamid grew up in Iran on the edge of the Caspian Sea and "learned about traditional Persian cuisine amid his father's citrus orchards and dairy farm." With those early culinary imprints ingrained in his culinary style, his "innovative approach to blending multicultural influences with traditional French fare" brought him much acclaim and awards. His cuisine is described as creative and soulful. Former executive chef at Diva at the Met, Hamid is spending his time now focusing on his role as captain of Culinary Team Canada (yeah!) and making flour with his girl. Hamid also operates as a culinary creative consultant and food photographer.

COMPANY Nextjen Gluten-Free   TWITTER @hamidsalimian
LOCATION Vancouver, BC   WEB chefhamid.com & nextjen.ca

SEA CIDER FARM & CIDER HOUSE 🍶 THE CIDER MAKER

THE CIDERHOUSE RULES!

Although she grew up in a family of farmers and ranchers and eventually ended up inheriting her father's apple orchard as a teenager, Kristen Jordan's plans for the future did not include farming. After attending school abroad, engaging in an internationally focused career, and raising a family, Kristen ended up planting an apple orchard by the sea and going to cider school. "The idea of starting a cidery had been percolating for several years but the 'aha' moment happened during a visit to my family's abandoned orchard on Shuswap Lake in August 2002. I went for a walk along the lakeshore to the site of our first orchard. It was a magical discovery and at that moment it felt like the cider idea was possible."—Kristen

CIDERY 2487 Mt. St. Michael Rd, Saanichton, BC   FB seacider   TWITTER @SeaCiderHouse   WEB SeaCider.ca

⭐ THE FARMER
Mary Forstbauer
Chilliwack, BC

🦑 THE BAKER
Mary Mackay
Vancouver, BC

🐬 THE ARTISAN
Marisa Goodwin
Cobble Hill, BC

···· FEATURED INGREDIENT ····
·Forstbauer Farms blueberries

1 Terra Breads sourdough loaf

5 large eggs

¼ cup honey

1 tsp pure vanilla extract

1 Tbsp orange zest

1 tsp ground cinnamon

½ tsp ground cardamom

2¼ cups whole milk

2 cups blueberries

¼ cup unsalted butter

¼ cup brown sugar

¼ tsp sea salt

1 cup whole hazelnuts, roughly chopped

BLUEBERRY HAZELNUT FRENCH TOAST BAKE

"Baked French toast can be topped with fresh or frozen blueberries. I love Forstbauer Family Natural Food Farm blueberries grown in Chilliwack, BC. Their certified organic farm has been using biodynamic principles since 1977. Biodynamics is a spiritual, ethical, and ecological approach to agriculture. This dish is perfect to prepare for a brunch gathering. The bread is soaked in the custard overnight and then baked in the morning to serve warm."—Mary Mackay

Butter a 10" diameter baking dish or 13 × 9-inch baking dish.

Slice loaf of sourdough bread in half lengthwise then slice into ½" thick slices. Arrange bread slices overlapping in the baking dish. In a large bowl whisk together eggs, honey, vanilla, orange zest, cinnamon, cardamom, and milk. Pour evenly over the bread slices. Press down on the bread slices to emerge in the liquid. Place the baking dish in the fridge, covered, until all liquid is absorbed by the bread, about 8 hours.

Preheat oven to 400°F.

Remove the baking dish from the fridge and spread blueberries over the top of the soaked bread slices.

In a small saucepan melt ¼ cup butter and stir in the brown sugar, sea salt, and hazelnuts. Stir to coat hazelnuts completely. Spread the hazelnuts over top of the blueberries to cover the surface of the dish.

Bake in oven until the custard is set, about 30 minutes. Serve warm with maple syrup.

···· DRINK PAIRING ····

Main Ingredient: Lavender Lemonbalm Lemonaid
Marisa uses her amazing Lavender Lemonbalm Lemonaid Soda Syrup in her Earl of Lavender Gin Fizz cocktail recipe. Lavender and lemonbalm both grow merrily on Marisa's farm. They are "two natural flavour friends" and have healing powers. As with all of her soda products, they do not need alcohol to make them bloom—just some sparkling water. Cocktail recipe on page 29.

MARY FORSTBAUER ✳ THE FARMER

MERRY MARY, QUITE CONTRARY
HOW DOES YOUR GARDEN GROW?

Biodynamically, naturally, and beautifully, that's how. Mary and her husband, Hans Forstbauer, own and operate their certified organic farm using biodynamic principals and they are certified through the Biodynamic Society of British Columbia (Demeter). Pioneers in organic farming since the 1970s, they have worked their land in cahoots with Mother Nature. Mary explains that "the idea of biodynamic farming is to be 100% self-sufficient, building soil health to build plant health to build healthy food." Biodynamic farming is allowing nature to control the plant growth and "careful attention is given to viewing the farm as a complete ecosystem." The Forstbauers also engage Soil Food Web techniques: "In this method of farming, special attention is given to the complex community of organisms living in the soil, known as the soil food web. With the use of a microscope, compost, and a compost tea brewer the farmer can observe the microbial life and encourage biodiversity and healthy soil activity."

Mary explains how they got into the organic farming movement, "We met people like Herb Barbolet (founder of Farm Folk/City Folk) through food co-ops and got involved in setting up the BC Association of Regenerative Agriculture." Not only do they grow a wide array of vegetables, in and out of greenhouse, they have also grown a village of 12 children—and are "Oma and Opa" to 37 grandchildren. "4 came with shoes on," Mary says lovingly of her adopted grandchildren. Many of the 2nd generation of Forstbauers still work on the farm or operate a business connected with organic farming.

The pristine products that are grown on the farm are mostly sold through local farmers markets. Mary loves attending market days so that she can talk to her customers and explains, "Consumers want to know where their food is coming from."

FARM Forstbauer Family Natural Food Farm
LOCATION 49350 Prairie Central Road, Chilliwack, BC
TWITTER @ForstbauerFarm FB forstbauerfarm WEB forstbauer.com

MARY MACKAY 🐙 THE BAKER

GIVING US OUR DAILY BREAD.

Mary Mackay and Terra Breads have been a huge part of the Vancouver food culture since they opened their first bakery in Kitsilano in 1993. This artisan bakery grew exponentially after locals got a taste of Mary's healthy baking and sourdough-based bread made from natural starters and baked in stone-hearth ovens. They are community minded, and thrive on being hubs for the locals.

As head baker and co-owner, Mary has strong values that she shares with the Terra Breads philosophy: "We source local and organic whenever we can. And for me, I look at ingredient sourcing as more of an education process, learning about the products and where they come from."

Mary explains her kinship with the local farmers, comparing her passion for artisan bread making to what farmers do: "Farmers are crafting nature. I craft bread. I love tradition, and organic farming, like making bread, is based on Old World traditions. I have respect for these people—these people that take care of the land." She was inspired by organic farmers early on, "I met Herb Barbolet when I was 19. I was working at a restaurant and he would pull up in his truck full of beautiful produce to deliver. It was the highlight of my week."

Mary first connected with Forstbauer Farms at the farmers' market and since then, it is her go-to stop on her market shop. "What interested me was that they were not just organic growers, they were biodynamic as well."

Mary looks for farms that practice biodiverse farming as well as farms where the animals are treated humanely.

BAKERY & CAFES Terra Breads HQ 107–35 West 5th Avenue, Vancouver, BC
FB terrabreads TWITTER @terrabreads WEB terrabreads.com

LEFT TO RIGHT: Mary Mackay and Mary Forstbauer

THE EARL OF LAVENDER GIN FIZZ

15 mL or 1 tablespoon Lavender
Lemonbalm Lemonaid

45 mL or 1.5 ounces Ampersand Gin
(Vancouver Island Distillery)

60 mL or 2 ounces cold strong brewed
Earl Grey tea—(full 5 minute steep)

100 mL or 3 ounces of sparkling water or club
soda—(use more soda for a lighter drink)

a min of 4 ice cubes per glass, a squeeze of
lemon, and 2 shakes angostura bitters

In the bottom of a 250 mL or 8 oz glass, combine the first 3 ingredients. Give them a quick stir, add ice, top with soda, finish with a squeeze of lemon, and a couple shakes of bitters. Garnish with lemon and sprigs of lavender if available. This is a great recipe to scale up for parties. Set up a drink station with all the ingredients pre-mixed in a chilled serving pitcher except the ice, bitters, and garnish. A little sign on the bitters saying "two shakes please" and an extra bottle of soda to top up the glass is all you need for an easy party drink. All ingredients should be chilled!

Recipe by Marisa Goodwin.

LEFT TO RIGHT: Jubilee and Mary

LEFT TO RIGHT: Kent, Nigella, Jasper, and Marisa (Violet is their third child, not shown)

MARISA GOODWIN 🐬 THE ARTISAN

EVERYTHING THAT SMELLS GOOD AND TASTES GOOD IS MADE HERE.

Marisa Goodwin is an herbalist by trade and explains, "I have been an advocate of organic food for nearly 20 years and believe in the power of food to help heal people. Having been an herbalist for 13 years now and a grower of medicinal plants for 10, the initial choice to formally learn about herbal medicine was the next step in living a healthy life after caring about what we eat. Herbal medicine is preventative healthcare, especially combined with food they are a 'natural' combination. Herbs are delicious and nutritious. My experience as both a food professional and an herbalist is what makes Organic Fair's soda syrups, chocolates, and spices so interesting and enjoyable."

She owns and operates Organic Fair with her husband, Kent Goodwin. When the two first met, he specialized in essential oils and was obsessed with chocolate and supporting fair-trade chocolate. And guess what? She *loves* chocolate, humanity causes, essential oils, and is also a great cook (which she says won his heart). And so, like mixing the essential ingredients to make a magic potion, these two were a match made in apothecary heaven. They married

and now live on their farm with their three children in a fairytale log cabin in the woods where they make yummy things.

Specializing in an array of delights, Organic Fair makes: gourmet quality herbs and spices, small-batch crafted spice blends, spice rubs, flavoured salts, certified organic seasonings, organic fair-trade chocolate, a soda syrup line, and more. "We have been serious about organic, fair-trade dark chocolate since 2005. Since then, we have also had some serious fun with flavours in our dark chocolate bars." They have a chocolate factory on the farm as well as other production facilities for their products—it is amazing. Marisa explains that with three small children, the only way they could accomplish what they've done was to work at home. The business has been a huge success with their product line being shipped to stores in the US. Marisa and Kent say, "We like to think that you can truly taste the love in our products."

FARM Organic Fair Farm & Garden   LOCATION 1935 Doran Road, Cobble Hill, BC
FB organicfairfarm   TWITTER @OrganicFair   WEB organicfair.com

Manifesto: "Organic Fair is all about sustainability and has been since our work first started in the mid 1990s. We believe in organic agriculture, direct fair-trade, and environmental responsibility are keystones of sustainability."

THE FARMER
Marc and Lisa Vance
Black Creek, BC

THE BUTCHER
Peter Jenney
Vancouver, BC

THE WINE MAKER
Fairview Cellars
Oliver, BC

······ FEATURED INGREDIENT ······
Island Bison Ranch bison

MEAT MIX

7 lbs Island bison, trimmed

1 lb suet or pork leaf lard/back fat

DRY MIX

20 g caraway seeds

30 g paprika

25 g brown sugar

15 g mustard seeds

12 g black peppercorns

60 g salt

300 g dried blueberries

WET MIX

¼ cup thyme leaves (or to taste)

1 large onion, minced onion

6–8 cloves garlic, minced (optional)

½ cup ice water

pork or sheep sausage casings

    (ask your butcher to buy some)

BISON, BLUEBERRY & THYME SAUSAGE

Time to get out the meat grinder and sausage stuffer attachments for your Kitchen Aid! "Originally developed as a breakfast sausage, this sausage offers a balance of sweet and savoury flavours. It is a versatile sausage that holds up as a dinner component or even braised in a hunters pot alongside other proteins"—Pete

DRY MIX Grind the seeds and the peppercorns finely, then mix all of the ingredients together.

Pete likes to rehydrate the blueberries with ½ cup of boiling water, then place the "tea" in the freezer until chilled but not frozen (you can add a few ice cubes to speed this up). Combine and grind the chilled meat through a course die. Whisk together wet and dry mix, then add to the ground meat. Mix thoroughly, blending the sausage until it has a uniform texture. Case the sausage in pork or sheep casings, or form into small patties or crépinettes (flat sausage patties that are characteristically wrapped in caul fat) cased in caul fat (a thin membrane of fat covering the intestines of a pig, cow, or sheep). Let the sausage hang refrigerated overnight or cover the crépinettes/patties on a resting rack set in a sheet tray.

Grill, fry, poach, bake, broil, or braise the sausage until desired doneness is achieved; let the sausage rest a few minutes before serving.

····· **DRINK PAIRING** ·····

2011 Fairview Cellars Bucket O' Blood
Named in honour of the Moffatt Saloon nicknamed "The Bucket Of Blood" by the miners of the 1890s. This saloon was situated up the "Reed Creek" draw above the Fairview town site. "This is a quintessential 'Fireplace Wine.' Rich and robust in nature, the Cabernet Sauvignon lends structure, cassis, and capsicum flavours while the Syrah offers weight, juiciness, and peppery spice to the blend. Full-bodied and easy to drink, this wine pairs well with friends around a fire, and equally well with BBQ meats and burgers or stew."—Mireille Sauvé, The Wine Umbrella

"I use dried blueberries because the sugars have been developed and the flavour is more intensified."—Pete

MARC AND LISA VANCE ✴ THE FARMER

A HOME WHERE THE HAPPY BUFFALO ROAM.

Located on a beautiful 360-acre ranch in Black Creek on Vancouver, Island, Marc and Lisa Vance, their four kids, and Grandma and Grandpa Watson are raising 100% free-range, grass-fed bison using no antibiotics or hormones. "All in keeping with our ranch vision of raising 'happy meat.'" They have also added water buffalo to the herd, purchasing some babies to raise from Fairburn Farm. Anthea Archer, owner and water buffalo farmer at Fairburn Farm, explains that she "had to check out the new home that her buffalo babies were going to before she made the deal." She was delighted with this wonderful family and their beautiful farm and happily let the little ones go. The mellow nature of the water buffalo has also had an effect on the more naturally aggressive personalities of the bison, and so the two herds are living happily ever after.

Marc and Lisa are responsible farmers and use as much of the animals as possible. Tendons become pet chews, bones are available for soup or dogs, and even the hair is collected for fly tying! I also love that they donate the hides to the local First Nations community to make drums.

Bison is an extremely healthy red meat and comes in the same range of cuts as beef. They say that buffalo meat is lower in fat than "beef, pork, skinless chicken, lamb, veal, venison, ostrich, and sockeye salmon." The family also offers a variety of smoked products ranging from smokies to salami.

"Both our bison and water buffalo enjoy free-ranging on our pastures, which include numerous natural spring water sources, stands of forest and brush, as well as mud wallows and dust pits that are enjoyed throughout the summer months. We focus on maintaining a low-stress environment and believe that raising happy animals equals healthy, high-quality meat."

Island Bison products are available to order online, at the Comox Valley Farmers' Market, and they offer sales from their farm store on the ranch. In Vancouver, you can buy them at Pete's Meat.

FARM Island Bison Ranch   LOCATION 3100 Hamm Road, Black Creek, BC
FB IslandBison   TWITTER @islandbison   WEB islandbison.com

PETER JENNEY 🦀 THE BUTCHER

MEET PETE!

Pete began working in the restaurant world at age 12 and ended up training as a chef. He spent some time up in Haida Gwaii cooking at a fishing lodge where he learned to improvise and create dishes from what was available. "I didn't know what I would get when my orders were delivered, I just had to deal with it." This is when he realized that he didn't know much about how to cut meats and became interested in butchery. In 2002, he became an apprentice at Windsor Meats and spent five years there learning the ropes. Four years ago the opportunity to open his own shop was presented and he jumped on it. Pete specializes in the highest-quality meats he can find, and "sources almost everything locally, except for the kangaroo," he laughs. He strives to "keep my products from BC. I like being able to interact directly with the farmer and BC farmers offer world-class meats. All our products are hormone and antibiotic free as well." Pete makes his own charcuterie and loves special requests from customers. "I like when people challenge me as a butcher. On Star Wars Day, a local fan called to order a steak cut into the shape of the Millennium Falcon, and I did it," he smiles. The deli counter offers delicious lunch items, including hot or cold sandwiches and salads to eat in or take out. Pete also loves consulting with his customers on dinner party ideas—and he also teaches classes. You will love him!

SHOP Pete's Meat Butcher Shop & Deli   LOCATION 2817 Arbutus Street, Vancouver, BC
FB petesmeats   TWITTER @petesmeats   WEB petes-meat.com

FAIRVIEW CELLARS 🍷 THE WINE MAKER

A VINE GUY.

Known as the "cab man" by many because of his top-notch Cabernet Sauvignon-based wines, Bill Eggert is a local wine guru. He is a vigneron, which means that he grows the grapes as well as makes the wine, but he likes to refer to himself as a farmer first because that is where great wines are made—in the vineyard. Bill is a former instructor in viticulture at the Okanagan College, and many of the Okanagan's young wine makers and/or viticulturalists count themselves lucky to have studied under him. He specializes in rich, terroir-driven red wines with one white, a Sauvignon Blanc, recently added to his portfolio.

WINE MAKER Bill Eggert   LOCATION 989 Cellar Road, Just off Old Golf Course Road, Oliver, BC
FB Fairview-Cellars   TWITTER @fairviewcellars   WEB fairviewcellars.ca

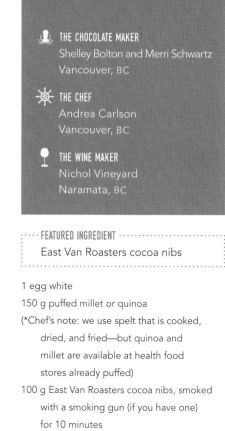

THE CHOCOLATE MAKER
Shelley Bolton and Merri Schwartz
Vancouver, BC

THE CHEF
Andrea Carlson
Vancouver, BC

THE WINE MAKER
Nichol Vineyard
Naramata, BC

···· FEATURED INGREDIENT ·················
East Van Roasters cocoa nibs

1 egg white

150 g puffed millet or quinoa

(*Chef's note: we use spelt that is cooked, dried, and fried—but quinoa and millet are available at health food stores already puffed)

100 g East Van Roasters cocoa nibs, smoked with a smoking gun (if you have one) for 10 minutes

2 Tbsp dried fruit such as lingonberry or cherry, cut into small pieces

2 tsp Maldon sea salt

2 Tbsp Turbinado sugar

EAST VAN ROASTERS COCOA NIB GRANOLA

Chef Andrea Carlson has created a delicious savoury granola that makes a unique accompaniment to meat dishes. As shown in the photo, she serves it with seared duck breast at her restaurant, Burdock & Co.

Whisk egg white until frothy.

In another bowl mix together grain, cocoa, dried fruit, sea salt, and sugar.

Add frothy whites to the grain mixture, one tablespoon at a time, until it is just moistened and lightly bound together.

Dry in dehydrator or on low in the oven on parchment or silicone paper until dry. *Chef's note: the temperature must be below 200 degrees because cocoa nibs will melt at 200 degrees!)

Serve as an accompaniment to game, such as venison or seared duck breast.

···· **DRINK PAIRING** ·····································

2012 Nichol Vineyard Syrah

100% Syrah, this full-bodied red wine is a fine example of the generosity of texture and flavour that comes from a single-vineyard Syrah. Ripe, rich flavours of blackberries and plums abound in this gem of a wine from the renowned Naramata Bench. Ageing potential reaches to about five years, but earlier drinking will also be enjoyed (with decanting) alongside such flavourful meats as venison, bison, lamb, or duck! —Mireille Sauvé, The Wine Umbrella

ANDREA CARLSON ✹ THE CHEF

LOCAL SOURCERESS.

A born and raised Vancouverite, Andrea trained at the local Dubrulle Culinary School and cut her teeth in some of the province's most celebrated, regionally focused restaurants: Raincity Grill, C Restaurant, Sooke Harbour House, as well as being chef for many years at the mothership of farm-to-table practices, Bishop's Restaurant. Her resume would qualify as a master's degree in sourcing local and working with community. Now with her new digs at Burdock & Co., Andrea has assembled a menu with conscience and great pride. She creates her dishes with as many locally sourced, organic ingredients as possible. She invests in forming relationships with her suppliers and is involved in many CSA (community sourced agriculture) programs that help support many farmers. The result? The best possible ingredients are served on her tables.

Andrea has been hailed as one of Vancouver's organic food pioneers. "Local, organic food has, for so long, belonged to the fine-dining experience. Burdock & Co. is about bringing that to the people," she says.

Choosing Merri and Shelley at East Van Roasters (EVR) to pair with speaks to her sourcing philosophies as well as her belief in empowering important local community philanthropic efforts like EVR's powerful work with the PHS Community Services Society.

Andrea is also involved with Harvest Community Foods, a hip little local grocery/community food shop in the Strathcona/Chinatown area. Andrea says, "I created the menu and we have an amazing chef, Gabe Meyers, who runs the kitchen and creates fantastic specials." This store project is another reflection of what this original locavorian lady is all about.

RESTAURANT Burdock & Co.   LOCATION 2702 Main Street, Vancouver, BC
TWITTER @BurdockAndCo   FB burdockandco   WEB burdockandco.com

SHELLEY BOLTON AND MERRI SCHWARTZ 🐙 THE CHOCOLATE MAKER

LADIES WHO ARE FULL OF BEANS AND GIVE BACK TO THEIR COMMUNITY IN A BIG WAY.

Chocolate and coffee are two of life's most delightful gifts and two things that many of us would put on our desert island list of must-haves. These two beans make a perfect pairing for good life and good vibrations at East Van Roasters. Shelley Bolton and Merri Schwartz have created a delicious business creating artisan bean-to-bar chocolate and in-house roasted coffee beans. They like to do stuff from scratch here—it's the real deal. What else makes this little 16-seat room extraordinary? The employees.

Chef Andrea Carlson explains it: "Shelley and Merri have created Vancouver's only bean-to-bar roastery under the umbrella of the PHS Community Services Society (PHS)—a nonprofit foundation for people in Vancouver's downtown eastside (DTES). The PHS supports various initiatives including East Van Roasters (EVR) that work with women of the DTES to provide job training and support. Merri and Shelley have done a remarkable job of researching and creating the business from the ground up. Their vision, and that of the PHS, has brought a truly unique and sustainable social enterprise business to our city and provides opportunities and some stability for the women who work with the program. Their chocolate has become so popular they can barely keep up with demand!"

The Rainier Hotel was an amazing project that offered a home, job training, and was a "radical new approach to treating addiction for marginalized women in Vancouver's Downtown Eastside." Sadly it lost funding in 2013 but it is still working to regain financial support.

East Van Roasters sources and uses organic fair trade and direct trade cacao beans and coffee beans, processing and handcrafting them in house under the tutelage of Doug Graf, coffee roaster extraordinaire. The cool thing is that you can enjoy your cuppa joe and chocolate treat while watching the ladies making their magic through the window into the chocolate factory.

"I don't think of EVR as just a job, I think of it as my support network, which has really helped my recovery. When I come to work I look forward to spending time with friends, women that I admire and women/mothers that I can talk to about anything without judgement and receive helpful advice if I ask for it. It's like a family here that supports me in many areas of my life and has helped me tremendously through important life changes I've had over the last year, such as moving out of the DTES and having my daughter come back to live with me."—Danielle, EVR employee

COFFEE SHOP AND CAFE East Van Roasters
LOCATION In the Rainier Hotel, 319 Carrall Street, Vancouver, BC
FB EastVanRoasters   TWITTER @Eastvanroasters   WEB eastvanroasters.com

NICHOL VINEYARD 🍷 THE WINE MAKER

HOME OF THE FAMOUS BLUSHING PINOT GRIS.

Owner/wine maker Ross Hackworth's Nichol Vineyard label is one of Naramata's most recognized and is celebrated for its fine wines. The vineyard that touches the Kettle Valley Railway is one of the first three pioneer vineyards on the Naramata Bench. "The Syrah vineyard was the first to be planted in Canada and consists of 17 rows planted on granite in the northeastern portion of the vineyard. We neither fine nor filter our red wines, use almost entirely used French barriques (neutral), and eschew the use of colour fixers, acidification techniques or 'flavour' and alcohol enhancers. Our wines are technically vegan."

Ross and Nicole Hackworth with son, Nate

WINE MAKER Ross Hackworth   LOCATION 1285 Smethurst Road, Naramata, BC
FB nichol-vineyard   TWITTER @nicholvineyard   WEB nicholvineyard.com

······ FEATURED INGREDIENT ·····················
Notch Cold Brew Coffee and
Apothecary Bitters

1 oz Los Siete Misterios Coyote Mezcal

½ oz Kong Yiji Shoaxing Rice Wine

1 oz Notch Cold Brew Coffee

1 oz Luo Han Guo tea/sweetened
    condensed milk

2 dashes of Apothecary Aromatic Bitters

CHINATOWN EXPRESS COCKTAIL

This rich concoction both relaxes you and gives you a nice kick in the pants! Keenan's cocktails are all unique and combine local ingredients whenever possible. This cocktail has more of an international spin, using Mezcal from a small-batch spirit maker in Mexico and rice wine from China, but it features local bitters and cold brew coffee. The name is in keeping with The Keefer's cool hood in Chinatown.

Shake it up and pour over ice.
    Kapow!

KEENAN HOOD ☵ THE DRINK MAKER

COCKTAIL CHEF.

The Keefer Bar in The Keefer Hotel lies on the edge of Chinatown. The place holds a certain mystique and rates around a 10 in the coolness department. The cocktails are epic and feature exotic herbs and tinctures highlighted by the menu, which is styled after an old apothecary list. Keenan is a manager there and is one of the creative forces behind that cocktail list.

The modern bartender has been referred to as a "liquid chef" because of the incredible usage of herbs, fresh fruits, vegetables, and other kitchen ingredients in their drinks. The time of the pop-and-booze highball is over.

Keenan says, "I felt like a 'born-again bartender' learning all these new drinks with these fresh ingredients. Muddling ginger and cilantro, lemon and peaches, mint, kiwis, and limes, infusing gin with cucumber and lavender, lemon grass and vodka. Man, I was cooking again and I loved it! Being asked by my dear friend Dani Tatarin to come open The Keefer Bar with her has been the most amazing experience of my industry career. Six years ago if I walked through Chinatown and went through some of these shops with smells, weird foreign fruits and spices, and crazy dried creatures it would make my stomach feel queasy, but now that I have worked with so many of the ingredients I have learned to love the smells and have found so many delicious flavours out there!"

"There is a huge amount of cool ingredients that come through our door that are locally made. We are all about supporting our local producers and I appreciate the door-to-door sales—it makes using their products so much more personal. So, hey, local producers! If you have any fun, tasty ingredients out there, come find me!"

BAR The Keefer Bar   LOCATION 135 Keefer Street, Vancouver
TWITTER @thekeeferbar   FB thekeeferbar   WEB thekeeferbar.com

DEVIN LILLY ☕ THE COLD COFFEE BREWER

COOL KID—HOPPED UP ON COLD COFFEE.

Too hot outside to order a cappo? Not into hot drinks? Don't feel like going to a café to order an iced coffee? Need a wicked ingredient to make a cocktail? Notch Coffee has solved these timeless questions by introducing a locally created cold coffee. Devin Lilly came up with the solution. Housed in a pop bottle, Notch Coffee is a smooth cold brew, ready to drink and keep in the fridge at home. Supreme smartness.

"Notch started late last May, when I was approached by a friend who wanted to start a local cold brew coffee company. He was frustrated with the only option for cold brew in Vancouver being from a company out of Portland called Stumptown. I started developing the product throughout the summer and launched it at the Hawkers market in late July," Devin explains.

Devin sources the coffee locally as well as using beans roasted by Bows and Arrows Coffee in Victoria. "Drew (the owner) shares the same passion and vision for coffee." Notch is created using seasonal, single-origin coffees that are exceptionally sweet and clean. The current coffee beans hail from a farm called Quebradón in Huila.

"What makes it unique is our focus on the coffee itself. My focus is brewing coffee to bring out its unique flavour with maximum sweetness. We are meticulous about quality and are always working to improve our product. We want to offer our customers a ready-to-drink coffee experience that's as good as, if not better than they can get at any café, in a convenient and aesthetically pleasing package," Devin says.

COMPANY Notch Coffee   LOCATION 1007 East Cordova St., Vancouver, BC
FB notchcoffee   TWITTER @notchcoffee   WEB notchcoffee.com

COLE BENOIT ⊻ THE BITTERS MAKER

MIXOLOGY NERD. SWEET GUY WHO MAKES BITTER REMEDIES FOR COCKTAILS.

The art of cocktailing continues to rise on the west coast drink scene. What's old is new again with lots of vintage libations coming back into fashion. What's not new is the use of bitters in these concoctions, but what is new is the use of local bitters. Cole Benoit is creating small-batch, craft bitters that are rocking the drink house.

"We're still very much in our infancy as far as ingredients being manufactured here and so that aspect of it is only going to get better and expand. I think it's a great place to be regardless of whether you're a manufacturer, a bartender, or a consumer and it's only going to continue to grow and improve from here on out," says Cole.

How does one get into making bitters?

". . . bitters really caught my attention not only because of the unique history and creative potential but also especially because of the extensive use of botanicals in them; my Dad has a degree in horticulture and when I was a teenager, we lived on an acreage with a massive garden, greenhouse, and extensive forest, so using plants and fresh ingredients is something that has always been a part of my life," says Cole.

"My ultimate favourite has to be our Mystic Caravan Smokey Pear Bitters. I love the use of smoke in all things culinary and beverage related in general, which is why I came up with these bitters. I think the smoke works especially well in these bitters with the tannic notes from the tea, the sweetness of the pears, and the dark spice notes creating a unique and delicious profile that adds a great accent and depth to drinks."

COMPANY The Apothecary Bitters Company   **LOCATION** Vancouver, BC
EMAIL cole@apothecarybitters.com   **WEB** apothecarybitters.com

····· FEATURED INGREDIENT ·····
Out Landish scallops

RICE CRACKER

1 cup white rice, overcooked

1 tsp turmeric

1 Tbsp seafood stock or clam nectar

salt to taste

APPLE CIDER GASTRIC

1 cup apple cider vinegar

2 bay leaves

¼ tsp each chili flakes, cayenne, cumin

1 cup sugar

COCONUT WATER MIXTURE

1 14-oz can coconut water (juice)

2 bay leaves

1 Tbsp peppercorns

BASE

1 14-oz can coconut milk

1 jalapeno pepper, roasted

1 aji amarillo chili, skin removed and deseeded

1 scallion, finely diced

½ red onion, finely diced

1 lime, zested and juiced

1 clove garlic, very finely diced

1 tsp ginger, finely diced

1 pound Ocean Wise scallops,
finely diced

1 15-oz can coconut meat, finely sliced,
    with syrup reserved

COCONUT SCALLOP CEVICHE
ON RICE CRACKERS

This dish tastes as beautiful as it looks! It's fun to make the rice crackers from scratch; there are layers of flavour in this dish. Only use the highest quality Ocean Wise scallops you can find—preferably ones from Out Landish Shellfish.

RICE CRACKER Purée ingredients in a blender until very smooth. Line a baking sheet with parchment paper and spread mixture out as thinly as possible. Leave out overnight to dry. Then another night in oven turned off to dry out more. Break into pieces fry at 350°C until they have doubled in size and are crispy.

APPLE CIDER GASTRIC Combine ingredients in a saucepan and bring to the boil then remove from heat and cool.

Combine Coconut Water Mixture ingredients in a saucepan and then bring to the boil. Remove from heat and let sit for 2 hours.

In a large bowl, combine all of the base ingredients up to the scallops. Then add the coconut water mixture and the scallops and the coconut meat. Drizzle with the apple gastric to taste—depending on how sweet you want it. Let scallops sit for 15 minutes before serving. To garnish, top with cilantro and black sesame seeds. Serve on rice crackers. Tip: Do not leave the scallops in the coconut mixture for any longer than 30 minutes as this dish is best served super fresh. Serve cold.

GARNISH ½ Tbsp cilantro, finely chopped, sprinkling of black sesame seeds

···· **DRINK PAIRING** ····································

Talisman West Coast Pale Ale
"The Siren of the Seas is a fickle creature: benevolent or spiteful, she can bestow a safe passage and a bountiful catch, or provoke storms and shipwrecks. Sailors have long cast gifts of flowers, food, or trinkets into the sea in exchange for good fortune. Talisman is a delicately dry-hopped and golden-hued ale with its tropical and citrusy aroma—may be just the thing to encourage the Siren's blessing."—from the brewery

LEFT TO RIGHT: Ian, Jules, Kathy, and Victor

OUT LANDISH SHELLFISH SEAFOOD GUILD ⛵ THE SEA FARMER

A MERRY BAND OF SHUCKERS.

This marvelous, outlandish band of merrymaking sea farmers is comprised of family-owned shellfish farms scattered around the Discovery Island and Desolation Sound areas in the beautiful west coast waters of BC. The gang includes: Jules Frank and Ian Mowat, Kathy and Victor McLaggan, Troy Bouchard, Michael Gibbons, and Stephanie Milne. A hardworking crew, dedicate to providing "the absolute highest quality shellfish product," they have become the chef and fishmonger's choice of companies to deal with.

If you are a seafood festival type of person, you will have seen some or a couple of the Out Landish crew; usually they are dressed up in fun costumes participating in oyster shucking competitions and generally having a good time (loved the shark outfits). "We love what we do, and we have a lot of fun doing it!" Together, the farmers are able to offer many different products to their customers, including oysters, mussels, clams, and scallops.

Their manifesto includes the promotion and protection of their local waters, and they all use sustainable fishing and harvesting methods, and they are Ocean Wise certified.

Each use different styles and methods of harvesting, which is really cool. For instance: Jules Frank and Ian Mowat own an oyster farm in Frederic Bay off Read Island. Here, they grew their oysters in trays with multiple shelves hung vertically in the water column. Troy Bouchard grows his mussels in socking that hang vertically in the ocean and Kathy and Victor McLaggan grow their oysters both on their intertidal leases and hung from rafts at deep water sites. They also have manila clams that can be dug at low tide.

I have to share this testimonial verse from Patrick McMurray of Pearl Diver Restaurant in Toronto—how many oyster farmers do you know that make chefs wax poetic about them?

"Plump, luscious, salty, sweet,
McLaggan grows shells without feet.
Frilly, beachy, pearly, round
Suck them back with sultry sound."

LOCATION PO Box 497, Heriot Bay, BC   FB outlandish.shellfish
TWITTER @Oshellfish   WEB outlandish-shellfish.com

LEFT TO RIGHT: Iain, Shelome, and Aaron

SHELOME BOUVETTE ✹ THE CHEF

PISCO SOURS ANYONE?

Shelome Bouvette is as delightful and colourful as the food she creates. The former executive chef of Davie Street's hopping Lolita Restaurant, she is now rocking her new digs, Chicha, on the east side of town. From Mexican cuisine to Peruvian, this lady stays ahead of the food trend curve. Shelome fell in love with Peruvian food for the same reason she fell for Mexican, "I love the colours and bright flavours." Before opening shop, she travelled to Peru for the real experience and discovered the fascinating food scene there. This country has such a unique and diverse food culture. Shelome says this is why Peru is estimated to be the next foodie destination, "it has so much to offer which is why Peruvian food is becoming a big thing around the world. Did you know that ceviche comes from Peru? There is a very large community of Peruvian-Japanese

there that created this dish (kind of makes sense right—raw fish prep.) There is also a large Peruvian-Chinese community with its own distinct cuisine."

Shelome says, "In Peru, ceviche is only really served at lunchtime. Fish is caught in the morning and prepared for lunch."

Shelome is one-third of a three-woman partnership at Chicha with Allison Flook and Kumiko Umeno. "Our menu is made from scratch and fresh by us with love," they say, and "it is important to us to feature local produce and go that extra mile to source and support our community." Go girls!

RESTAURANT Chicha Restaurant   LOCATION 136 East Broadway, Vancouver, BC
TWITTER @chichavancouver   FB chicharestaurant   WEB chicharestaurant.com

STRANGE FELLOWS BREWING 🍶 THE BEER MAKER

THE PARTICULARIST AND THE WANDERER MAKING OLD WORLD BREW.

Iain Hill and Aaron Jonckheere are two beer-loving guys that happened to share the same dream of opening a cool brewery.

Iain: A pioneer of BC's craft brewing industry, he has been a professional brewer for over 20 years. He was THE guy that brewed the first traditional Hefeweizen in Canada when he was at Yaletown Brewing.

Aaron: "A passion for craft beer is in my DNA as I am of Belgian

decent and a third-generation home brewer, so you could say I was motivated from an early age to be part of the craft beer scene." Manifesto: A commitment to unique and unapologetic beer, crafted for those who aren't afraid to stand out in the crowd and celebrate that which is strange.

BEER MAKER Iain Hill and Aaron Jonckheere   LOCATION 1345 Clark Drive, Vancouver, BC
FB strangefellowsbrewing   TWITTER @Strange_Fellows   WEB strangefellowsbrewing.com

THE CANNED SALMON MAKER
Don Millerd
Vancouver, BC

THE CHEF
Barbara-jo McIntosh
Vancouver, BC

THE WINE MAKER
Sea Star Vineyards
Pender Island, BC

······· **FEATURED INGREDIENT** ·········
Local canned salmon

1 lb (500 g) package puff pastry

2 7.5 oz (213 g) tins salmon, drained

1 package Uncle Ben's Wild Rice,
    cooked according to directions

2 Tbsp chopped parsley

2 Tbsp chopped dill

3 green onions, finely chopped

zest of 1 lemon

sea salt and freshly ground
    black pepper, to taste

4 eggs, hard-boiled

1 egg, well beaten

SALMON COULIBIAC

"Coulibiac, a hot fish pie, is an innovation of Russian cuisine with worldwide appeal. So, from St. Petersburg, Russia, to St. Petersburg, Florida, this delicious dish is almost as fun to pronounce as it is to eat." —Barbara-jo McIntosh **MAKES 6 SERVINGS**

Prehat oven to 425°F (220°C).

Roll out puff pastry into 2 triangles 6 × 10 in (15 × 25 cm). In a large bowl, combine salmon, wild rice, parsley, dill, green onions, lemon zest, and salt and pepper.

Place 1 pastry triangle on an oiled baking sheet. Spread ½ of rice-salmon mixture over pastry, leaving a ½ in (1 cm) border. Arrange hard-boiled eggs in centre, end to end. Spread remainder of rice mixture in an even layer over eggs. Brush border of pastry with beaten egg. Cover with second pastry triangle and crimp edges to form a tight seal. Chill in refrigerator for 1 hour.

Cut 4 small slits in top. Brush top with beaten egg.

Bake for 10 minutes. Reduce heat to 375°F (190°C) and bake for 30 minutes more, until golden brown.

*Recipe and photo from Barbara-jo's cookbook *Tin Fish Gourmet* reprinted with the permission of Arsenal Pulp Press.

········ **DRINK PAIRING** ···································

2014 Sea Star Vineyards Blanc de Noir
Made with Pinot Noir grapes grown close to the winery by Clam Bay Farm, the fruit is whole-cluster pressed, embellishing the wine with an appealing colour. With hints of strawberry, cranberry, and rhubarb, it also stands proud as a delicious wine to enjoy on its own. "Love this wine and the labels!"—Jennifer Schell

BARBARA-JO MCINTOSH ✳ THE CHEF

THIS COOKBOOK QUEEN WHETS YOUR APPETITE FOR WORDS.

Barbara-jo's original plan did not include owning a cookbook store. Before that vision was realized; she was involved in various capacities of the Vancouver food scene. She recalls, "If you count working in the Marine Room at the legendary Eaton Department store as the beginning of a culinary career, then this is where it began for me, back in highschool. I went on to work five years for Umberto Menghi, attended Dubrulle Culinary School, was catering director at the Mandarin Hotel, and then decided to open my open special events and catering business. A restaurant soon followed."

That restaurant was Barbara-jo's Elegant Home Cooking, and for many years it was a beloved neighbourhood haunt with a menu dedicated to the local farm and fishing scene. When the restaurant was shuttered, Barbara-jo developed a new dream and opened a cookbook shop that had a kitchen. "This new venture filled both the void left from no longer having the restaurant I loved, while also providing my community with a place where people could be entertained, educated and nourished," she explains.

Barbara-Jo's Books to Cooks was an instant success. The original location opened in Yaletown in 1997, and relocated to West 2nd Avenue, Armoury District, in 2005. Cookbook authors and chefs from around the world have crossed the store's threshold to promote their books. "The events take many forms," she explains, "from author chats, to demonstrations to convivial and informative dinner parties, but are always about the book. Such joy can be derived from the stories of chefs and cooks".

As a hub for Vancouver's chefs and foodies, Barbara-jo's bookstore offers much more than just cookbooks; she has crafted a space that encourages and celebrates the culinary arts on every level. Her desire has always been to see people cook more, eat well, and read their cookery books just as they would a novel.

Barbara-jo is an author with three books penned to date. *Tin Fish Gourmet*, *Great Chefs Cook at Barbara-Jo's*, and *Cooking for Me and Sometimes You: A Parisienne Romance with Recipes*. Recently, *Tin Fish Gourmet* was revised and made new.

Barbara-jo too has shared a romance with the sea. She holds close the fishing industry and is an advocate for sustainable oceans, "my romance with the sea has been long, sweet and sad."

SHOP Barbara-Jo's Books to Cooks   LOCATION 1740 West 2nd Avenue, Vancouver, BC
FB Barbara-Jos-Books-to-Cooks   TWITTER @bookstocooks   WEB bookstocooks.com

THE WALLED CITY
WEST VANCOUVER
B.C.

MILLERD AND CO CANNERY ⛵ THE TIN FISH MAKER

PRESERVING THE OCEAN.

The tinned fish business was once was a booming industry on the west coast. Back in the day, Vancouver coastlines were lined with canneries. Technology advances in history like refrigeration hugely affected the demand for tinned fish as consumers no longer had to rely solely on preservation techniques to keep their food. Who knows though, there may just be a renaissance for these canned fish products. In Europe, countries like Spain and France are leaders in canning high-end seafood products.

Francis Millerd was born in Cork, Ireland and arrived to the west coast of Canada in 1907 literally by mistake. He was planning to go to Australia but the ship had to make an emergency stop in Canada. He stayed, got a job at a cannery, and went on to become a giant in the canning industry after purchasing the Great Northern Cannery in the early 1920s.

More than just canning salmon, grandson Don Millerd says, "They canned many products as well as salmon: herring, sardines, clams, smoked salmon. They processed fresh, local shrimp and salted herring for Asia." After many long successful years, with the second generation running the business, the Great Northern Cannery was taken down in 1968. Don Millerd explains, "The cannery was a victim of time and progress. West Vancouver had grown up around it, and the expensive residential real estate was not partial to an old fish cannery. The salmon business in the 1960s was tough. Competition from small companies freezing salmon for export to Japan drove prices up. Canners found it hard to compete. The industry was changing fast, and the long-established companies had a large investment in infrastructure that was no longer as productive."

The cannery was unique in that it was part of a walled village where the employees lived, including Francis Millerd and his family (where Don's father grew up). Don says, "There was a vibrant Japanese community that lived within the cannery walls. There was a general store and a café. It was a walled self-contained community. Dad had loved the business, but was starting to get tired."

TINNED FISH MAKER Don Millerd (Grandson of Francis Millerd)
CANNERY Great Northern Cannery   LOCATION West Vancouver, BC

SEA STAR VINEYARDS 🍷 THE WINE MAKER

AN ISLAND PARADISE WITH DELICIOUS ROSÉ AND CUTE SHEEP—WHAT MORE DO YOU WANT?

Not new to the magic of making wine on the islands, Ian Baker has been in the island wine industry for a long time and was one of the founders of Mistaken Identity Vineyard on Salt Spring Island. Sea Star Vineyards, owned by David Goudge, is located on gorgeous Pender Island with one of the vineyards actually cascading down to the beach (sigh). Both vineyards here were planted in 2002. The Bakers have some wonderful furry (or shall I say wooly) employees. The furry one is the vineyard maintenance supervisor, Hudson and the woolies, the crazy-cute Babydoll Southdown miniature sheep, are the maintenance crew keeping the lawns in manicured form.

Ian and Wendy with Hudson the dog

LOCATION 6621 Harbour Hill Drive, Pender Island, BC   FB seastarestatefarmandvineyards   WEB seastarvineyards.ca

······· ⚓ ·······

STARTERS

★ THE FARMER
Bruce Miller
Pemberton, BC

✳ THE CHEF
James Walt
Whistler, BC

🍶 THE SPIRIT MAKER
Tyler Schramm
Pemberton, BC

········ FEATURED INGREDIENT ········
Across the Creek Organics
Organic German Butter or
Yukon Gold potatoes

100 mL extra virgin olive oil
    or 75 g whole butter

1 medium leek, white part only,
    sliced and rinsed

1 medium white onion, sliced

1 rib celery, sliced

sea salt to taste

2 cloves garlic, sliced

1 bay leaf

3 lbs (1.2 kg) Across the Creek Organics
    Organic German Butter or Yukon Gold
    potatoes, peeled and ¼ inch dice

75 mL dry white wine

2½ litres vegetable or chicken stock
    (brought to a boil)

juice of 1 lemon

60 mL heavy cream or 3 Tbsp crème fraiche
    (can be omitted if need be)

GARNISH

6 slices cold smoked wild salmon

micro herbs or baby salad greens

1 Tbsp wild salmon or trout caviar

CHILLED PEMBERTON POTATO SOUP

In celebration of the potato farming history of Pemberton and of his friend Bruce Miller's fine organic potato farm, Chef Walt created this beautiful soup that makes for a perfect lunch or an elegant starter to a meal. The soup pairs perfectly with a shot of Schramm Organic Potato Vodka, also made with Bruce's spuds! **MAKES APPROXIMATELY 3 LITRES**

In a medium saucepot, add the butter or olive oil with the leeks, onions, celery, small pinch of sea salt, and garlic on medium to low heat. Cook gently until softened and translucent or with very little colour, approximately 7–10 minutes.

Add the bay leaf, potatoes, small pinch of sea salt, and white wine; stir then cook until the wine has reduced almost completely, approximately 4–5 minutes.

Add the heated stock of your choice and simmer (don't boil) until the potatoes have softened; check every 5 minutes with a fork, they should be quite tender.

Once cooked, remove from the heat and add lemon juice and cream and stir.

Let cool slightly, remove the bay leaf, then in a food processor or blender, purée in small batches and strain into a bowl. Check the seasoning and add sea salt if necessary. Place in the fridge to chill for at least four hours or overnight.

To serve, ladle 6–8 ounces (200–250 mL) of soup into chilled bowls. Place the smoked salmon slices on a cutting board and roll them up into rose shapes and place in the soup. Garnish salmon with micro herbs or baby salad greens and top with salmon caviar. Drizzle with extra virgin olive oil if desired.

········ DRINK PAIRING ········

Schramm Organic Potato Vodka
Smoooooth. Nose: Fresh aroma with floral complement. Notes of green mint, chocolate, nougat, and candy. Palate: Bold and round, full body. Distinctively complex. Coffee, vanilla, caramel, peely spiciness, subtle roasted and smokey notes. Finish: Smooth, lengthy finish with a hint of spice.

LEFT TO RIGHT: Bruce and James

BRUCE MILLER ✶ THE FARMER

HANDSOME FARMER GROWS ORGANIC POTATOES AND STRAPPING SONS.

Bruce and his wife, Brenda Miller, own and operate Across the Creek Organics, a fourth-generation family farm (established 1912) that produces the highest quality organic table potatoes on the Lillooet river flood plains. Over the years the Millers have raised five sons on this land and now offer 50 acres of organic potatoes, of which they are one of the largest BC providers.

"My grandfather left his home in Scotland at the age of 17 working his way around the world on merchant ships," says Bruce. "He came to Pemberton in 1896 and carved this farm out of the swamps and wilderness—imagine, no roads, no rail. My father was born here in 1919 and farmed here all his life clearing this land and learning which crops could be grown. I was raised here following my dad around potato fields and chasing cows in alpine pastures. Soon after Brenda and I were married, we started farming

organically and converted the entire farm to certified organic. We raised five amazing boys who were free to breathe the air and splash in any puddle they fancied. There is a river here in the valley named after my grandfather as well as a mountain, which is kind of cool. The history of Pemberton is interesting but the excitement is in the days to come with the new young farmers experimenting with organic farming. Buying food from local farms is definitely growing—there is so much more environmental awareness now, people are choosing a local living lifestyle; it makes them happy and gives them a feeling of fulfillment knowing the farm that grew their food."—Bruce

FARM Across the Creek Organics   **LOCATION** RR#2 Meadows Road, Pemberton, BC
FB Across-the-Creek-Organics   **WEB** acrossthecreekorganics.ca

JAMES WALT ✳ THE CHEF

SPEAKS LOCAVORIAN, PIONEER, FRIEND TO F'S (FARMERS, FORAGERS, FISHERS).

Currently executive chef at Whistler's world-class restaurant, Araxi, James has worked at some of British Columbia's most celebrated restaurants—Sooke Harbour House on Vancouver Island and Blue Water Cafe in Vancouver. James is also author of the bestselling cookbook *Araxi: Seasonal Recipes from the Celebrated Whistler Restaurant*, winner of a Gourmand World Cookbook Award—Best Chef Book in Canada. He was inducted into the British Columbia Restaurant Association Hall of Fame in 2011.

A truly beloved local chef, pioneer, and advocate for sourcing and supporting local farmers and producers, Chef James Walt has created a strong, trusted personal brand from living his legend. His cuisine embodies his philosophy of sourcing direct from BC land and sea and building relationships with local farmers, fishers, foragers, and producers.

"Over the years there have been many fun encounters with the farmers, producers, and foragers. I remember an eighty-plus-year-old, Ernie Knott, carrying a sixty-pound Hubbard squash to the back door of Sooke Harbour House. We offered to carry it, but he was too proud. In Whistler we see a lot of mushroom foragers in the spring and in the fall. It is always hard to say no when the product is really good, so we generally take some from everyone."

James and his wife, Tina, love living in Pemberton. He says, "Being an agricultural community, you meet some of the nicest people and the pace of the town is exactly what we want. My wife and I really wanted our kids to grow up in a friendly small town. It helps being able to go to the farms and pick produce up for the restaurant as well; it keeps us inspired."

Potato farmer Bruce Miller explains, "I met Chef Walt at the Farmers' Market in Whistler. Soon he came to visit the farm to get the dirt on everything we grow. James has always been very supportive of our organic farming efforts. We have a few chefs who source directly from us, but it takes a very dedicated effort to reach the level of local farm support that Chef Walt maintains."

RESTAURANT Araxi Restaurant + Oyster Bar   FB AraxiRestaurant
LOCATION 4222 Village Square, Whistler, BC   TWITTER @araxirestaurant   WEB araxi.com

TYLER SCHRAMM 🍶 THE SPIRIT MAKER

THE SECRET LIFE OF PEMBERTON POTATOES.

In the summer of 2002, brothers Tyler and Jonathan Schramm had an epiphany. While discussing innovative ideas on what to do with Jonathan's potato farm in "potatoland" Pemberton, they came up with a brilliant idea: "Pemberton's fine potatoes and the pristine glacial waters from the mountain creeks would provide the perfect ingredients for an ultra-premium vodka." Hell, yeah! Famous for its potatoes and affectionately known as Spud Valley, Pemberton is a small farming community nestled beneath the snow-capped coastal mountains north of Whistler. After formulating the Schramm plan to build a distillery using local potatoes to make a premium vodka, Tyler set off to learn the craft at Scotland's Heriot-Watt University, a world leader in the field of distilling. In 2009 he and his brothers, Jonathan and Jake, built the distillery together by hand, carefully ensuring that only environmentally friendly systems like a geothermal and cooling system were in place to protect the land. Potato farmer Bruce Miller, who lives up the road, provides organic potatoes from Across the Creek Organics farm as the main ingredient for the vodka, and definitely the secret ingredient as well. The high quality of the organic potatoes makes for an extra silky and smooth textured vodka. A lesson in recycling and a form of composting, Bruce's culled potatoes are the "vodka line" potatoes—nothing goes to waste. Schramm Vodka is made from 100% BC agricultural product and is incredibly smooth—made to be a sipping vodka. They use an all-natural fermentation process without the use of chemicals, synthetic anti-foaming agents, or additives and follow the traditional Scottish methods used in many fine single-malt scotch distilleries.

COMPANY Pemberton Distillery   LOCATION 1954 Venture Pl, Pemberton, BC
TWITTER @pembydistillery   FB Pemberton.Distillery.Inc   WEB pembertondistillery.ca

····· FEATURED INGREDIENT ·········
Vancouver Island Sea Salt

4 lbs frozen cassava (Vij says that frozen whole
   cassava works just as well as fresh cassava,
   and means less work.)
10 cups water
1 Tbsp Vancouver Island Sea Salt
6 cups oil for deep-frying
½ tsp Vancouver Island Sea Salt
½ tsp ground cayenne pepper

CASSAVA FRIES

Cassava is also known as mogo or yucca and comes from Central and South America. You can substitute potatoes in this recipe if you wish. The story of the Cassava Fries—"I was dating an Ismaili girl for a brief time and whenever I went to an Ismaili function, I would have mogo or cassava with tamarind chutney. Years later, when Vij's was open, I took inspiration from her mom's mogo recipe and added my own twist to it. Our menus are always inspired by our experiences in life." —Vikram Vij

Combine frozen cassava, water, and 1 Tbsp salt in large pot. Bring to boil on high heat, then reduce heat to medium, cover, and boil for 25 minutes, or until tender. Drain cassava and cool for 15 minutes.

Cut cassava in half. With a paring knife, remove the tough, string-like fibre that runs the length of the cassava. Discard the fibre, and then cut the cassava in pieces 3 to 4 inches long, about ½ inch wide and ½ inch thick, similar to the size of french fries.

Line a baking tray with paper towels. Preheat a deep fryer to high heat or heat oil in a large heavy-bottomed pan on high heat for 5 minutes.

Drop a small piece of cassava into the oil. It should immediately float to the top and sizzle. Once the oil is hot enough, place fries in the pan and fry for 3 to 4 minutes, or until golden.

Using a slotted spoon, transfer fries to the paper towels to drain any excess oil. Sprinkle fries with the ½ tsp of salt (or black salt) and the cayenne while they are still hot.

···· DRINK PAIRING ····································

caution: *intense*
hand crafted beer

Hurricane IPA (aka Vij's On Tap)
India Pale Ale dates back to the 1700s when the British needed a way to ship beer across the seas to troops in India. The answer—copious amounts of hops and a higher alcohol content to prevent spoilage and maintain the flavour of their ales. The result is a rich, golden, intense beer with bitterness in perfect balance with residual sweetness—7% ABV.

···

"I always like to work with people who
have crazy ideas—if they're crazier than
mine, that's even better!"—Vikram

···

LEFT TO RIGHT: Andrew and Vikram

VIKRAM VIJ ✲ THE CHEF

THE FOOD MAHARAJAH OF THE WEST COAST.

The legend—Vikram Vij is one of the brightest culinary stars and heroes of the west coast and Canadian food scene. He achieved the highest success in the restaurant business when Vij's, the flagship restaurant belonging to Vij and his wife and partner, Meeru Dhalwala, was described by Mark Bittman in the *New York Times* as "easily among the finest Indian restaurants in the world." Over the years they have significantly expanded their brand, opening a more casual-style eatery next door called Rangoli, which also offers their gourmet pre-packaged Indian cuisine, as well as their latest endeavour, Vij's Railway Express, a Vancouver-based food truck! They also have a successful new restaurant in Surrey, My Shanti, as well as Meeru's own new US venture, Shanik Restaurant, which has made a fiery splash onto the Seattle food scene.

Aside from being a restaurateur, Vikram became a television celebrity as a "dragon" on the Canadian reality show *Dragons' Den* in 2014. He is also an award-winning author, a chef, a sommelier,

and an overall incredible force of personality. Bursting at the seams with energy, Vikram has a sense of humour and booming laugh that also make him the stuff of legends.

Vikram was born and raised in India and, after completing his studies in hotel management, chef, and sommelier training in Europe, he arrived in Vancouver in 1989 where he worked under iconic Chef John Bishop. "My first memory (after arriving in Vancouver) is of eating from a buffet in the Punjabi Market at 49th and Main. Everything about it—the spices, the jewellery, the smells, the colours—reminded me of home. It's such a vivid memory for me." Vikram opened his tribute to home, Vij's, in 1994 with the help of his parents who, "In the early days would make the curry at their home and deliver it by bus to the restaurant."

RESTAURANT Vij's Restaurant   LOCATION 1480 W 11th Ave, Vancouver, BC
FB Vijs   TWITTER @Vijs_restaurant   WEB vijsrestaurant.ca

ANDREW SHEPHERD ⛵ THE SEA SALT MAKER

IN SALT WE TRUST.

Chef Andrew Shepherd, a self-proclaimed "proud Maritimer" grew up in Halifax on the rugged east coast. "I always remember my first look at the Pacific when I was about 18, it's so different than the Atlantic, it's way more inviting and I immediately wanted to throw myself in! To live on this island now and make my living from the Pacific (which I jump in all year long) gives me an incredible feeling of having found my place and my calling . . . call it super salty zen."

After moving to Vancouver Island Andrew wondered why Canada did not make a sea salt? A friend remarked, "If it could be done, it would be done." Andrew took that as a challenge and bet his friend a case of beer that it could be done. He set up camp on the beach and spent the night boiling down seawater over a fire. In the morning, the first ever batch of Vancouver Island Sea Salt was harvested.

"I always knew I'd win the bet," says Andrew, "as a chef, the principle that water evaporates while salt concentrates was burned into my brain by Chef Higgins at George Brown College when I was a student. What blew me away, and continues to blow me away is the reaction I received when I showed my first batch to other chefs and foodies. It was the strong reaction of chefs that gave me the idea that there was more to this salt thing than a night at the beach and some beers."

Vancouver Island Sea Salt now creates a variety of flavoured sea salts—from smoked and spiced to the coveted flakes of Fleur de Sel (flowers of salt), the first layer of sea salt that are hand-harvested from the salt vats. "Nothing is added," explains Andrew, "(no chemicals, no additives, no anti-caking agents)—just all the best our clean ocean has to offer!"

HEADQUARTERS Vancouver Island Salt Co.   LOCATION 4235 Telegraph Road, Cobble Hill, BC
TWITTER @vanislesalt   FB vancouverislandsaltco   WEB visaltco.com

"A complex, flavourful and fascinating
ale lies just on the edge of being totally
out of control."—Stephen Beaumont,
Celebrator Beer News

STORM BREWING 🍶 THE BEER MAKER

THERE IS A STORM A BREWING IN EAST VAN.

In the newly cool East Village neighbourhood of Vancouver, you will sense notes of hops in the air as you enter the graffiti-covered alleyway leading you into the eye of Storm. The place is rockstar-chic and infested with rats—plastic rats that is, a symbol of the rebellious nature of Vancouver's first microbrewery. The sign on the wall says, "We put rats on things."

Brewmaster/owner James Walton, who is known to sport KISS-style platform shoes to accessorize his spiky hair and multi-piercings, opened up shop in the hood back in 1995 (before the area became cool), and actually lived at the brewery while he grew the now super prosperous business. Storm brews are unfiltered and additive free.

LOCATION 310 Commercial Dr, Vancouver, BC   FB StormBrewing
TWITTER @stormbrewingvan   WEB stormbrewing.org

⭑ THE FARMER
Donna Plough
Abbotsford, BC

☸ THE CHEF
Quang Dang
Vancouver, BC

♀ THE WINE MAKER
Terravista Vineyards
Naramata, BC

········· FEATURED INGREDIENT ·········
Glen Valley artichokes

ARTICHOKES

6 Glen Valley artichokes

1 lemon, cut in half

6 Tbsp white wine vinegar

6 Tbsp kosher sea salt

PARSLEY SAUCE

1 bunch Italian parsley, picked

1 tsp salt

1 tsp sugar

2 Tbsp grapeseed oil

DUNGENESS CRAB AND LEEK STUFFING

2 Tbsp butter

1 leek, julienned

½ lb Dungeness crabmeat, picked fresh

1 Tbsp flat leaf parsley, roughly chopped

1 lemon, juiced

½ tsp togorashi chilli powder

salt and pepper

GLEN VALLEY
ARTICHOKES STUFFED WITH DUNGENESS CRAB,
LEEKS & PARSLEY SAUCE

This dish is a beautiful celebration of two west coast treasures: glorious Dungeness crab and Glen Valley's beautiful artichokes. This is a perfect starter dish or serves as part of an elegant brunch or lunch menu. Quang explains, "Glen Valley Artichokes is a farm that is unique to the Fraser Valley; artichokes are a challenge to grow and they are one of the few farmers in BC willing to grow them." SERVES 4

ARTICHOKES Wash the artichokes. To obtain the flesh from the heart of the artichoke, start by tearing off the first three layers of leaves working your way up from the stem to the top. Chef's note: wear latex gloves on one of your hands to help prevent the tips of the leaves from poking you. Remove the green leaves only—once you see yellow on the leaves, stop. Using a sharp knife, cut the top of the artichoke off about 1 inch down. Holding the artichoke in your hand and using a paring knife, cut around the artichoke carefully until you reach the heart. Trim off all of the green skin leaving the yellow colored artichoke heart. Immediately rub the heart with fresh lemon juice to prevent it from oxidizing. Store in acidulated cold water (a few good squeezes of lemon juice added to a container of water) until you are ready to cook them. Place the artichokes into a pot large enough to fit all of the artichokes and water to cover them. Add the vinegar and salt. You may need to add a bit more of the salt and vinegar, so taste the poaching liquid (it should be quite seasoned, yet balanced). Place a small kitchen towel on top of the artichokes to help keep them submerged. Cook on medium heat until fork tender. Remove from heat. Let the artichokes cool in the liquid. Once cool, using a sturdy spoon scoop out the middle of the artichoke heart (the choke, the furry fibrous stuff in the middle) and discard.

PARSLEY SAUCE Bring a pot of water to boil, blanch the parsley for 30 seconds. Strain it through a fine sieve. Place into a high powered blender, add salt, sugar, and oil and blend until you have a smooth purée. Strain though a fine mesh sieve and set aside.

DUNGENESS CRAB AND LEEK STUFFING In a sauté pan over medium heat, add the butter and leeks and sweat until the leeks are tender. Add the crabmeat and mix well and heat until the crabmeat is warm. Fold in the parsley, lemon juice, and togorashi. Season to taste. Stuff into the hollowed out artichokes and serve immediately with parsley sauce.

········· DRINK PAIRING ·········

2012 Terravista Vineyards Fandango
A blend of two white grape varieties, Albarino and Verdejo, this is the only wine of these grapes produced in Canada! Complex, yet delicate aromas of crushed herbs mingled with scents of early summer pear, peach, and melon. Freshness reigns over the palate with energy and balanced tension that lasts well after the last drop.

TERRAVISTA VINEYARDS ♀ THE WINE MAKER

DO THE FANDANGO!

Terravista is owned and operated by wine country veterans Bob and Senka Tennant. Bob and Senka are the legendary original owners/creators of Black Hills Winery in Oliver, Senka as wine maker and Bob as vineyard and business operator. The couple sold in 2007 to seek a smaller vineyard and build a new label, happily landing on the beautiful Naramata Bench. Making only two labels, both blends, the wines are delightful and complex, each achieving an instant fan club. Not surprising, as Senka is known for creating cult wines (ahem . . . *nota bene!*).

WINE MAKER Senka Tennant   **LOCATION** 1853 Sutherland Road, Penticton, BC
TWITTER @terravistavines   **WEB** terravistavineyards.com

QUANG DANG ✳ THE CHEF

LOVE ON A PLATE.

Quang Dang is a culinary star of Vancouver's food scene and a champion of west coast cuisine. Originally from Calgary, he serendipitously began has career at celebrated West Restaurant as sous chef to David Hawksworth and, after many years of honing his skills, he returned in 2011 to become executive chef.

He has trained for the Olympics, studied engineering, competed at the Bocuse d'Or—this guy is impressive and unique. With a background that includes Scottish and Vietnamese influence, it is not a surprise that his palate would have experienced a range of flavours and ingredients at a young, impressionable age. On his choice of career Quang articulates, "Cheffing is the kind of career that is more of a lifestyle than a job; everything that you do is relevant to being a chef."

Quang's personal beliefs and philosophy on sourcing locally and ethically make him a leader in this style of cooking. The West Restaurant website has a list of the local purveyors used in the menu—it is a remarkable and long list. "Throughout my career I have maintained great relationships with my farmers, fishermen, purveyors etc. From a final plate point of view, great products make great dishes. With great products it becomes my duty as a chef to showcase all of the farmer's passion and love onto a plate. Farmers and chefs tend to have similar outlooks on life: both work hard, work long hours and money is not the primary reason why chefs/farmers do what they do. Supporting the local food producers is very important as well. The best part of our local food production is the quality of ingredients our farmers produce. Maintaining the chef to farmer relationship is a key to maintaining the local food movement. At the end of the day we all want people to eat as best as possible."

RESTAURANT West Restaurant   LOCATION 2881 Granville Street, Vancouver, BC
FB WestRestaurantVan   TWITTER @westrestaurant   WEB westrestaurant.com

⚓

DONNA PLOUGH ✳ THE FARMER

CHOKED UP ABOUT ARTIES.

Long have artichokes been the symbol for gourmands and foodies, they are actually a perennial in the thistle group of the sunflower family. The artichoke has also gained a reputation as a sexy veggie, thanks partly to Marilyn Monroe, who became California's first Artichoke Queen in February 1948.

Donna and John Plough own and operate a 20-acre farm in the Fraser Valley featuring artichokes (or as Donna affectionately calls them "arties"). They start 35,000 artichoke plants each year in their greenhouse and plant them out in the field in the spring and each plant can bear about five to ten artichokes. A bucolic farm setting, they are bordered by commercial blueberry and cranberry operations to the west and north, and hayfields and an organic dairy farm on the other sides. The use of pesticides, fungicides, and herbicides are not employed on the farm. Instead, natural insect predators are encouraged, such as birds and ladybugs. They have also dedicated five acres of the farm's forested area to the Land Conservancy—"firmly believing in the need to preserve our forest lands."

"We went into the farming business quite naturally," Donna shares. "My hubby John has a diploma from the West of Scotland Agricultural College and I come from a family with strong farming backgrounds. We raised beef cattle for a while, then wanted to grow a different crop. John met Pat Bowman at the Agassiz Research Centre. She was working with artichokes at the time and we were looking for a niche crop, and that is how the farm started. They are one of the best vegetables for antioxidants, full of minerals and vitamins, and are well documented as a liver detoxifier. You will notice that they mainly grow along coastlines due to the mist from the ocean, and Glen Valley has a lot of morning mist so they do quite well here."

FARM Glen Valley Artichoke Farm LOCATION 28182 Marsh McCormick Road, Abbotsford, BC
FB glenvalleyartichokes   TWITTER @bcartichokes   WEB glenvalleyartichokes.com

⭐ THE FARMER
Julia Smith
Burnaby, BC

☸ THE CHEF
Adrian Beaty
Langley, BC

🍷 THE WINE MAKER
Kettle Valley Winery
Naramata, BC

····· FEATURED INGREDIENT ·····
Urban Digs veggies

1 lb Urban Digs organic salad greens

SALAD DRESSING
150 m hazelnut oil
150 mL apple cider vinegar
10 assorted Urban Digs radishes
    (save greens for radish top oil),
    thinly sliced (approx. 2 bunches)
60 mL shallots, minced
5 mL sea salt

RADISH TOP OIL
1 bunch Urban Digs parsley,
    tough stems removed
Reserved greens from 2 bunches
    of Urban Digs radishes
1 cup vegetable oil

BEET MARMALADE
1 kg Urban Digs red beets
28 grams unsalted butter
2 medium red onions, peeled and julienned
75 mL balsamic vinegar
75 mL brown sugar
10 mL sea salt

HERBED CHÈVRE
454 grams chèvre
5 mL sea salt
2.5 mL fresh ground black pepper
10 grams shallots, minced
6 grams Italian parsley, minced
5 grams thyme, minced

HERBED CHÈVRE ⟨with⟩ PICKLED RADISH
ORGANIC GREENS & BEET MARMALADE

Chef Beaty sources many ingredients from Julia at Urban Digs—both animal and vegetable. He chose to celebrate her beautiful, organic vegetables in this recipe, leaving the piggies as friends—only for the photo op. SERVES 4–6

RADISHES AND SALAD DRESSING Combine all ingredients. Allow to sit a minimum of 2 hours or as long as overnight.

RADISH TOP OIL Rinse parsley and radish tops; blanche in boiling water for 1 minute. Remove and shock in ice water. Squeeze dry and purée with vegetable oil. Allow to sit overnight, then strain through a fine strainer.

BEET MARMALADE Boil beets till tender, peel, and grate. Set aside. Heat butter in heavy bottomed saucepot, add onion, and gently cook for 20–30 minutes until caramelized. Add vinegar, sugar, salt, and grated beets and reduce until thick and jam-like, then cool. *Makes more than you need for this recipe, will keep 7–10 days in the fridge.

HERBED CHÈVRE Combine all ingredients. *Can be made several days in advance.

TO ASSEMBLE Remove radishes from the vinaigrette. Lightly toss greens with some of the hazelnut vinaigrette (reserving any extra dressing for another use). Place some of the herbed chèvre on plate and top with dressed greens. Make a quenelle (an oval shape by using two spoons) with beet marmalade and place off to side. Place radishes around plate and finish with a drizzle of the radish top oil. Enjoy.

···· DRINK PAIRING ·········

2011 Kettle Valley Riesling
This is a classic German style Riesling that exhibits honey, peach, pineapple and spicy notes with nice crisp acidity and a touch of residual sugars to add richness and weight to the finish. The grapes were de-stemmed, but not crushed, and allowed to sit on their skins for 2 days to extract more flavour compounds. After pressing, the juice was clarified and fermented cold to add complexity and build mouth-feel. "We choose Kettle Valley's Riesling because the balance of acidity and residual sugars go very well with the complexity of this recipe," says Adrian.

LEFT TO RIGHT: Julia, William, and Adrian

ADRIAN BEATY ☸ THE CHEF

GUARDIAN OF LOCAVORISM. COOKS FOR LOVE.

Chef Adrian was actually planning to study law, not food, when he had an epiphany. Throwing himself headlong into the world of cookery came about in an effort to woo his now-wife, Shannon. He describes his awakening as "going from being an inspiration to obsession," and he decided to drop out of university to enroll in "restaurant kitchen 101."

Adrian now happily operates his catering business, Seasonal Experience, and restaurant, Seasonal 56, from his space on 56th Avenue in Langley where he has "fulfilled his passion for working with local growers and producers."

A recent blog post of his called "No more Mr. Nice Guy" wonderfully embodies his philosophies. From the blog post: "Something that is really starting to piss me off is the whole 'local' thing. I go to many restaurants that say they are 'local.' Buying and supporting local is something that I really believe in. In fact, it is the idea that

drives our business. It is NOT a buzzword that we use to get asses in seats. So many restaurants say they support local. But what is local? Is it buying inhumanely raised animals from a nearby animal factory? Or buying produce from a big international food distribution company that buys 'local' produce from large producers who sell genetically modified products? Or is 'local' meeting farmers, learning about their practices, and supporting them directly? As you can see, 'local' means a lot of things to different people . . . For years now, I have told people to get to know your farmer; well, maybe it's time to get to know your restaurateur!"

Read the rest of this blog post and others on his website. Bravo, Adrian.

RESTAURANT Seasonal 56 Restaurant   LOCATION 201–26730 56 Avenue, Langley
FB Seasonal56   TWITTER @seasonal56   WEB seasonal56.ca

JULIA SMITH ✳ THE FARMER

URBAN FARMER WITH A BIG HEART AND CONSCIENCE. FRIEND OF PIGS.

Julia Smith is one of the most passionate, ethical farmers you will ever meet. Her strength of principle, passion, and her heartfelt farming ethics are admirable. She is a food hero who has the gumption to speak freely of her values and demands of the farming industry and educates consumers about ethical farming practice. Her goal is to bring forth to her customers the most healthful vegetables and happy animals and to support her community. Yay for Julia! She stumbled into the farming lifestyle by chance and is a first-generation farmer. Julia explains, "I always tell people that I think it's a virus. Neither my partner, (Ludo Ferrari) nor I had any family history of farming or personal experience when we started farming. We live in uncertain times. The global economy is unstable. Our reliance on fossil fuels makes us vulnerable. Climate change is upon us. Our food system is in crisis. A career in agriculture seemed more likely to give me any control or influence over these challenges." Julia is well educated in farm-speak and the state of livestock production, and explains what solutions and measures she is taking at Urban Digs: "Many well-meaning consumers would be shocked to learn that much of the meat being marketed as 'sustainable' or 'ethical' is produced indoors using GMO feed, antibiotics, and confinement systems like gestation crates. There are organizations certifying animal welfare, like the SPCA for example, so asking if a farm is SPCA certified is a good place to start. Consumers have to do their homework and use their best judgment. At Urban Digs we choose to feed as little commercial feed as possible, taking advantage of the abundant food waste generated as a byproduct of the human food system. Spent brewery grains, over-ripe and imperfect fruits and vegetables, stale bakery goods, and whey from cheese making make up a large component of our animal's diets. I believe that giving animals liberal access to a natural, outdoor environment is the only way to meet their unique physiological needs." The farm offers a Beasty Box for sale, which is a "nose to tail" butchery box. The meat is sourced locally from small-scale farms that practice sustainable farming methods. Animals are naturally and ethically raised without antibiotics or hormones in an environment that allows them to express their unique physiological distinctness. "We bring in whole animals and use every part of them."

company Urban Digs Farm   LOCATION 4992 Byrne Road, Burnaby, BC
FB urban.digs   TWITTER @UrbanDigsFarm   WEB urbandigsfarm.com

"Food should be produced in a balanced agro-ecosystem. The system should be both economically and environmentally sustainable and provide a healthy, nurturing environment to the people, soil, plants, and animals that make up the system."—Julia Smith

KETTLE VALLEY WINERY ♀ THE WINE MAKER

WINE ON THE RIGHT SIDE OF THE TRACKS.

This family farm winery began as a hobby for brothers-in-law Bob Fergusson and Tim Watts. The two started their winemaking careers in Tim and wife Janet's apartment in the '80s. Soon the hobby turned to passion and a need to grow their own grapes. So they, along with their wives, sisters Janet and Colleen, bought some land in the still orchard-heavy area of Naramata and planted their first vines in 1987. The dream became reality with their first vintage released in 1992, after applying for and receiving the third winery license for the area!

The winery's name is a celebration of the history of the area, specifically the Kettle Valley Railway that ran through Naramata between 1915 and 1961, connecting the Southern Interior of British Columbia to the markets of the Pacific Northwest.

WINE MAKERS Bob Fergusson and Tim Watts   LOCATION 2988 Hayman Road, RR#1, Site 2, Comp. 39, Naramata, BC
FB kvwinery   TWITTER @kvwinery   WEB kettlevalleywinery.com

THE SEA FARMER
Steve Pocock
Quadra Island, BC

THE CHEF
Wayne Sych
Vancouver, BC

THE WINE MAKER
Church & State Wines
Saanich, BC

······ FEATURED INGREDIENT ······
Sawmill Bay oysters

2 Tbsp butter

1 celery stalk, chopped

1¼ cups fennel bulb, cleaned and chopped

¾ cups leeks, white part only, chopped

1 Tbsp fresh parsley, chopped

½ tsp fresh thyme leaves

2 cloves garlic, minced

4¼ cups fresh spinach leaves, lightly packed

2 Tbsp Pernod

½ tsp salt

¼ tsp fresh ground pepper

2–3 drops Tabasco sauce

16 Sawmill Bay large size fresh oysters

⅔ cups Grana Padano Parmesan
    cheese, grated (for baking)

Paprika to garnish

HOLLANDAISE SAUCE

(MAKES A LITTLE MORE THAN A CUP)

1 cup clarified butter

8 large egg yolks

pinch cayenne

1 Tbsp fresh lemon juice

2–3 drops Tabasco sauce

1–2 drops Worcestershire sauce

1 Tbsp white wine

salt to taste

OYSTERS ROCKEFELLER

Chef Jules Alciatore created this luxurious baked oyster dish recipe at Antoine's Restaurant in New Orleans in 1899, and that original recipe remains a secret to this day. It is named for the super-wealthy Rockefeller family because of its glorious richness. Chef Wayne Sych has created his own lush spin using beautiful oysters from Sawmill Bay Shellfish Co.'s sea farm located on the crystal-clear waters of Read Island. MAKES 4 LARGE APPETIZER PORTIONS

Over medium heat melt the butter. Add the celery, fennel, leeks, parsley, thyme, and garlic. Sauté until the vegetables are soft about 4–5 minutes; be careful not to brown them. Add the spinach, Pernod, salt and pepper, and toss until the spinach is wilted— 2–3 minutes. Remove from heat; add the Tabasco. While the mixture is still warm, purée in a food processor until smooth. This can be prepared a day ahead—store in refrigerator. Shuck the fresh oysters and gently remove the meat. Save the bottom shells and wash thoroughly removing any excess oyster meat. If the shells are in too poor shape to use as the base to bake with, use ovenproof ramekins. Bring a large pot of water to a rolling boil. Plunge the oyster meat into the water and let simmer for 1 minute. Remove oyster meat from pot with a slotted spoon and place on absorbent towels. Do not place in ice water. This can be done a day ahead. It is important to pre-poach the oysters; otherwise the finished recipe will be runny.

TO ASSEMBLE THE ROCKEFELLERS Preheat oven to 375°F. On the bottom of each oyster shell or ramekin place about a tablespoon of the vegetable mixture, place a pre-poached oyster on top and sprinkle with Parmesan cheese. Place on a baking sheet and bake uncovered for 10–12 minutes until hot. Remove from oven; spoon hollandaise sauce over each one (recipe follows), sprinkle with paprika, serve immediately. *A trick to keep the oysters from rocking around on the plate is to pour coarse salt on the plate and sit the baked oysters on top of the salt.

HOLLANDAISE SAUCE To clarify the butter, begin with about ¾ lbs of butter. Melt butter in a saucepan over medium heat; skim off any solids that float to the top. With a ladle carefully remove the butter leaving any of the milk solids on the bottom of the saucepan. It is important that you end up with 1 cup of clarified butter. Set aside and keep warm. Place egg yolks, cayenne, lemon juice, Tabasco, Worcestershire sauce, and white wine in a stainless steel bowl. Place egg yolk mixture over a pot of low simmering water. Whisk constantly until egg yolks thicken and are at the ribbon stage. Remove egg yolks from the double boiler and slowly pour in melted butter until incorporated. Season with salt. If hollandaise is thick, add a few drops of warm water. It is important to whisk the egg yolks constantly and to add the warm butter slowly as it will separate the sauce. Serve immediately.

······ **DRINK PAIRING** ···

2012 Church & State Gravelbourg Chardonnay
This truly memorable chardonnay features aromas of golden delicious apples, lemon crème fraîche, vanilla bean, and subtle notes of peach and apricot.

LEFT TO RIGHT: Steve and Wayne

STEVE POCOCK ⛵ THE SEA FARMER

HE SELLS SEA SHELLS BY THE SEA SHORE.

A family-run sea farm, Sawmill Bay Shellfish Company is owned and operated by Steve and Linda Pocock out of Heriot Bay on Quadra Island. The couple explains: "We have no history of fishing/sea farming, but have always been involved in farming of one sort or another—we were drawn solely by the love of the coast and of course farming!"

Their oyster farms (or, as they are officially referred to, leases) are both operated in the pristine, glacier-fed waters off of Read Island. This tiny island has a year-round population of approximately 50 people, doubling in the summer, and it is boat access only. This allows favourable, unpolluted conditions to grow the shellfish with less human contamination. Steve says, "One farm is in Dunsterville

Bay and is a deep water farm of roughly 10 acres where we grow mussels and oysters—this is where juvenile oysters are raised. The other farm is in Sawmill Bay—a beach lease of 12 acres—where we grow oysters and clams."

The Pococks pride themselves on delivering the freshest shellfish possible and offer direct delivery after harvest—no holding tanks are used here. They operate in an environmentally sustainable and ethical manner. Steve explains, "We use a homemade lifting gantry to lift stacks of trays out of the water for sorting—an environmentally friendly device, hand operated with a rope pulley."

SEA FARM Sawmill Bay Shellfish Company **LOCATION** Box 233, Heriot Bay, BC
FB Sawmill-Bay-Shellfish **WEB** sawmillbay.ca

WAYNE SYCH ☀ THE CHEF

A PEARL OF A CHEF.

For over twenty-nine years, Joe Fortes has remained a favourite hangout for Vancouverites and visitors. It has outstanding service, delicious food, and the gorgeous digs don't hurt either—including a most magical rooftop garden bar.

Chef Wayne, as he is affectionately known, is part of the welcome vibe at Fortes. His wide smile and enthusiasm for his food and his restaurant are contagious and what makes guests return again and again (if you have more than a few agains, you might even get a plaque at a bar stool as a thank you for your loyalty). He says, "Being a part of The Fish House, The Cannery, and now Joe's, I am fortunate to have had the opportunity to work in such great iconic seafood restaurants."

The anchor of the restaurant is the oyster bar, featuring a wide selection of east and west coast oysters. They serve over 500,000 oysters a year! Chef Wayne likes dealing with his local suppliers like Sawmill Bay Oysters and explains, "I like Steve's oysters because I like dealing directly with him, the farmer. He delivers them himself most of the time; twice a week he stops in here at Joe's. Knowing that his oysters are harvested and delivered right away makes me feel good about serving them to our guests."

This local legend of a restaurant is named for another local legend and hero, Joe Fortes. Yes, he was a real man—a very special man who was a lifeguard, swimming instructor in English Bay, and friend to all, especially children. In the early 1900s he devoted his time to the local waters, teaching children to swim and patrolling the beach, and over that time became a hero by saving many lives. The self-appointed unpaid lifeguard continued to support himself by working odd jobs until one day in 1900 when the City appointed him its first official lifeguard.

RESTAURANT Joe Fortes Seafood & Chop House LOCATION 777 Thurlow Street, Vancouver
FB JoeFortesVan TWITTER @JoeFortesVan WEB joefortes.ca

> "Joe Fortes serves over
> 500,000 oysters per year."

CHURCH & STATE WINES ♟ THE WINE MAKER

CLASSY, SASSY, SMART-ASSY

With vineyards and wineries both on properties in Vancouver Island and Oliver, Kim Pullen with wine maker Jeff Del Nin and team have been creating a wide range of red and whites for over 10 years. Their winemaking philosophy focuses on the concept of balance "a balance between the head and the heart, between change and tradition."

This balance is apparent through their new line of Lost Inhibitions labels that are crazy fun as opposed to the more, serious classic style of their original Church & State line. And, to borrow from one of their rad new label series, THIS IS EFFING EPIC!

LOCATION 1445 Benvenuto Avenue, Central Saanich, BC FB churchandstatewines
TWITTER @churchstatewine WEB churchandstatewines.com

John Pullen, marketing manager

THE SEA FARMER
Northern Divine Sturgeon
Sunshine Coast, BC

THE CHEF
Chris Whittaker
Vancouver, BC

THE WINE MAKER
Covert Farms Family Estate
Oliver, BC

······ **FEATURED INGREDIENT** ······
Northern Divine white sturgeon

¾ cup bacon, cut into batons

⅓ cup salted butter

2 cups celeriac, diced

2 cups onion, diced

1 cup leeks, diced

1 cup carrots, diced

¼ cup flour

½ cup white wine

3 cups sturgeon (or white fish) stock

1 ½ cups heavy cream

2 cups tomato, diced

1¼ cups potato, diced

½ tsp Riesling vinegar

1 tsp Italian parsley, finely chopped

1 tsp thyme, finely chopped

1 pound Northern Divine sturgeon

salt and white pepper to taste

CHICHARON GARNISH

1 pound pork skin (fat removed and diced)

3 cups water

1 tsp salt

1 egg

CREAMY NORTHERN DIVINE STURGEON CHOWDER
WITH POACHED EGG & SMOKEY CHICHARON

Chef Whittaker is known by many as the Chowder King for his multiple wins at the annual Chowder Chowdown fundraiser in Vancouver. Chef says to feel free to substitute other sustainable seafood in place of the sturgeon—local spot prawns, salmon, halibut, or sablefish—they will all work wonderfully, as the base of this incredible chowder will make any seafood sing! **SERVES 4–6**

CHOWDER Heat a saucepan over medium heat and add the bacon and butter. Once the butter has melted and the bacon has begun to render, add celeriac, onion, leeks, and carrots. Sauté until the vegetables become translucent and then add the flour and mix until incorporated. Cook for about 5 minutes on low heat and then deglaze the pan with white wine. Once alcohol has cooked off (about 1 minute) add the fish stock and turn the heat back up to medium. Add the heavy cream, diced tomatoes, and potatoes. Cook for an additional 30 minutes on a gentle simmer and then add the Riesling vinegar, parsley, and thyme. Stir in the raw sturgeon and cook for an additional 2 minutes. Season with salt and white pepper.

CHICHARON GARNISH Place first three ingredients in a pot and bring to a boil. Cook for at least 30 minutes. Strain and dry in 180°F oven for 6 hours or until completely dry. Place in 350°F frying oil until they puff nicely. Remove and season with salt. At this point, lightly smoke with Applewood chips for 10–15 minutes (optional). Bring water to boil in a saucepan, add egg and poach until soft (2–3 minutes depending on egg size), remove to paper towel to drain. Place chowder in bowl of your choice and garnish with soft poached egg and chicharon—fried pork rinds. Eat!

······ **DRINK PAIRING** ······

2013 Covert Family Estate Amicitia White Blend
A Roussanne, Viognier, Semillon blend, the name (ah-mee-CHEE-tee-ah) is Latin for friends, which also wonderfully reflects the relationship of the varietals in this blend. Opulent and juicy, with flavours of dried apricots, preserved lemons, and white peach, it offers a generous yet complicated finish.

Justin

NORTHERN DIVINE STURGEON ⛵ THE SEA FARMER

A PLACE WHERE CAVIAR MEISTERS AND SHARK WRANGLERS HANG OUT.

Northern Divine Sturgeon are farmed at Target Marine Hatcheries on the beautiful Sunshine Coast and are Canada's only producer of certified organic, farmed Fraser River white sturgeon. The farm raises sturgeon from egg through to full-size fish, each weighing in at around a hefty 300 lbs.

In August 2006, the Canadian federal government officially listed the Kootenay, Nechako, Upper Columbia, and Upper Fraser rivers white sturgeon populations for protection under the Species At Risk Act (SARA). White sturgeon are a prehistoric breed and one of the largest fish species in the world. Native to the Fraser River, they can grow a maximum size of six metres (19 feet) and 800 kilograms (1,800 pounds) and can live over 100 years.

In 1999 Vancouver Island University donated Fraser River sturgeon to Target Marine Hatcheries and the owners took on the challenge to raise these prehistoric fish. Using a land based water recirculation system that uses fresh ground water from the surrounding lakes and streams close to their 60-acre farm, they were successful in the relocation project. 2011 marked a momentous occasion when the hatchery was able to produce its first batch of Northern Divine Caviar, which is currently rated as one of the best sustainable caviars in the world.

Target Marine Hatcheries has many interesting employees, from a caviar meister to a shark wrangler. Justin Henry is a fish farmer and a self-proclaimed "fish nerd." Justin studied aquaculture at UBC, and aquaculture biotechnology at Aalborg University in Denmark. Justin also chairs the Canadian General Standards Board Committee, which developed the Canadian Organic Aquaculture Standard.

SEA FARM Northern Divine Sturgeon/Target Marine Hatcheries
LOCATION 7333 Sechelt Inlet Road, The Sunshine Coast, BC
TWITTER @CanadianCaviar   FB NorthernDivineCaviar   WEB northerndivine.com

CHRIS WHITTAKER ✴ THE CHEF

"FORAGE IS ABOUT GOODNESS, ABOUT TAKING CARE OF EACH OTHER, AND BRINGING TOGETHER OUR COMMUNITY OVER GOOD FOOD."

The restaurant's manifesto shares the values of its chef, Chris Whittaker, who is the ultimate hands-on chef. In the garden, into the woods, out to sea, the guy is serious about foraging and sourcing local.

Chris was raised to appreciate the offerings from Mother Nature and explains, "Ever since I was a child, the outdoors were a huge part of my life. As I hunted and fished and just generally explored . . . knowing that you can eat a lot of what was around you made me curious."

BC has faced some controversy recently regarding hunting licenses. Chris hunts—it too is a form of foraging—but shares his thoughts on this issue: "I think we have to educate a lot of people that hunting is a limited resource, although well managed, people need to respect that and be aware of that when they set foot in our great Canadian wilderness. It is a lot of work and takes a lot of resources, but having my freezer full of moose and deer that I have handled with my own hands as opposed to a bunch of Styrofoam vacuum-packed packages of commodity meat is a sense of pride and a source for great stories at the dinner table. Canadians have a proud and long hunting heritage, I think that it is sad (through the new hunting regulations favouring foreigners) that we are giving up the potential to show a new generation of hunters in Canada this tradition. The other part of it is that I am a meat hunter . . . not a trophy hunter. This is not a 'sport' to me, it is a way of putting healthy, sustainable meat in my freezer."

RESTAURANT Forage Restaurant LOCATION 1300 Robson St Vancouver, in the Listel Hotel
FB foragevancouver TWITTER @foragevancouver WEB foragevancouver.com

COVERT FARMS FAMILY ESTATE WINERY ♀ THE WINE MAKER

A COVERT ORGANIC REVOLUTION.

Covert Farms is literally a 600-acre utopia of organic living in the Okanagan. Gene and Shelly Covert take pride in specializing in certified organic growing. Their sprawling third-generation farm has every kind of vegetable you can imagine, plus berries and an organic vineyard that feeds their Covert Farms Family Estate winery; they also run a Salmon Safe operation and are in every way conscious caretakers of an exceptional piece of nature.

WINE MAKER Gene Covert LOCATION 107th Street Oliver, BC FB covertfarmsorganics
TWITTER @covertorganics WEB covertfarms.ca

THE SEA DIVER
Dan Larsen
Vancouver, BC

THE CHEF
Stephen Wong
Vancouver, BC

THE WINE MAKER
JoieFarm Winery
Naramata, BC

········· **FEATURED INGREDIENT** ·················
  Canadian geoduck

large geoduck from Canada, shelled, skinned,
    cleaned, and very thinly sliced

BROTH FOR HOT POT

8 cups (2 L) chicken stock or water

5 slices fresh ginger root

dried Chinese (shiitake) mushrooms

1 clove peeled garlic, smashed

green onion, smashed

1 cup (250 mL) shredded siu choy
    (Napa cabbage)

DIPPING SAUCE

½ cup (125 mL) light soy sauce

2 Tbsp (30 mL) unsalted chicken stock,
    or to taste

pinch sugar, to taste

1 to 2 fresh red chilies, sliced

1 Tbsp (15 mL) sesame oil

EXTRA GARNISH FOR GEODUCK SASHIMI

2 Tbsp (30 mL) grated wasabi

½ cup (125 mL) Japanese soy sauce

¼ cup (60 mL) XO sauce (see Chef's Notes)

CANADIAN HOT POT WITH GEODUCK SASHIMI

A hot pot is a traditional Chinese meal in which the ingredients are cooked in a pot of simmering broth directly at the table. This style of cooking makes the meal more fun and allows the chef to hang out with the guests. SERVES 4

CHEF'S NOTES: "XO sauce is essentially a premium chili-spiked Chinese condiment enhanced with dried scallops, shrimps, garlic, and sometimes even dry-cured ham. There are commercial versions available in Chinese supermarkets or you can buy some from your favourite Cantonese or Hong Kong-style seafood restaurants as many restaurants make their own version of it. As they often vary in flavour profile, I recommend tasting the sauce you choose and adjust seasoning and amount to your taste."

In a large saucepan, combine all broth ingredients and bring to boil. Transfer to a hot pot and bring to the table and set on an electric or butane burner. Set burner to high initially to start broth boiling and adjust the heat to medium simmer when serving.

In a small saucepan, combine all dipping sauce ingredients and bring to a boil. Adjust amounts to taste for intensity and spiciness. Transfer into small serving bowls for individual diners to use as dipping sauce for blanched geoduck.

Set out each of the extra garnish ingredients in separate saucers or bowls and provide each diner with a small sauce plate to mix their own sauce for dipping the sashimi-style geoduck. Geoduck can be eaten sashimi style (raw) or blanched lightly (about 15 seconds) in boiling broth and dipped in dipping sauce.

Other hot pot ingredients such as sliced raw fish, meats, jiaozi, and noodles can be added to broth and served as a complete meal if desired. Enjoy the rich broth as a soup to finish the meal. Arrange geoduck slices attractively on a platter. Garnish with extra leafy vegetables such as sliced Napa cabbage or leaf lettuce if desired.

··· **DRINK PAIRING** ·····································

2014 JoieFarm A Noble Blend
The 2014 A Noble Blend is a blend of Gewürztraminer, Riesling, Pinot Blanc, Pinot Auxerrois, Schoenberger, and Muscat. This aromatic wine exhibits an intense nose of guava, nutmeg, and clove. This spiciness continues onto the palate and opens up with unctuous flavours of lychee and guava carrying through to a fresh lime finish.

Underwater Harvesters Association

DAN LARSEN ⛵ THE SEA DIVER

DIVING FOR GOLD.

These unique saltwater creatures hail from the clam family and are prized as a delicacy in Asia. Now becoming more familiar on the current culinary scene, the geoduck ("gooey duck") is native to the west coast of North America and is one of the largest clams in the world. Also known as a King Clam, interestingly, the geoduck is also one of the longest-lived animals on the planet!

Dan Larsen, a former geoduck diver, current license holder, and director of the Underwater Harvesters Association, became involved in this pioneering industry in the late 1970s. "I came from Denmark, and I fell in love with the ocean and the nature on the west coast. When geoduck diving started I found it an interesting opportunity to be involved in a new dive fishery as an owner/operator/diver. This was in 1977–1978 and the fisheries issued 55 experimental licenses as a pilot program and I qualified for one."

Contrary to common belief, these giant clams are not found on shore but rather in deep waters and can only be accessed via diving. Specially trained divers, after reaching the ocean floor, will carefully loosen the substrate around the clam with pressurized water supplied by a pump on the fishing vessel on the surface. Dan explains, "The clams are then placed in a large mesh bag which, when full, is pulled by the diver to a weighted line back at the vessel where it is replaced with an empty bag. The full bag is hoisted onboard the vessel. The crew onboard then band and pack the geoducks for transport." The geoducks are now transported whole, while in the past they were cut up and vacuum packed.

The Canadian geoduck harvests are sustainably co-managed by the Underwater Harvesters Association and the Department of Fisheries and Oceans (Canada), and also controlled under strict standards set by the Canadian Food Inspection Agency (CFIA). Waterproof tags follow the clams from the fishing grounds to the table in China and other markets. In 1989, a milestone was reached by all license holders to divide the coast quota into individual license quotas to best meet market demand.

COMPANY Underwater Harvesters Association   LOCATION Vancouver, BC   WEB geoduck.org

STEPHEN WONG ✳ THE CHEF

KEEP CALM AND CLAM ON.

Born in Hong Kong, Stephen moved to BC at a young age and enjoyed a career as a chef, manager, and owner of a number of top restaurants in Vancouver throughout the 1980s and 1990s. He is now a well-known Vancouver-based freelance journalist and consulting chef involved in so many levels of the culinary culture of the west coast. From organizing city festivals and events to hosting tourism groups, he writes for various local and national magazines and newspapers and is the author of many cookbooks. Stephen sits on the critics panel for the annual *Vancouver Magazine* restaurant awards and also co-founded the Chinese Restaurant Awards.

As a food and beverage consultant, Stephen provides services to a number of local food producers and seafood harvesters on the development and promotion of specialty food and beverage products. His services range from recipe development/formulation, food industry/consumer market research, product promotions, photo food styling, trade seminars and on-site chef services for international trade shows, exhibitions and agri-food missions both on this continent and in Asia.

Stephen became involved with the Underwater Harvesters Association (UHA) and Geoduck from Canada (pronounced GOOEY-duck) as their consulting chef and has enjoyed representing this unique sea creature and its allure as a culinary delicacy. Stephen has created many recipes using this almost "blush-worthy" looking clam, but what does it taste like? Stephen explains: "Geoduck has a sea-sweet clam flavour that is clean and rich, and a crunchy-snappy texture, making it delicious for sashimi and sushi. Its siphon and its mantle have different textures and tastes, so it's fun to come up with diverse ways to cook geoduck that yield different results."

Becoming more popular now on the west coast, it is beloved by the foreign Asian community. Stephen explains, "First and foremost Asians seem to love the texture of geoduck and its 'fresh' 'sweet' flavour (the two Chinese words most often used to describe the taste of geoduck). The clam's size and dramatic shape also seem to impress (wink). Chinese and Asians take the concept of 'you are what you eat' quite literally, believing that in the act of eating one takes in the quality of what is eaten . . . and the associations can be diverse, from nutritional to symbolic. So geoduck's size, shape, and price are all part of the magic that elevates it to its prized top-table status."

COMPANY Underwater Harvesters Association   LOCATION Vancouver, BC   WEB geoduck.org

JOIEFARM WINERY ♀ THE WINE MAKER

JOIE TO THE WORLD!

Heidi Noble, owner/wine maker/chef/published cookbook author/mom, first transformed her farmhouse into a cooking school, guesthouse, and dreamy location where she hosted dinners in the orchard. Also a sommelier, Heidi took her love of wine to the next level and began winemaking—JoieFarm Winery was born in 2004 (co-wine maker Robert Thielicke joined her in 2009). Heidi has just opened a tasting room on the property, so wine lovers are now able to visit and stay for some "farm-to-table" snacks from the wood fire oven if they like. The cooking school is no longer open, but you can always buy her book, *Menus from an Orchard Table*, for inspiration.

LOCATION 2825 Naramata Road, Naramata, BC   TWITTER @joiefarm   FB joiefarm-winery   WEB joiefarm.com

⭐ THE FARMER
Barbara Ebell
Nanoose Bay, BC

⚓ THE CHEF
Lisa Ahier
Tofino, BC

🍶 THE BEER MAKER
Hoyne Brewing Co.
Victoria, BC

········ FEATURED INGREDIENT ········
Nanoose Edibles organic veggies

BROTH

1 bulb fennel, white only, thinly sliced

30 mL (2 Tbsp) olive oil

2 leeks, whites only, thinly sliced

½ medium red onion, diced small

50 mL (¼ cup) garlic (10 to 12 cloves), minced

5 mL (1 ts saffron threads

500 mL (2 cups) tomatoes (2 to 3 medium
      tomatoes), small-diced

125 mL (½ cup) dry white wine

1 L (4 cups) fish stock

STEW

6 medium red potatoes, cut into 2.5-cm
      (1-inch) cubes

50 mL (¼ cup) butter

Salt and pepper, to taste

15 mL (1 Tbsp) olive oil, plus extra for drizzling

4 pieces (each 175 g/6 oz) halibut,
      ling cod, or combination

500 g (1 lb) live mussels, scrubbed and
      debearded

500 g (1 lb) live clams, scrubbed
      and free of sand

8 large raw shrimp or prawns,
      peeled and deveined

1 Dungeness crab cleaned and
      steamed for 12 minutes (optional)

LEFT COAST SEAFOOD STEW

This rich stew is a celebration of the west coast "in all its glory," and can be served as a sharing starter or a main. It uses vegetables from Barbara at Nanoose Edibles. The "Left Coast" is Lisa's way of describing the location and lifestyle in Tofino. Lisa says to "mix and match the seafood to your own taste." **SERVES 4**

BROTH In a medium saucepan over low heat, sauté fennel in olive oil for 2 minutes. Add leeks, red onion, and garlic and sauté for another 3 to 4 minutes. Add saffron threads and sauté for 2 minutes, then add tomatoes and sweat until all vegetables are tender.

Increase heat to medium, add white wine and reduce for 1 minute. Add fish stock and simmer broth, uncovered, for 20 minutes.

STEW Preheat oven to 190°C (375°F). In a small saucepan, place potatoes and add just enough cold water to cover them. Bring to a boil, reduce heat and simmer, uncovered, for 5 minutes. The potatoes should be just cooked through, tender enough to be easily pierced by a fork but not mushy. Strain potatoes and make sure they are as dry as possible before roasting.

In a small saucepan over low heat, melt butter. Add potatoes with salt and pepper, and toss in butter until coated. Place potatoes on a baking sheet and bake in centre of oven for 10 to 15 minutes, until they are golden-brown, crispy croutons.

Meanwhile, lightly oil another baking sheet with 15 mL (1 Tbsp) olive oil. Season both sides of the halibut with salt and pepper. Place fish on baking sheet and drizzle a little more olive oil over top. Bake for about 10 minutes or until opaque throughout (try to time this so potatoes and fish finish at the same time; the fish should be on a higher rack than the potatoes).

While potatoes and fish are baking, increase heat under broth to high and add mussels and clams to pot. Cover and steam them for 1 to 2 minutes, then reduce heat to medium and add prawns for another 1 to 2 minutes. Discard any mussels or clams that do not open. The prawns should be pink but not overcooked.

Divide baked fish pieces among 4 bowls. Ladle shellfish and broth over top. Top with crispy potato croutons.

If you are using crab, evenly divide crabmeat among bowls of stew once plated. For visual effect, lay a few of the legs and claws on top. There is also an aioli recipe that you can serve with this and you will find that recipe in Lisa's cookbook, *The SOBO Cookbook*, by Lisa with Andrew Morrison (Appetite by Random House, 2014).

Serve with lots of bread to mop up the sauce!.

····· **DRINK PAIRING** ·······································

Hoyne Brewing Co., Helios
"Earthy bitterness, heavenly body, out of world experience." In the tradition of the robust beers of the Ruhr district, this export golden lager is malt forward and moderately hopped. It's described as a "hearty brew for a hardy people!"

BARBARA EBELL ✳ THE FARMER

GROWING NURTURING FOOD AND NURTURING GROWING FARMERS.

Barbara and Lorne Ebell bought their beautiful 23-acre farm as a retirement project 25 years or so ago. Row upon row, this glimmering farm offers a spectacular array of organic vegetables—around 50 varieties or so, plus herbs and 12 different fruits. This good earth is also scattered with young farmers, eagerly learning from their learned teachers; this is a truly inspiring place to visit.

Barbara emanates her nurturing nature, both to humans and to plants, and is a fountain of information and wonderful stories. "We specialize in growing nutrient-rich food, especially greens," Barbara says after sharing her story of her time living in Africa where she observed and learned the power of a greens-rich diet. Barbara believes that food heals, and that "If people can understand which nutrients their bodies need to eat, they wouldn't have to visit the doctor."

The produce and grains at Nanoose Edibles are grown without synthetic pesticides, herbicides, fertilizers, or GMOs (genetically modified organisms). Their animals are never fed with by-products of other animals, and are not constantly caged indoors without

access to fresh air or opportunities to socialize with other animals. When we were visiting, Barbara commented on the chicken standing by the till inside the on-site vegetable stand joking that, "she has decided that she no longer wants to be a chicken, but a shopkeeper." This is a farm where everything thrives—the farm exudes love and beauty.

Besides growing nutrient-rich food for our good health, she is also working on making sure there is a next generation of conscientious young farmers who will carry on this important job. "We have apprentices on the farm, we want to train young farmers." Instead of hiring workers without passion for the land or an interest in the land's future, she chooses those who want to learn and go into the business of organic farming. The soil here is well moralized—digging down you will find seashells. 15,000 years ago, this land was under the sea.

FARM Nanoose Edibles Organic Farm   LOCATION 1960 Stewart Rd, Nanoose Bay, BC
FB Nanoose-Edibles-Organic-Farm-BC-Certified-Organic   WEB nanooseediblesfarm.com

LISA AHIER ✳ THE CHEF

FOOD TRUCK PHENOM. MAMACITA. GOOD HUGGER.

Exchanging Texas cowboys for Tofitian surfers, this gal has wrangled taste buds from the east coast to the west (with a ranch in the Chihuahuan Desert in between). Lisa Ahier, a legend on the BC (actually, the Canadian) food truck scene, birth mother of the fish taco craze, SOBO (Sophisticated Bohemian), brought the mouths of the international culinary world to Tofino. She and her New Brunswick-bred hubby, Artie, opened up her purple food truck behind a surf shop in 2003, it was named one of the top 10 Canadian restaurants in *En Route* magazine that very first year.

Obviously, Lisa's gourmet spin and Texas taste caused a downright frenzy for food lovers. Fish tacos have been around the coast of Mexico for like, forever. But up here, nay, we hadn't tasted anything like it. Not to mention, she used fresh local fish to make the tacos—double points for that. She was now creating truly west coast-style cuisine.

In 2007 they parked the truck and set up shop in a real restaurant and business has been booming ever since. She still sports her trademark purple bandana to keep her hair back too. Lisa's gorgeous *SOBO Cookbook* was released in 2014 and was named one of the World's Top 20 Cookbooks that year. The book shares many of her favourite recipes and stories of some of her favourite local suppliers. It is a taste and celebration of the super-cool Tofino lifestyle. Her staff lovingly refer to her as "mamacita" because she "is the first one to reach out to take care of anyone in need." Even Sarah McLachlan provided these kind words for the foreword: "Lisa's food is infused with the perfect combination of love, fresh healthy ingredients, and a subtle but sophisticated magic."

RESTAURANT SOBO Restaurant   LOCATION 311 Neill Street, Tofino, BC
FB SOBO   TWITTER @chef_lisa   WEB sobo.ca

HOYNE BREWING CO 🍶 THE BEER MAKER

GOOD BEER.

Brewmaster Sean Hoyne credits one of North American's pioneers in the microbrewery movement for his success, "Frank Appleton taught me what it means to make great beer, and I am truly grateful for that." Frank and Sean set the brewery up together in 1989 with a goal to "create interesting and thoroughly enjoyable beer. Beer that looks good in the glass, feels good in the mouth, and lifts the spirit—and for that, I am proud."

LOCATION 101–2740 Bridge Street, Victoria, BC   TWITTER @hoynebeer   FB Hoyne-Brewing   WEB hoynebrewing.ca

····· FEATURED INGREDIENT ··················
Moses Martin halibut

SALSA

3 fresh cobs of corn

3–4 medium sized beefsteak or Roma
    tomatoes, diced

1 small red onion, diced

2–3 medium jalapeno peppers (more if
    you like it hot!), seeded and diced

½ bunch of cilantro, roughly chopped

4 limes, juiced

salt

1 small can of black beans, rinsed

SRIRACHA MAYO

250 g mayonnaise

50 g sriracha hot sauce (rooster on the bottle)

25 g fresh lime juice (about 1 lime's worth)

JICAMA SLAW

1 small jicama, peeled and julienned
    (use a mandolin to make it easier)

2 limes, juiced

½ bunch of cilantro, chopped

salt and pepper

FISH

vegetable oil/butter

1˙(1 kg) large piece of halibut, divided into
    12 equal pieces around 10 cm long

salt and pepper

BUILDING THE TACO

12 corn or wheat tortillas

4 avocados, sliced

limes for garnish

cilantro for garnish

HALIBUT FISH TACOS WITH ROASTED CORN SALSA

Chef Matty Kane's lip-smacking fish tacos are on the day menu at Shelter Restaurant in Tofino, and make for the perfect recharge between surf sessions. They pair perfectly with a cold pint of Tofino Brewing brewsky. **FEEDS A CREW OF 12**

SALSA Using a hot grill, or your oven's broiler, roast the peeled corn cobs until the corn takes on some color and is tender. Cool the corn and cut the kernels off. Combine all ingredients thoroughly in a bowl.

MAYO Combine all ingredients using a whisk. Chef tip: transfer the mayonnaise to a squeeze bottle to deploy.

JICAMA SLAW Combine all ingredients thoroughly and season to taste with salt and fresh cracked pepper.

FISH Heat a large skillet over medium high heat. Once it is hot, oil the pan using a flavourless oil, such as canola, peanut, or grapeseed. Season the fish with salt and pepper and place in the hot pan. Turn the heat down a little and cook on that side without moving until a crust starts to form. Once one side of the fish has been seared, turn the fish over, turn the heat down, and add some butter to the pan. Baste the fish a little with the hot butter using a spoon. Allow the fish to continue cooking slowly for several minutes. If you aren't sure when it's done, break a piece (you're making tacos remember). It should be juicy, but no longer translucent. It won't take long. Remove the fish from the pan, and reserve someplace warm.

Feel free to put all the ingredients out and allow your guests to build their own tacos. This is how we do it: toast your tortillas on a hot pan, turning once. Slice the avocados (about a ¼ of an avocado per taco). Lay the avocado on the shell. add a piece of fish, top with the slaw and some corn salsa, garnish with sriracha mayo and some chopped cilantro. Serve with fresh lime wedges on the side.

··· **DRINK PAIRING** ·······································

Tofino Brewing Blonde Ale
Blonde ale, pale, straw colour. Light, biscuity malt body. Earthy hop notes. Crisp finish. A must to follow on Instagram (/tofino-brewco), where the posts will give you an idea of how good life is in Tofinoland . . . with Tofino Brewing beer. Good times.

Chef Matty Kane

LEFT TO RIGHT: James, Moses, and Jay

MOSES MARTIN ⚓ THE FISHERMAN

THE PEACEFUL WARRIOR.

Elder Moses Martin, who was Chief of Tla-o-qui-aht First Nation for 23 years, has built a legacy of protecting land and sea. A gentle spirit, he is the seventh-generation descendant of War Chief Nookmiis (famous for sinking the Tonquin in 1811 after a previous ship destroyed over 200 houses in the ancient village of Optisaht). This is the village where Moses was raised on Meares Island.

Moses is a hero for organizing a peaceful protest against MacMillan Bloedel's plans to clearcut and destroy the island. On April 21, 1984, "the Tla-o-qui-aht first declared the area a tribal park and five months later, Martin and hundreds of people, native and non-native, stood shoulder to shoulder to stop the clearcut of 90% of the island in Clayoquot Sound." Moses says it was the "most rewarding thing I've ever done."

He is a commercial fisherman, like his father before him, "honouring the First Nations tradition" and passing on "family knowledge" to his children who are also in the business. He loves providing fresh fish to his community, "local family to local family,"

he smiles. His two boys, James and Gary, were fishing with Moses as soon as they could stand. Moses himself started fishing when he was six years old and "never left it," he says. "The first day out of school I was out on the boat."

His father taught him how to make his first canoe at eight years old. Moses recalls someone asking his brother who his best friend was. "The ocean," he earnestly replied.

The Martin family lives with the principle that everything, from land to sea to sky, is spiritual. Moses says, "We are all one." Moses and his wife, Carla, and two sons operate Clayoquot Wild, which offers wildlife and custom tours based on the dock off Main Street in Tofino. Visitors can sign up to go deep-sea fishing, whale or bear watching, visit the local hot springs, or go on a local history tour with Moses himself. All tours are lead by local and First Nations guides of Tofino and Clayoquot Sound.

COMPANY Clayoquot Wild   LOCATION 316 Main Street, Tofino, BC
FB clayoquotwild   WEB clayoquotwild.com

LEFT TO RIGHT: Mattie, Sam and Jay Gildenhuys

JAY GILDENHUYS ✴ THE RESTAURANT MAKER

"COME IN," HE SAID, "I'LL GIVE YOU SHELTER FROM THE STORM."

Gimme, gimme Shelter! To many Tofinians, Shelter is the hub, the hangout, or as the surfer's dictionary, the Riptionary (I kid you not) might call it, the shredquarters for locals in Tofino. Known as the "end of the road," Tofino is a stunning little town on the west coast of Vancouver Island. A truly magnificent setting, it is Mother Nature at her most alive. Surrounded by lush rainforest, it offers long beaches dotted with shells and sand dollars, a gift from the majestic waves that crash to shore from this emotional, tumultuous ocean that makes it a lusty destination for surfers and storm watchers.

Shelter's owner, Jay Gildenhuys, created his well-loved eatery in 2003 and offers gastronomic cuisine that will appeal to the palates of both surfer and sophisticate.

"At Shelter, we use local, organic ingredients and ethically raised, all-natural meats whenever possible. The salmon, halibut, and prawns are caught by Tofino fisherman, the poultry is free run and farmed on Vancouver Island. We offer hormone-free, grass-fed beef, as well as antibiotic and hormone-free pork, including bacon from the Fraser Valley." They also have also planted a kitchen garden out back to source from.

Jay is a surfer, his wife, Mattie, is a world champion surfer, and their extremely adorable kid, Sam, is a surfer in training. So, um yes, they encompass all of the island's philosophies—source local, eat local, be local, and live to surf.

Shelter gives back to its community big time. Founders of TUCG (The Tofino Ucluelet Culinary Guild—more next page) and FEAST Tofino (annual celebration of local food and drink culture), Jay and his crew are leaders in supporting and promoting the local culture. Eat, drink, surf.

RESTAURANT Shelter Restaurant   LOCATION 601 Campbell Street, Tofino, BC
FB shelterrestaurant   TWITTER @foodwineshelter   WEB shelterrestaurant.com

Bobby

TOFINO UCLUELET CULINARY GUILD ➤ THE FOOD CONNECTION MAKER

HONEST FOOD FROM PASSIONATE PEOPLE.

Vancouver Island has an amazing organization called TUCG (Tofino Ucluelet Culinary Guild), a group co-op that formed in 2010 with a mission to "help their region's farmers, fishermen, and foragers to provide unique food experiences that rely on sustainable farm/boat-to-table practices and the freshest local ingredients prepared with integrity and passion." The cool thing about this program is that because they are group buying and shipping, they can make the best local food more affordable and for the small producer, they "create a strong market with established distribution." It is a win-win for everyone.

Jay Guildenhuys, the founder of TUCG explains, "This has mostly been driven by the passion for food in the community," Jay says, "Why start the Guild? We all have a passion for sourcing the best ingredients from the Island. By coming together as a group we could also afford to hire someone to source the best local food for us and coordinate delivery."

This program allows its members to go online each week and choose to shop by product or by farm. Whether it be seasonal fruit or vegetables, fish, meats, or foraged goods, it is delicious farm shopping online. The membership includes restaurants, resorts,

farmers, product partners, as well as other community support members. It allows consumers a portal into the best Island sourced produce and meats without having to source for themselves.

The TUCG also offers a weekly box program from June to October allowing consumers to receive a box full of a variety of local treasures that are in season chosen by them. The Food Lover's Box includes a variety of greenery, ground crops, fruits, greenhouse crops, and other special items that they "find special but not too weird." The Heat of the Summer Box is a "picnic style" box with items that require no cooking to help locals out during the crazy summer surf season in Tofino.

Bobby Lax is the community food coordinator for TUCG and a beloved, active member of the food scene on the Island. He is that cute guy with a huge smile that roars around in his red TUCG van (sadly not the old VW anymore, he needed more space and something more reliable). Bobby is passionate about his role representing both the farmer and the consumer, and "is dedicated to providing quality products to local residents and chefs."

TWITTER @TUCGuild   FB tofinouclueletculinaryguild   WEB tucg.ca

LEFT TO RIGHT: Brewmaster Bryan, Kieran, and Andy

TOFINO BREWING CO. 🍺 THE BEER MAKER

GROWLENATORS AVAILABLE FOR BEER FREAKS.

Making nine different brews to satiate the Tofino surf culture and now the world beyond, this brewery has a conscience. "Our brewery was built around a few basic ideas: brewing great beer, being a positive addition to our town, and operating in a sustainable and locally focused manner." The brewery is happily locally owned and operated by Dave McConnell, Chris Neufeld, and Bryan O'Malley.

To protect their precious land and sea, they developed a water recovery system that "allows them to recapture all of the water used in the heat exchange process for use in subsequent brews." They promote recycling and offer cool glass bottles-Growlers, Growlitos, and Growlenators—that are refillable at the brewery. They also recycle their spent grain by offering it to Collins Farm in Port Alberni to use as livestock feed. I wonder if the cows get a buzz?

LOCATION Unit C & D, 681 Industrial Way, Tofino, BC
TWITTER @TofinoBrewCo   FB TofinoBrewCo   WEB tofinobrewingco.com

······· FEATURED INGREDIENT ·················
Matsutakes and local rice

FOR THE FISH

½ tsp cumin seeds

pinch chili flakes, ground

2 tsp fine sea salt

16 oz sashimi grade Albacore tuna

½ cup sesame seeds

FOR THE MATSUTAKE

4 oz matsutake or chanterelles

1 tsp butter for frying

2 Tbsp soy sauce

FOR RICE

½ large onion, diced fine

2 med cloves garlic, diced fine

2 tsp parsley

2 tsp tarragon

1 cup rice, uncooked

2 cups chicken stock

2 Tbsp butter

¼ tsp white pepper

PONZU SAUCE

1 cup soy sauce

⅓ cup rice vinegar

1 cup yuzu (or citrus) juice

2 Tbsp tamari

2 Tbsp mirin

2 Tbsp katsuobushi

2 inch square piece of kombu

1 tsp ginger, grated

MATSUTAKE & SEARED ALBACORE TUNA TATAKI

Matsutake and pine mushrooms are the same variety—the *Tricholoma magnivelare*—matsutake is the Japanese word for pine. These sexy, biggie mushrooms are found hiding under moss in forests around BC, and are a treasure to find. **SERVES 4**
"If you don't have matsutakes, use chanterelles in this recipe," says Chef Robin.

PONZU SAUCE Mix, bring to a boil, and then let soak in fridge for 24 hours, strain and then let age for 3 months in fridge for best flavour, though you can use it right away. Or just use a good store bought ponzu as most home cooks may not want to wait.

DIRECTIONS The key to this recipe is very fresh fish and not over garnishing, making sure the matsutake is the dominant flavour, which usually isn't that hard as fresh matsutake are very aromatic.

Make your fish salt: Toast cumin in a dry pan to bring out flavour, grind with the chili flakes, and add to salt. Then, liberally salt your fish with this mixture, roll in sesame seeds, and set aside.

Chop or prep all your garnishes: onion, garlic, and herbs and set aside. Make the rice. Rinse rice really well in a strainer under cold water. In a saucepan large enough to hold the cooked rice, fry onions, garlic, and butter in a pan till the onions are translucent, around 3 minutes on medium heat. Add your rice and cook for another 2 minutes. Add stock, salt to taste, and bring to a boil, then simmer for around 15 minutes with the lid on. Test the rice for tenderness and keep cooking if it needs another few minutes. Remove from heat and add herbs, fluff the rice. Set aside covered.

TIP If you need to clean your matsutake you can peel the outer dirty layer off, don't rinse in water. Slice the matsutake thin (around 2 mm thick) and chop into 3 inch long slices. Sprinkle slices with soy sauce. Melt butter in a hot pan and add matsutake slices as soon as the butter is browned. Turn slices to brown the other side after a minute, this should be a quick fry. Remove the mushrooms, taste one, and add a little salt to your taste. Add the fish to this hot pan, sear for 1 minute per side until just the outer edges are cooked and the sesame seeds are browned. Remove the fish and slice with a very sharp knife into 1 cm thick pieces. Place on rice and arugula, zest orange over the fish, and then artfully add your beautiful matsutakes. Place a bowl of ponzu sauce with a dash of chives in it for dipping.

FOR GARNISHING Arugula (about a handful), 2 tsp chives (chopped fine), orange for zesting, ½ cup ponzu sauce (for dipping).

······· **DRINK PAIRING** ·······················

Osake Junmai Nama
Light, crisp and dry. Lively and bright with pear, melon, citrus notes; it is a refined sipping sake and ideal companion to seafood. Kampai!
Light, crisp and dry. Lively and bright with pear, melon, citrus notes; it is a refined sipping sake

MASA SHIROKI ✳ THE SAKE MAKER AND FARMER

A RICE STORY.

Masa Shiroki is a revolutionary drink maker and farmer. He not only makes local sake, he is growing local rice in the Fraser Valley! How cool is that? It is the "first sake rice production in Canadian history and the most northerly rice production region in the world."

Sake is a Japanese beverage made from fermented rice and the Artisan SakeMaker's dream was to create 100% Canadian sake using 100% of his local rice production. Masa Shiroki opened Artisan SakeMaker in 2007 and in 2008, "I made up my mind to do it and I went to Japan's most northerly rice growing region to find the variety grown there and brought it back. I started experimenting in different growing regions from 2009–2010—including the Okanagan and Vancouver Island and found that the Fraser Valley was best." Masa's yields have increased steadily from the first harvest in 2011 and in 2014 he met a local cattle farmer, Ralph Gough, who was interested in trying out the rice in his Surrey field. That too was successful—Masa went from growing rice on 2 acres to 14 acres in 4 years. "In May 2013, we produced our first Fraser Valley Junmai Sake—Series One. It was the first of Artisan SakeMaker's (ASM) regional Osake series made from 100% organically grown sake rice in Abbotsford, BC."

Masa's career in sake began at age 50, and he explains, "I wanted to do something culturally meaningful to me." He first began importing premium sake for sale before he decided to make his own. His high-quality, small-lot sake is all pressed and bottled by hand, it's unfiltered and free of preservatives.

The importance of rice crops: "Local rice production is pertinent to the pressing global need for food security and the national issue of food sovereignty. Namely, local production of food and beverage products is of immediate and long-term importance to the sustainability of Canadian agricultural production, environmentally, socially, and economically. Specifically, reducing the food miles attached to products that are consumed in Canada is primarily of importance to the environment, but it is also of importance to society as a whole, since increased awareness of environmental issues continues to drive demand for local products."

The tasting room for Artisan SakeMaker is located on Granville Island. You can purchase his brown and white rice at the shop and at some farmers markets. What's next, a sake chateau in the Okanagan?

COMPANY Artisan SakeMaker   **LOCATION** 1339 Railspur Alley, Vancouver, BC
TWITTER @ArtisanSake   **FB** ArtisanSakeMaker   **WEB** artisansakemaker.com

ROBIN KORT ✴ THE CHEF AND FORAGER

SHROOM LOVER. FUN, CREATIVE, EDGY, AND INNOVATIVE. ENCOURAGES PLAYING WITH FOOD.

What does a matsutake mushroom smell like? "Red hots and dirty socks . . . or if you want a more pleasing descriptor . . . cinnamon and earth."—Robin

Robin Kort is a native Vancouverite who has always been involved in the local restaurant scene, she also studied art, which is actually a natural pairing for most chefs. Also a sommelier, she has created a "culinary circus" around her Swallow Tail business that embodies all of her creative instincts and is a celebration of her passions for wine, art, and "cooking, drinking, foraging, friends, and the great outdoors."

She was one of the first to bring the super cool pop-up restaurant concept to the Vancouver food scene. She explains them as "flash in the pan" culinary moments: "We're here today, you come, eat and drink with us. Poof! We're gone."

Robin is the queen of the Vancouver foraging world and has encyclopedia knowledge of all things mushroom as well as other rainforest edibles. Offering tours that explore "everything you need to know to safely gather, prepare, and cook the unique flavours found only in nature," her Wild Edible Identification Trips are a super cool way to discover the gifts from the land in BC.

How she got hooked on foraging:

"My first taste experience: eating hedgehog mushrooms for the first time, picked while hunting for deer with my grandfather in the Okanagan. The creamy, butter notes of this mushroom along with its crispy texture when fried were a revelation."

"I love foraging because it's like looking for treasure, when you find a $100 matsutake in the forest you feel like a pirate. One that's going to eat like a king."

Cheers to Mother Nature and her gifts!

COMPANY Swallow Tail Culinary Adventures for Food & Wine Lovers
LOCATION Vancouver, BC **FB** SwallowTailCanada
TWITTER @theswallowdive **WEB** swallowtail.ca

⭐ **THE FARMER**
Heather Pritchard
Aldergrove, BC

⚙ **THE CHEF**
Dave Gunawan
Vancouver, BC

🍷 **THE WINE MAKER**
Summerhill Pyramid Winery
Kelowna, BC

······ FEATURED INGREDIENT ······
Glorious Organics rhubarb

FOR SMOKED SOCKEYE OR TROUT

1 fish, 5–6 lbs

CURE

70 g sugar

30 g salt

zest from 1 orange, 1 lemon, and 1 lime

RHUBARB DASHI

300 g rhubarb, chopped

2 L water

18 g dried kelp (konbu)

1 thumb size piece of ginger root, sliced thinly

20 g sugar

25 g bonito flakes

2 tsp organic soy sauce

salt to taste

LACTO FERMENTED SEA ASPARAGUS

1 L water

30 g salt

50 g unpasteurized whey

RHUBARB DASHI WITH SMOKED FISH,
SEA ASPARAGUS & RADISH

This rhubarb dashi recipe was created the day I arrived to photograph the dish. Chef Dave Gunawan received the first order of rhubarb of the season that morning and whipped up something to celebrate its tartness. It was both delicious and beautiful, like all of Dave's creations. The combination of flavours creates a serious party in your mouth. *Pickling or using the lacto-fermenting process is a great way to utilize sea asparagus, yet another wonderful gift from the sea.

Mix cure ingredients together and then cover the fish in the mixture. Cure the fish filet for 14 hours in the refrigerator and then wash off cure mixture. Pat dry with a paper towel and let dry overnight in the refrigerator to form the pellicle. A pellicle is a skin or coating of proteins on the surface of meat, fish, or poultry, which allows the smoke to better adhere to the surface of the meat during the smoking process.

Move to smoker and smoke with alder chips at 30°C for 20 minutes.

RHUBARB DASHI Combine ingredients in a saucepot and cook together a low simmering temperature for 30 minutes, not to exceed 80°C.

LACTO FERMENTED SEA ASPARAGUS Brine the sea asparagus in the salt and water combination. Add 50 g of unpasteurized whey and stir to combine. Ferment at room temperature for 1 week.

TO SERVE Chop the fish to ½ cm cubes and dress with chives and olive oil. Spoon 4 tsp of dashi around the plate. Garnish with fresh and fermented sea asparagus and top with shaved radishes (optional).

······ DRINK PAIRING ······

Summerhill Pyramid Winery Organic Cipes Rosé
100% Pinot Noir cuvee grown at multiple vineyard locations around the Okanagan Valley. The vines were planted and are maintained specifically for sparkling wine production to express a crisp, bright style. Notes of raspberry, strawberry, kiwi, blood orange, vanilla, almond, and white toast.

DAVE GUNAWAN ✳ THE CHEF

THE THOUGHTFUL CHEF.

In 2012, Dave Gunawan left us swooning after we licked up his riotously wonderful Wildebeest menu. In 2013, we were stressed when he left, but cheered when he dove into his own passion project opening Farmer's Apprentice with partner Dara Young. This menu is a manifestation of his cooking philosophy and hyper-local dedication to the farmer. Offering revolutionary flavour combinations, he creates dishes directly from the products that are delivered to the door. On his relationships with his suppliers, Dave explains his modus operandi, "Human connection is important. Understanding where, how, and why they do what they do, allows us to understand how to transform their product. Without proper understanding of climate and all of those variables, how do we know which technique to apply? Kale is not just a kale, different farmers produce different kale based on the soil conditions and weather system—some might be tough, some might be spicy, so by understanding the intrinsic property of our vegetables we then know the appropriate technique to apply."

Grapes & Soda, their unique new wine bar next door, will be open by the time this book hits the press. Like his strong food philosophies, Dave's views on winemaking are uber ethical: "The focus is on natural, biodynamic wine and pairing each individual wine with a dish. The whole idea is to enable a dialogue with the sommelier and the chefs, creating an educational facility. What we are offering are phenomenal wines devoid of monetary incentives. These wines are made using a philosophy of dedication and love and not controlled with chemicals to create a predictable market outcome. It takes years of experience and care for the earth in order to produce this style of wine and an understanding of the microbiology and natural enzymes that occur during the process. They are guiding nature to take control, rather than trying to control nature. The whole mindset of these vintners is very parallel to what we do here."

RESTAURANT Farmer's Apprentice   LOCATION 1535 West 6th Avenue, Vancouver, BC
FB farmers-apprentice   TWITTER @gunawan_dave   WEB farmersapprentice.ca

HEATHER PRITCHARD ✴ THE FARMER

THE MOTHER OF THE ORGANIC GREEN SALAD MIX.

Co-founder of Farm Folk/City Folk, co-founder/farmer of Glorious Organics Co-op, food activist, local farm hero, and pioneer in the organic farming movement, Heather Pritchard is a leader in the west coast food and farm scene.

Heather is the creator of the now-essential packaged organic mixed greens! Not raised in farming or gardening, Heather explains, "My buddy, Herb Bartolet (co-founder of Farm Folk/City Folk and Glorious Organics) and I lived in a housing co-op in Kits and when he went to work at a farm, he left me in charge of his herb garden and I immediately became smitten with gardening." Heather became involved with the farm in 1985, "after a year of experimenting with different mixes." Her salad mixes are legendary—they are delicious and nutritious, they contain herbs and flowers, and the different colours and textures make them beautiful. Heather says, "My idea was to put greens together in a salad using foraged ingredients to add different flavours and balance . . . to make it colourful and unique. We were the first people in Canada to do this. The Glorious Garnish and Seasonal Salad Company was formed in 1986. When it dissolved 20 years later in 2006, five members founded the Glorious Organics Co-operative."

FARM Glorious Organics Co-op   LOCATION 1374 256th Street, Aldergrove, BC
TWITTER @gloriousfarmers   FB glorious-organics-cooperative   WEB gloriousorganics.com

SUMMERHILL PYRAMID WINERY ♀ THE WINE MAKER

ORGANIC CHAMPIONS.

The Cipes family, led by father Stephen Cipes, purchased their Kelowna vineyard back in 1986 always with a crystal clear vision to transform the property to certified organic vineyards and to create certified organic wines. Organic winemaking is overseen by master wine maker Eric von Krosigk and the winery operations are now in the gentle hands of one of Stephen's sons, Ezra. The vineyards are being raised biodynamically, allowing the most natural occurrence of vine management along with the touch of Mother Nature, which allows the ultimate terroir to be expressed through the grapes.

LOCATION 4870 Chute Lake Road, Kelowna, BC   TWITTER @summerhillwine   FB summerhillwine   WEB summerhill.bc.ca

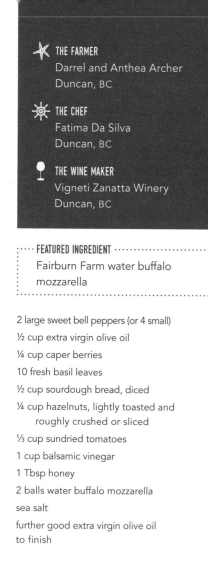

★ THE FARMER
Darrel and Anthea Archer
Duncan, BC

⚓ THE CHEF
Fatima Da Silva
Duncan, BC

🍷 THE WINE MAKER
Vigneti Zanatta Winery
Duncan, BC

······· FEATURED INGREDIENT ········
Fairburn Farm water buffalo
mozzarella
·····························

2 large sweet bell peppers (or 4 small)

½ cup extra virgin olive oil

¼ cup caper berries

10 fresh basil leaves

½ cup sourdough bread, diced

¼ cup hazelnuts, lightly toasted and
    roughly crushed or sliced

⅓ cup sundried tomatoes

1 cup balsamic vinegar

1 Tbsp honey

2 balls water buffalo mozzarella

sea salt

further good extra virgin olive oil
to finish

WATER BUFFALO MOZZARELLA WITH ROASTED PEPPERS & CRUMBLY HAZELNUT CROUTONS

This gorgeous salad will send your taste buds into mambo mode. A unique combination of flavours and textures, this is one of my favourite salads ever.

To fire roast the peppers, you can use an open flame from a gas stove or BBQ, or use the broiler in your oven; they are done when all sides are charred. Let them cool off and then remove the skin with your hands or a spoon. Cut the peppers in strips, remove the stem and seeds, and set aside.

In a small pot, warm up most of the olive oil (save a couple of tablespoons to drizzle at the end) and fry the caper berries until crispy. Remove from the pan and set aside.

In the same oil, fry half of the basil leaves (warning, no need for body armour, but keep in mind that they do splatter and pop and it only takes a few seconds) until they get translucent, which means they are ready. Set aside.

In a frying pan, drizzle 2 tablespoons of the oil that was used to fry the basil leaves and then sauté the bread until crispy golden. Add the hazelnuts and chopped sundried tomatoes, toss a couple of times, and remove from heat. Spread on a plate to cool.

MAKE BALSAMIC REDUCTION In a frying pan bring balsamic vinegar to a boil, turn down the heat, and simmer for about 15 minutes. The best way to check that it is done is that it should coat the back of a spoon when stirred. Be careful not to overcook as it will burn and taste bitter. Remove from heat, add the honey, and let cool. It will thicken further as it cools.

TO SERVE Spread the bread mixture on a platter and drizzle with olive oil and balsamic reduction. Slice the buffalo mozzarella into rounds and sprinkle with sea salt and place on top of bread mixture. Top with the crispy caper berries and fried basil and surround with the sliced charred peppers. Sprinkle with chopped fresh basil and a drizzle olive oil. Enjoy every bite!

····· DRINK PAIRING ·············

Vigneti Zanatta Allegria Brut Rosé
Aged on the lees for a minimum of 18 months, this Champagne-method sparkling wine boasts a raspberry hued cuveé of Pinot Noir with a very rich, fruity body and gentle aromas of strawberries and raspberry.

Anthea and her son, Richard

THE ARCHER FAMILY ✷ THE FARMER

FAIRBURN FARM—WHERE EVERY WATER BUFFALO HAS A NAME.

Fairburn Farm is a third-generation family affair located in a bucolic setting in the lush core of Cowichan Bay. Rolling hills and pastures house a herd of water buffalo under the care of the Archer family. Darrel Archer's parents purchased the property in 1955 from the Jackson family, the original homesteaders of the property who came over from Scotland. Mary Jackson named the farm Fairburn, which in Scots means "beautiful stream."

Darrel and Anthea took over operations in 1980 and made the remarkable decision to import a herd of river water buffalo from Denmark—the first in Canada! Tragically after hearing of a case of BSE (Bovine Spongiform Encephalopathy) in a cow in Denmark, the government ordered that the herd be killed. The Archers fought the order but after two years of court battles they lost and were only allowed to keep the offspring born on the farm. There is a marker listing the names of the water buffalo that perished on the property, a testament to the caring nature of these special farmers, kindness I was to witness many times in watching Anthea talk and handle the baby water buffaloes—it is a beautiful thing.

Two of the Archer's six children returned to the farm to work—Richard, who is heavily involved in the ranching, and Maryann, who with her husband and two wee children, has been running the guesthouse operations.

The water buffalo milk is a prized commodity and rare to our country. In Italy, this milk is used to make their luxurious Mozzarella di Bufala, a much richer, silkier version of bocconcini. The Archers sell the milk to make their version of water buffalo mozzarella, which Fatima has used in this delicious recipe, at Natural Pastures Cheese Company. The water buffalo also provide lean and healthy meat that is a delicious alternative to beef. The Archers are currently selling their male calves to Island Bison Ranch in Comox to raise and sell as meat products. See page 34 for contact information. Water buffalo are a unique and loving species, I dare you not to fall in love.

FARM Fairburn Farmstay and Guesthouse   LOCATION 3310 Jackson Rd, Duncan, BC
FB fairburnfarmstayandguesthouse   WEB fairburnfarm.bc.ca

FATIMA DA SILVA ✳ THE CHEF

PRAISE FATIMA.

Born and raised in Mozambique, Fatima Da Silva is a well-loved local source of beautiful farm- and sea-to-table cuisine. Fatima is not only a natural, self-trained chef, she is a force of good energy and one of the best huggers around. There is always laughter and giggles when this woman is around—notoriously flying by the seat of her pants—she laughs when she tells tales of the staff inquiring what the specials of the day are . . . at 10:30 AM before opening. Laughing, she throws up her arms. "I don't know yet!" And off she disappears into her kitchen to create magic.

Her family background is as colourful as she is: her roots consist of Mozambican, Portuguese, Goan, Arabic, and Pakistani with a sprinkle of Spanish. She giggles when she says, "Well, every few years we discover another influence; I like to think of myself as a crazy work in progress."

"As a child growing up in Mozambique in a multiracial/multicultural family, I was privileged to be exposed to a wide range of ethnic cuisines, but none had as much impact as the rituals of East Indian cooking. As we gathered in my mother's kitchen, the toasting and grinding of different colourful spices with their pungent nutty aromas were always an intriguing prelude to an amazing meal. Once in a while my mother would get rice still in its shell, and we would help with the hulling process that was done by gently pounding it in a large wooden mortar. The result was this absolutely to die for aromatic rice, which you could smell from around the block; nothing else better accompanied her fish curry." She sources from the large kitchen garden on the property and from local farmers and fishers. The experience of wining and dining on the wide back porch of Vinoteca set in the original 1903 farmhouse, glass of bubbly in hand, plate of Fatima's cuisine in front of you while overlooking the vineyard is simply sublime.

RESTAURANT Vinoteca Restaurant and Wine Bar   LOCATION 5039 Marshall Rd, Duncan, BC
FB vinoteca.zanatta   TWITTER @cheffatima   WEB zanatta.ca

VIGNETI ZANATTA WINERY 🍷 THE WINE MAKER

A SPARKLING ROMANCE

The story of the Vigneti Zanatta Winery is as romantic as the venue itself.

Known as the "First Family of Vancouver Island Wine" family patriarch, Dionisio (Dennis) Zanatta arrived in Canada in the 1950s from his home in Treviso, Italy. Daughter Loretta Zanatta followed in her father's footsteps and went on to study wine in Italy at the University of Piacenza in Enology where she was inspired to learn the champagne method of winemaking and brought that knowledge home to the island. When the family officially opened up their farm gate winery in 1992, they became the first sparkling wine producers on the island. In 1996 Loretta and her husband, Jim Moody, took over Vinoteca and Jim also became principal wine maker. "We are proud to make uniquely Vancouver Island wine."

WINE MAKER Loretta Zenatta and Jim Moody   LOCATION 5039 Marshall Rd, Duncan, BC   FB zanatta-winery   TWITTER @zanattawinery   WEB zanatta.ca

···· FEATURED INGREDIENT ·····················
Oyama Sausage and
The Farm House Cheese

MODERN DOG ROASTED YAM TREATS

2 medium-large yams or sweet potatoes (or as
many as you want to make)

A PICNIC FOR MODERN DOGS
& THEIR PEOPLE

One of the wonderful attributes of west coast culture is its unabashed love for man's best friend. Dogs are everywhere and are able to enjoy some of the most beautiful beaches and parks with their humans. Here are some treats to serve for both the "furs and the skins" on a picnic by the sea.

MODERN DOG ROASTED YAM TREATS These treats for your furry pal are both healthy and easy to make. Best thing is, you will enjoy these bites too!

Preheat oven to 250°F. Scrub the sweet potato or yam, no need to peel. Cut it into thin slices (the thinner the slice the shorter the cooking time) and place on a cookie sheet in a single layer. Bake at 250°F for about 3 hours for slightly chewy treats or bake slightly longer to get them crunchy. Note: timing will vary according to the thickness of your slices; just keep an eye on them. Or, better yet, if you have a dehydrator, pop them in there instead of the oven.

Note from *Modern Dog*: sweet potatoes are a source of dietary fiber and contain vitamin B6, vitamin C, beta carotene, and manganese. Most dogs love the chewy sweetness of a delish dehydrated sweet potato treat. And you can rest easy knowing there's no additives, preservatives, or anything extraneous added.

FOR THE HUMANS: SAUSAGE AND CHEESE PLATE

OYAMA SAUSAGE OH-YEAH-MA SAUSAGE! For your picnic, make a sausage stop at Granville Island's Oyama Sausage—it is a destination for charcuterie lovers. All of their products are amazing, so choose some lovely pâté and an array of sausages to slice up, including the Beautiful British Columbia Saucisson Sec made with sea salt from Vancouver Island Salt Co., seaweed from Haida Gwaii, and the pastured rare breed BC pork from North Thompson Heritage Ranch.

As for a cheese selection, I suggest a soft and hard cheese: perhaps the Brie and the Goat Peppercorn Gouda from The Farm House Natural Cheeses in Agassiz! Shops at Granville Island carry it or if you can visit the farm—do that. They also make butter, which is a must.

···· **DRINK PAIRING** ···································

Wayward Distillation House Unruly Gin
This gin is a beautifully balanced blend of organic, locally sourced botanicals delicately infused into their 100% BC Honey Spirit. Unlike traditional juniper-heavy London Dry gins, Unruly Gin is a refreshingly alternative Canadian-style gin that has balanced and complemented its juniper with a hint of cedar and citrus, a dash of fragrant lavender and sarsaparilla root, and vibrant notes of coriander.

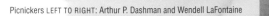
Picnickers LEFT TO RIGHT: Arthur P. Dashman and Wendell LaFontaine

DEBRA AMREIN-BOYES 🐬 THE CHEESE MAKER

EATING HER CURDS AND WHEY.

The Boyes' pastoral farm is located in the farm-rich Fraser Valley region, and makes an ideal home for the family to raise healthy cows and goats for milk to make cheese.

This crew has high standards and ethics, "It is our wish to nurture and preserve the increasingly threatened values and traditions of the family farm, and give visitors the opportunity to connect with the farmer and the animals who produce their food."

This is a world-class cheesemaking operation. Debra is one of only 12 people in Western Canada and the US who has been inducted into the prestigious French Cheese Guild, the "Guilde des Fromagers Confrérie de Saint-Uguzon," which recognizes those who protect and continue the tradition of cheesemaking around the world. She has also written a book for home cheesemakers called *200 Easy Homemade Cheese Recipes: From Cheddar and Brie to Butter and Yogurt*—you can pick up a copy at their farm shop! Grab a baguette from Terra Breads and you are all set . . . except for picnic cocktails. Congratulations to Debra for winning Best Aged Cheddar Cheese in Canada for two years in a row!

COMPANY The Farm House Natural Cheeses   LOCATION 5634 McCallum Road, Kent, BC
TWITTER @thcheeses   FB the-farm-house-natural-cheeses   WEB farmhousecheeses.com

WAYWARD DISTILLATION HOUSE 🍯 THE SPIRIT MAKER

WAYWARD AND UNRULY.

Although Dave and Andrea Brimacombe are newbies on the local drink scene, spirit enthusiasts are buzzing about their bee-autiful new products! Using 100% BC honey and locally sourced botanicals, the two wanted to "do something different and stand out in this industry," explains Andrea. And that they did! "All of our honey comes from the far-reaching wild clover fields of Northern BC, unpasteurized and all-natural."

With no background at all in the industry—he in the military for 14 years and she an artist and commercial painter—the two think their new career is "absolutely fantastic" and their success story, extra sweet.

PEOPLE Dave and Andrea Brimacombe   LOCATION 2931 Moray Avenue, Courtenay, BC
TWITTER @waywarddh   FB waywarddistillation   WEB waywarddistillationhouse.com

JOHN AND CHRISTINE VAN DER LIECK 🐬 THE SAUSAGE MAKER

EURO WONDERLAND.

Oyama Sausage at Granville Island is one of my favourite food stops in Vancouver. I love the wide variety of charcuterie, meats, and rich pâtés (omg, the foie gras is unreal). I am a disciple of their perfect, house-made sauerkraut and German sausages (yes, I am a German girl!). They have a Choucroute (baked sausages and sauerkraut from Deutsche heaven) Festival each year and offer prepared takeaway. Same goes for another Euro-comfort food favourite from France, cassoulet, the rich bean stew (they have it frozen too).

John and Christine van der Lieck have built a loyal following to their brand because of their highest-quality crafting and ingredients. John is a fifth-generation charcuterie craftsman with a German and Dutch background, so it is no wonder this guy knows his craft and is passionate about it. Christine is so warm and welcoming, and greets every customer like an old friend. I adore their bustling business at Granville Island, and even though one has to wait in line, it feels so European and is worth every second.

"If there is one thing I hope to achieve at Oyama, it is to instill the same enthusiasm for the wonders of the culinary universe that I feel every day," says John.

SHOP Oyama Sausage   LOCATION Granville Island Market   TWITTER @oyamasausage
FB oyama-sausage-co-on-granville-Island   WEB oyamasausage.ca

---

3 ounces Unruly Gin
3 ounces fresh lemon juice
4 tsp superfine granulated sugar
1½ cups ice cubes
1 cup chilled BC sparkling rosé

PINK FRENCH HEINZ 57

A delightful combination of gin and bubble, this cocktail is perfect to enjoy on a picnic or on any patio under the summer sun. Cheers to your fur pals and to *le bon vivre!*

In a cocktail shaker, combine all ingredients except bubbly and shake to chill. Strain into two glasses and top bubbly with a twist of lemon rind to make it pretty.

⛵ **THE SEA FARMER**
Paul Simpson
Salt Spring Island, BC

☸ **THE CHEF**
David Robertson
Vancouver, BC

🍷 **THE WINE MAKER**
Upper Bench Estate
Winery & Creamery
Penticton, BC

···· **FEATURED INGREDIENT** ·················
Salt Spring Island mussels

10 mL grapeseed oil

2 garlic cloves, minced

1 tsp fresh ginger

30 mL green curry paste (recipe to follow)

250 mL coconut milk

15 mL fish sauce

2 kaffir lime leaves, fresh

1 lb mussels, cleaned

salt and pepper to taste

½ red pepper, julienned

2 Tbsp cilantro, chopped to garnish

3 springs Thai basil, to garnish

GREEN CURRY PASTE
MAKES ¾ CUP

1 lemongrass stalk, finely chopped

1 kaffir lime leaf (torn into pieces)

1 shallot, chopped

1 tsp fresh ginger

2 cloves garlic

½ tsp black peppercorns

1 tsp coriander seeds

8 small fresh green chilies

½ cup cilantro leaves, stalks, roots

½ lime, juiced

1 tsp grapeseed oil

¼ tsp salt

THAI GREEN CURRY MUSSELS

Mussels are such an incredibly diverse shellfish and so easy to prepare at home. It is hard to go wrong with mussels, whether they are steamed open in a variety of sauces or even just in some white wine and garlic. The richness of this gorgeous green curry coconut sauce takes the mussels to another exotic level. Make sure to serve with bread or a spoon to devour every last drop of the sauce!

Rinse and scrub mussels and remove beard before starting. Place a small, wide-bottom pot over medium heat. Add grapeseed oil, garlic, and ginger. Sauté over a gentle heat, constantly stirring. Add green curry paste (see recipe) and sauté to ensure the paste does not burn—approximately 20 seconds—until aromatics are released. Add coconut milk, fish sauce, kaffir lime leaves, and bring to a gentle simmer. Add mussels and cover pot with a lid. Simmer for approximately 2 minutes. Do not remove lid to see how the mussels are cooking! Once the mussels are cooked, season to taste with salt and pepper and additional fish sauce if required. Garnish with red peppers and cilantro.

GREEN CURRY PASTE With the back of your knife, bruise lemongrass and slice as finely as you can. Also coarsely chop kaffir lime leaves, shallots, ginger, and garlic.

In a mortar and pestle, start grinding the lemongrass until finely broken down. Add kaffir lime leaves, black peppercorns, coriander seeds, and chilies. Continue to pound away with pestle. Add shallots, garlic, and ginger. Lastly, add the cilantro, lime juice, and oil.

Paste should be fine and smooth.

*If you don't have a mortar and pestle, put all of the ingredients in a food processor and process to a thick paste. Transfer the paste to an airtight container. Store in the fridge for up to three weeks.

···· **DRINK PAIRING** ·································

2012 Upper Bench Winery Pinot Blanc
Nose: nectarine, canned pear, and pineapple with a hint of elderflower. Palate: guava, tangerine, and lychee along with a bright, clean minerality. "This has a freshness that recalls Sauvignon Blanc, with lightly grassy aromas, flavours of apples and limes and a lively, refreshing acidity. 90 points."—John Schreiner

PAUL SIMPSON ⛵ THE SEA FARMER

FLEXING THEIR MUSSELS.

Paul Simpson, the president and founder of Island Sea Farms, has been in the shellfish biz his whole life. He began shucking and packing oysters on Salt Spring and selling them door-to-door at age 10! His farming business truly began in 1996 when, while diving near Salt Spring, he discovered a variety of Blue mussels called Mediterranean mussels—a variety previously unknown in British Columbia waters. After a year of government research, Island Sea Farms received the first aquaculture license to grow this mussel in British Columbia. In 2005 their hatchery team created a hybrid of the "Gallo" or Mediterranean ("Med") Mussel with the Atlantic Blue or "PEI Mussel," the new hybrid having the best characteristics of both varieties. Island Sea Farms is the only mussel farming company in the world to be 100% reliant on hatchery seed.

These plump and perfect mussels are grown in the ideal waters surrounding beautiful Salt Spring Island and Cortes Island. The hatchery, nursery, and administration are located on Salt Spring Island—from there, the mussels are moved to Cortes Island waters "to grow up." The waters offer ideal conditions, where "rich oceanic waters collide with the warmer waters of the protected bays and sounds, causing an explosion of phyto-plankton."

"The unique blend of these single cell plants produce a sweetness measured by a very high glycogen content, a sweet starch, as well as omega 3 levels approaching those of salmon," explains Paul. "Our rope-grown deep-water farming methods are 100% natural, use no chemicals or any other additives and only biodegradable materials. In awe of the pristine beauty of the islands they farm, Island Sea Farms is active in the movement to establish best aquaculture practices and supports organic standards for British Columbia aquaculture."

SEA FARM Island Sea Farms/Salt Spring Island Mussels   LOCATION PO Box 445, Ganges, Salt Spring Island, BC
WEB saltspringislandmussels.com

UPPER BENCH ESTATE WINERY & CREAMERY 🍷 THE WINE MAKER

AND THE WINE AND CHEESE MAKER LIVED HAPPILY EVER AFTER.

Gavin (the wine maker) and Shana (the cheese maker) Miller own and operate Upper Bench Estate Winery & Creamery. This couple's love and passion for their individual crafts is steeped into the luxurious flavour and refinement of their creations. And there is a romance in their artistry—it manifests in the wine and cheese pairings—each offering the perfect marriage of flavours on the palate. Gavin is originally from the UK and Shana from Nova Scotia, and they always shared the dream of owning their own winery and creamery one day, and now they do. And it is an Okanagan treasure.

WINE MAKERS Gavin and Shana Miller   LOCATION 170 Upper Bench Road South, Penticton, BC
FB upperbench   TWITTER @upperbench   WEB upperbench.ca

LEFT TO RIGHT: David and Sara

DAVID ROBERTSON ✳ THE CHEF

GETTING DIRTY IN THE KITCHEN.

The Dirty Apron is a magical place. Visually stunning in a heritage building with high ceilings and grand doors, the dining room features tall windows and antique chandeliers hanging over a long harvest table—it is like walking into a French chateau. And then there is the kitchen! Never will you see such elaborate cooking stations for students, suited up with the best appliances and tools, this place will make you feel like you are studying at Le Cordon Bleu.

Owners David and Sara Robertson are gracious hosts. David is a natural teacher and he shares technique without ego, is encouraging and gentle as he leads students through the steps of a recipe.

While working as the sous chef at Chambar Restaurant next door, David realized that he loved to teach and The Dirty Apron Cooking School & Delicatessen opened its doors in August of 2009. David recalls, "The name of 'The Dirty Apron' came about when we found out that we were also expecting our first child in the same year that the cooking school was to open. We joked that the year

of 2009 was going to be the year of dirty diapers, to which Sara added: '. . . and dirty aprons!' The rest is history."

David shares: "The food culture in Vancouver is enthusiastic, excited for new things, and thirsty for more knowledge. Foodies in Vancouver are no longer happy to just have a tasty meal . . . they want to be able to entertain at home and create tasty and cutting-edge dishes in their own kitchens. Our clientele has become increasingly younger. Cooking over the past few years has become approachable, fun, and even cool, so a lot of kids who come out of high school want to learn how to cook now. On any given night I have students ranging in age between 19 years and 70 years old—all sharing the same culinary experience and excitement."

SCHOOL Dirty Apron Cooking School & Delicatessen
LOCATION 540 Beatty Street, Vancouver, BC   TWITTER @Dirty_Apron
FB thedirtyapron   WEB dirtyapron.com

⛵ **THE SEA FARMER**
Bob Hegedus
New Westminister, BC

☸ **THE CHEF**
Frank Pabst
Vancouver, BC

🍷 **THE WINE MAKER**
50th Parallel Estate Winery
Lake Country, BC

···· FEATURED INGREDIENT ····················
Pacific sea urchin

2 ripe avocados, crushed with a fork to
　　a chunky purée, seasoned with one
　　tablespoon of olive oil, sea salt and
　　a pinch of cayenne.
8½ inch slices of ciabatta bread,
　　toasted to golden brown
extra virgin olive oil—the finest
　　you are willing to buy
16 pieces of freshest sea urchin roe,
　　cut into 3 pieces each
½ lemon
4 red radishes, cut into thin julienne on
　　a Japanese mandolin and seasoned
　　with a pinch of salt
1 green onion cut into very thin slices
6 oz baby arugula
16 grape tomatoes cut into halves

SEA URCHIN BRUSCHETTA
WITH AVOCADO, RADISH & ARUGULA

If you have been afraid of tasting or making sea urchin at home, this recipe is the perfect one to try. The rich textures of the avocado and the sea urchin blend beautifully to accent each other's luxurious features. The peppery notes from the radish atop the bruschetta with the arugula salad and the little kick of cayenne offer that perfect palate dance.

Spread the avocado purée evenly on top of the ciabatta toasts and drizzle with olive oil.

Place six chunks of sea urchin roe on top of each avocado ciabatta and squeeze a little lemon on top. Sprinkle the radish julienne and green onion slices on top of the bruschetta.

Toss baby arugula and grape tomatoes with olive oil and lemon and season with a pinch of sea salt.

Serve two sea urchin bruschetta per person alongside some arugula and grape tomato salad.

Enjoy your taste of one of the unsung heroes of the sea!

···· **DRINK PAIRING** ····································

2014 50th Parallel Estate Winery Gewürztraminer
Lychee, peach, candied ginger, honeydew, and exotic Indian spices. Richly aromatic. The palate is lush and mouth filling, with abundant exotic melon fruits. Generous and sweet fruit on entry, the finish is rich, long, and refreshingly dry with a touch of acidity to complement a hint of cardamom spice.

Diver: Ryan

BOB HEGEDUS ⛵ THE SEA FARMER

FISHING FOR PRICKLY THINGS.

Bob Hegedus' career in commercial fishing began with an interest in diving. "As a kid I loved Jacques Cousteau (the famous underwater explorer) and watched him on TV all the time." So when old enough, Bob took a commercial diving course in West Vancouver. He says, "it took a long time to break into the industry back then. One day a friend invited me to come along on a commercial dive for geoduck in 1987—and I went and my career continued from there."

Bob sails his Westport 1 boat and crew out to dive for red sea urchin and sea cucumbers from the Gulf Islands area all the way up to Haida Gwaii. "I love being on the ocean and under the water," he says. During their season they will dive all day, bringing up bags of sea urchin. Bob explains the process, "One of the divers will go down to survey the area, and if it looks like a good spot, the diver will bring an urchin up to quality check it. To harvest, we use a metal rake to pull them off the rocks, etc., and then bag them."

The red sea urchin they harvest is the largest sea urchin in the world and found only along the rocky sub-tidal Pacific shores of North America. Export to Japan and China is a large part of their business, but sales off the docks in Steveston have significantly increased. This local treasure is best enjoyed fresh from the sea, and I can attest to that. One of Bob's diving crew (shown in picture) Ryan Griffith offered me a taste from the sea urchin. It is mildly sweet and super fresh tasting with notes of honeydew melon. Most people will be familiar with sea urchin as 'uni,' a popular dish in sushi restaurants.

Pacific Urchin Harvesters Association (PUHA) was incorporated in 1994 and is composed of eligible license-holding sea urchin divers. It currently has 110 members in the fishery.

HQ Westport 1 Pacific Urchin Harvesters Association (PUHA)
LOCATION 902–4th Street, New Westminster, BC
FB Pacific-Urchin-Harvesters-Association TWITTER @puhaorg WEB puha.org

FRANK PABST ✷ THE CHEF

A CHAMPION FOR THE UNSUNG HEROES OF THE SEA.

Celebrated executive chef Frank Pabst has a most extraordinary restaurant history. His career began as an apprentice in a small one star Michelin French restaurant in Aachen, Germany. From there he went on to work under an array of culinary superstars (all Michelin rated) in France. Onward to Canada where he was chef de cuisine at Vancouver's legendary Lumière Restaurant and opened the award-winning Pastis Restaurant. All that before 2003 when he joined the Blue Water Cafe, creating yet another star on the Vancouver food scene.

Multi-award winning, both chef and restaurant, Frank creates sumptuous menus that feature west coast seafood at its freshest. The concept for his Unsung Heroes Festival, this year in February it celebrated its 11th anniversary, was to educate consumers about the more under-utilized species available locally from the sea, therefore curbing the danger factor of the more popular species being overfished. It also provides the unique opportunity to taste these delightful unusual creatures available from our local waters like sea urchin, herring, and jellyfish, which many have not had the opportunity to experience.

Chef Pabst remains a leader in promoting and utilizing responsible, sustainable seafood practice and Blue Water Cafe is a founding member of the Vancouver Aquarium's Ocean Wise program.

Frank and Blue Water Cafe also have their own award-winning cookbook that celebrates the waters of the Pacific Northwest and "draws on the freshest fish and an East meets West style that allows the seafood to shine."

RESTAURANT Blue Water Cafe   LOCATION 1095 Hamilton Street, Vancouver, BC
FB BlueWaterCafe   TWITTER @bluewatercafe   WEB bluewatercafe.net

50TH PARALLEL ESTATE WINERY
☥ THE WINE MAKER

MEET YOU AT THE 50TH!

This is a rockstar winery team (seriously, and they all look like rockstars). As friendly and passionate about their winery as they are glamourous, Sheri-Lee Turner-Krouzel, Curtis Krouzel, and wine maker Grant Stanley are building a colossal new winery in Lake Country. The winemaking facility and tasting room itself are amazing—modern and meticulously planned, but the plans for restaurant, lakeview accommodation, and event facilities will take the 50th over the top.

LOCATION 17101 Terrace View Road, Lake Country, BC   FB 50thparallelestate   TWITTER @50thparallelwin   WEB 50thparallel.com

LEFT TO RIGHT: Grant, Sheri-Lee, and Curtis

WARNING
PROTECT YOUR FOOD FROM
SEAGULLS

⚓

MAINS

THE FARMER
Bob Mitchell
Pemberton, BC

THE CHEF
Randy Jones
Pemberton, BC

THE WINE MAKER
Rolf de Bruin and
Heleen Pannekoek
Lillooet, BC

······ FEATURED INGREDIENT ······
Pemberton Meadows
natural beef short ribs

SHORT RIBS

3 lbs Pemberton Meadows
natural beef short ribs

4 Tbsp canola oil

1 large onion, cut into 1" dice

1 large carrot, peeled and cut into 1" dice

2 stalks celery, cut into 1" dice

4 garlic cloves, peeled

1 Tbsp black peppercorns

1 large sprig fresh thyme

1 bottle (750 mL) Fort Berens
    23 Camels Cabernet Merlot

salt and pepper

MAC 'N' CHEESE

3 cups elbow noodles, cooked al dente
    (cooked but still firm)

2 large Pemberton carrots, peeled
    and cut into ¼-inch dice

10 garlic cloves, peeled

2 Tbsp canola oil

3 cups seasonal mushrooms, chopped
    ½" dice, thick but chunky

3 Tbsp butter

1.5 liters, 36% whipping cream

1 cup aged white cheddar cheese, grated

1 cup mozzarella cheese, grated

2 sprigs fresh thyme

2 cups kale, roughly chopped

salt and pepper

FORT BERENS WINE-BRAISED

PEMBERTON MEADOWS NATURAL BEEF SHORT RIBS

WITH EXTRA CHEESY MAC & CHEESE

Comfort food like no other, this is the richest, most delicious mac 'n cheese you will ever treat your taste buds to. Make this at home but do plan to visit Pemberton and Mile One. It is a very special place with GOOD FOOD.

SHORT RIBS Season short ribs with salt and pepper; in a heavy-bottom pot heat oil, sear short ribs until brown on all sides, remove from pot. Add onions, carrots, celery, and garlic to pot, gently browning in the remaining oil. Place short ribs back into pot, add black peppercorns, thyme, and cover with red wine. Gently simmer on the stovetop until meat is tender and starts to pull away from bone. Allow short ribs to cool in the refrigerator in the braising liquid overnight. The next day pull meat off rib bones in rustic chunks and set aside. Strain the braising liquid and reduce by half.

MAC 'N' CHEESE Boil the pasta and set aside. Preheat oven to 400°F (200°C). Toss the carrots and garlic cloves together with canola oil in a baking pan, season with salt and pepper, and then roast in the oven until the garlic is lightly browned and the carrots are golden and tender. Remove from oven.

On the stovetop, melt butter in heavy-bottom pot, add mushrooms, and cook lightly. Then add the roasted carrots and garlic and continue to cook for a couple of minutes before adding the braising liquid and reducing it by half. Then add the pulled short rib meat and 1-litre of whipping cream and simmer until the cream reduces by half. Add the cooked pasta to the simmering cream sauce to coat pasta then add both cheeses, folding them in and stirring until well simmering. If pasta is too dry add remaining cream, if too wet reduce slightly. Add thyme leaves from sprigs then add the kale, gently stirring it in to wilt. Season with salt and pepper to taste. Dive in!

······ DRINK PAIRING ······

2012 Fort Berens 23 Camels Cabernet Merlot
A delightful blend of 55% Cabernet Franc and 45% Merlot. A medium-bodied wine with pleasing red juicy fruit, to be enjoyed on its own, or with dinner.

LEFT TO RIGHT: Bob, Erin (sous chef), and Randy

BOB MITCHELL ✱ THE FARMER

COW WHISPERER.

Farmer Bob whistles and "his girls" come running. It is evident that these cows are treated well, even lovingly, at Pemberton Meadows. They are beautiful looking beasts and they live with a staggeringly beautiful mountain vista surrounding them. They are calm and quiet—a clear sign of happiness, says Temple Grandin, America's foremost animal behaviour expert. "Treat 'em nice" is Temple's key message in low-stress cattle handling. And these girls are treated exceptionally well. Green grass, misty mountains, glacial water to drink—this is kind of like a cow paradise.

Cattle rancher Bob Mitchell was born and raised on the family farm that his parents cleared and cultivated before the road even reached Pemberton.

Bob grew up farming potatoes and raising cattle. His neighbour Don Millerd moved onto the farm next door in 1968 when his family changed their livelihood from ocean to land based. The Millerds came from the coast where they were pioneers in the salmon canning business with Francis Millerd & Co., which was the second biggest cannery in BC in its time. In 2004, Don and Bob decided to go into business together and began to raise and finish their herds on their own, land–raising them naturally on homegrown hay and grain. They believed that with the emphasis on healthy eating, food traceability, and local products, this beef would find an appreciative market. This has proven to be the case.

"Our cattle are raised as nature intended—living outdoors, in a herd, on pasture. In the winter, when snow covers the ground, they stay in a large treed area where they can take shelter from harsh weather. The cattle are free to spread out under the trees at night. We have found that the cattle stay cleaner and drier than they would if confined to a barn or feedlot, where bacteria and pathogens might flourish."

"Our experience has been that animals that are not confined to a barn or feedlot remain healthy, and do not require drugs." Isn't it nice to know where your food comes from and how it was raised? All of Pemberton Meadows beef is sold through Two Rivers Specialty Meats—see more on them page 153.

FARM Pemberton Meadows Natural Beef   LOCATION Pemberton, BC—c/o Two Rivers Meats, 180 Donaghy Avenue North Vancouver, BC   WEB pembertonmeadowsbeef.com

RANDY JONES ✳ THE CHEF

PROWLS FOR MUSHROOMS IN THE DARK.

"My culinary training was upper-scale French Culinary School and very structured hotel kitchens, so there's still some of that in me; but uncomplicated preparations using great quality seasonal BC products is what inspires me these days!" explains Chef Randy Jones.

And BC-centric he is. This guy does local comfort food in a big way. Randy and his wife/partner Cindy Yu focus on making the Mile One Eating House experience comfortable and delicious. "We love bringing things full circle and connecting our amazing farmers, fisherman, ranchers, wine makers, brewers, distillers, craftspeople, and artisans to our daily offerings."

Over the years Randy's kitchen experience took him from literally sea to sky (Tofino to urban Vancouver to Whistler) sourcing local purveyors along the way and building relationships. From featuring a local Pemberton beef farmer on the menu all the way to sea level with Albacore tuna from Captain Ian Bryce in Tofino, Randy sources direct. Randy says, "For over three years now Ian, and now recently his son, have been delivering hundreds of pounds of Albacore Tuna to us, directly from their home base on Vancouver Island. All of our Albacore Tuna offerings come from this single Fishing Vessel and Family (Natural Gift Seafoods)."

So clearly this is not the usual, sometimes boring, comfort food—this place ain't boring. Mac n' Cheese becomes pure luxury in Randy's hands. He'll throw in some white chanterelles foraged from the Pemberton woods nearby, or make it a little wild by adding local elk chorizo–every way he spins it, this is good grub. His menu was designed to feed the people of his village—the farmers, the ranchers—people who are working hard that "need to get fed" he says. And Randy works hard to feed them.

RESTAURANT Mile One Eating House   LOCATION 7330 Arbutus Street Pemberton, BC
FB MileOneEatingHouse   TWITTER @MileOnePemby   WEB MileOneEatingHouse.com

FORT BERENS ESTATE WINERY ♟ THE WINE MAKER

DOUBLE DUTCH WINEMAKING IN THE MOUNTAINS.

Heleen Pannekoek and Rolf de Bruin moved to BC from the Netherlands in 2008 with a plan to start a winery. They discovered that the climate and soil conditions in Lillooet were similar to that of the South Okanagan and decided to become pioneers in this budding new wine region. A good choice—the awards have been coming in ever since! The featured short ribs are braised in the Fort Berens 23 Camels Cabernet Merlot. What the heck do camels have to do with BC wine? Rolf explains: "In 1862, John Galbraith, who was a prospector in town decided that camels would be better suited for working in the hot dry climate in Lillooet. So he went down to San Francisco, where apparently camels were for sale, and bought 24 camels; one died en route. Things didn't go as planned and at some point, John decided to let the camels roam. Sightings of camels have been reported as late as 1908, when a First Nation chief was photographed on a camel!"

LOCATION 1881 Hwy 99 North Lillooet, BC   FB FortBerns   TWITTER @FortBerens   WEB FortBerens.ca

⛵ **THE FISHERMAN**
Organic Ocean Seafood
Vancouver, BC

⚙ **THE CHEF**
David Hawksworth
Vancouver, BC

🍷 **THE WINE MAKER**
Meyer Family Vineyards
Okanagan Falls, BC

···· FEATURED INGREDIENT ·····················
Organic Ocean salmon fillets

4 × 5 oz Organic Ocean salmon fillets, skin on

2 Tbsp unsalted butter

2 shallots, minced

¼ of a small butternut squash, peeled
    and cut into ¾-inch (2 cm)cubes

1 garlic clove

4 sprigs of fresh thyme

1⅓ cups chicken stock

sea salt

4 oz wild mushrooms, cleaned and sliced

4 tsp extra-virgin olive oil

1 Tbsp lemon juice

12 cherry tomatoes, cut into quarters

4 sage leaves, finely chopped

PAN-SEARED WILD SALMON
WITH BUTTERNUT SQUASH & WILD MUSHROOMS

This recipe is a celebration of treasures sourced from the farm, sea, and forests of the west coast. Chef Hawksworth works closely with Organic Ocean to source his seafood, and Mikuni Wild Harvest, which provides the wild mushrooms.

Melt 1 Tbsp butter in a large pot over low heat. Add the shallots and cook until they are soft but not brown, about 4 to 5 minutes.

Add the squash, garlic, and thyme. Cook for 5 minutes, stirring frequently, without browning. Add the chicken stock and bring to a gentle simmer. Season to taste. Cook covered until the squash is tender but not falling apart. Remove the garlic and thyme. In a medium frying pan, melt the remaining 1 Tbsp butter over medium-high heat. Add the mushrooms and sauté until soft. Season to taste and add to the squash mixture.

Preheat the oven to 400°F/200°C. Heat the oil in a large, preferably nonstick frying pan that can go into the oven. Season the salmon and place in the pan skin side down. Cook without turning for 3 to 4 minutes until the fish is lightly browned around the edges. Flip the salmon and then place the frying pan in the oven and cook the fish for 7 to 10 minutes until cooked through.

Re-warm the sauce mixture and add the lemon juice, cherry tomatoes, and sage. Spoon into warmed bowls and top with the salmon fillets. Serve immediately.

···· DRINK PAIRING ····································

2011 Meyer Family Vineyards, Okanagan Valley Pinot Noir
"Expect an overt earthy nose with bits of strawberry and racy acidity and what we can now term the Meyer elegance. The palate is soft but not flabby with wild raspberry fruit, spice, Worcestershire, dried herbs, and some stony minerality."—Anthony Gismondi

LEFT TO RIGHT: Jak, Steve, and David

MEYER FAMILY VINEYARDS ♀ THE WINE MAKER

MEYER MANIA.

Meyer Family Vineyards arrived onto the Okanagan wine scene back in 2006 with a huge splash. Focused on producing world-class Chardonnays and Pinot Noirs, it has been a multi-award winner since its inception. It now has vineyards in both Naramata and Okanagan Falls, and owners Jak Meyer and Janice Stevens now live at the Okanagan Falls vineyard with their two girls. Born and raised in Alberta, the Meyers quickly became well-loved members of the local wine community, bringing with them their contagious friendliness and welcome smiles. The Meyers produce single vineyard wines, which are an excellent example of how terroir affects the expression of varietal character. Wine maker Chris Carson is a graduate of Lincoln University, Canterbury, New Zealand with a bachelor of viticulture and oenology. His traditional training focuses on handcrafting classic wines to display the unique characteristics derived from this Okanagan Valley terroir.

LOCATION 4287 McLean Creek Rd, Okanagan Falls, BC   FB MeyerFamilyVineyards
TWITTER @mfvwines   WEB mfvwines.com

DAVID HAWKSWORTH ✳ THE CHEF

CULINARY EXCELLENCE.

In 2008 David Hawksworth was named to *Western Living*'s Top 40 under 40 and became the youngest chef inductee into the BC Restaurant Hall of Fame. Destined for greatness, this locally raised, European-trained chef has created a reputation for elegant, contemporary Canadian cuisine based on the finest local ingredients he can source. David Hawksworth became one of Canada's leading culinary talents as executive chef of West restaurant in 2000 where he remained for seven years, receiving critical acclaim from opening day on. Now at his celebrated namesake restaurant in the Rosewood Hotel Georgia in Vancouver, Hawksworth continues his legacy of fine dining and commitment to local food and drink producers, fishers, and foragers. A mentor to many of Vancouver's best chefs that have worked in his kitchen, Hawksworth passed on his knowledge and "Rolodex" of local suppliers. Founder of the Hawksworth Young Chef Scholarship Foundation, David Hawksworth created this culinary arts nonprofit organization to recognize and inspire young Canadian chefs while promoting professionalism and culinary excellence within the hospitality industry. The scholarship program provides a platform for talented young chefs to get a head start with an unparalleled opportunity to work in the country's leading restaurants.

David Hawksworth is a true culinary visionary.

RESTAURANT Hawksworth FB HawksworthRestaurant
LOCATION 801 W Georgia St, Vancouver/Rosewood Hotel Georgia
TWITTER @HawksworthRest WEB hawksworthrestaurant.com

⚓

ORGANIC OCEAN SEAFOOD ⛵ THE FISHERMAN

3 SALTY GUYS WHO SPEAK FLUENT FISH.

Independent fishermen, Steve Johansen, Dan Chauvel, and Frank Keitsch banded together to create a company and a brand, and it has become the west coast's strongest liaison between land and sea. Passionate spokesmen and advocates for healthy oceans, these three friends have been fishing since they were kids and, following in the footsteps of their fathers, they are making a living from the sea.

Working with OceanWise™ and other local causes, Organic Ocean has been a force of education, teaching the community about safe and sustainable fishing practices and how to shop for sustainable species as well as leading by example. Steve is happy to report, "Our oceans are healthy and we are finally making a difference. From the chefs to the consumers to the fishermen—everyone has been changing their ways by adopting ocean-friendly, sustainable, and responsible harvesting practices."

Organic Ocean is also a pioneer in seafood traceability, becoming the first seafood supplier in the world to provide DNA certification of authenticity to their products.

As one local chef explained, "Steve (Organic Ocean) brings the fish to the people. He's the guy behind the food." He's also the guy behind the wildly successful Annual Spot Prawn Festival! "The whole point was to let people know about this beautiful product and the best part was how the community in Vancouver rallied around it." From a crowd of around 300 in its first year (2016 will be the 10th year of the festival) to around 3,000 in 2014, Steve and his original spot prawn partner in crime, local chef Rob Clark, hit the mark. Steve says, "Spot prawns have really become the most celebrated ingredient in Vancouver now." This explains the hike in the prices—but it's a good thing. It's all supply and demand. And we are demanding spot prawns! The annual spot prawn boil is the signature event of the festival and is held at False Creek's Fishermen's Wharf. www.spotprawnfestival.com

FISHERMAN Organic Ocean Seafood FB organicoceanseafood
LOCATION HQ Fisherman's Wharf, Granville Island
TWITTER @OrganicOcean WEB organicocean.com

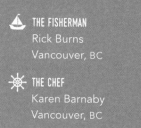
···· FEATURED INGREDIENT ········
Pacific Provider pink salmon

4 Tbsp (60 mL) soy sauce

4 cloves garlic, mashed to a paste

1 Tbsp (15 mL) fresh lemon juice

1 Tbsp (15 mL) honey

4–6 oz. (170 g) boneless pink
    salmon filets, skin on

8 tsp (40 mL) freshly and coarsely
    ground black pepper

2 Tbsp (30 mL) vegetable oil

CAST-IRON

PEPPER-CRUSTED PINK SALMON

"Pink salmon is sweet and nutty, and I've been a fan of pinks since meeting Rick Burns and Lynn Prestash of Pacific Provider. Their pink salmon (as well as their coho and spring) is lovingly taken care of, from the fishing to the delivery. This is one of their family's favourite recipes of mine—according to Rick, his children devour and demand it."—Karen **SERVES 4**

The key to cooking pinks is cooking them quickly, and serving them medium or medium rare. If you want a simple sauce for this dish, warm thinly sliced green onions in butter and serve overtop.

Combine the soy sauce, garlic, lemon juice, and honey in a baking dish that can hold the salmon snugly in a single layer. Add the salmon, flesh side down. Refrigerate for 30 minutes. Remove the salmon from the marinade and pat dry. Press 2 tsp (10 mL) of the pepper onto the flesh side of each piece of salmon, coating it evenly. In a cast-iron frying pan, heat the oil over medium high heat until it is hot but not smoking. Place the salmon in the pan, pepper side down. Cook for 2–3 minutes. Turn and cook for another 2–3 minutes. The salmon should be medium in the centre. Serve immediately.

···· DRINK PAIRING ···

2013 Bella Wines Sparkling Rosé Brut Natural
The colour of this rosé is a pretty, soft pink. Tiny bubbles tickle your nose and offer up lovely notes of strawberry and rhubarb. The fresh strawberries and rhubarb follow through on the palate with a little kick of spice to put you in the party mood.

BELLA WINES 🍷 THE WINE MAKER

BUBBLING OVER IN NARAMATA.

Wine maker (and chef!) Jay Drysdale and wife Wendy Rose have made a wonderful addition to the Naramata community and have brought with them their great passion for food and wine along with a little urban sparkle. Bella Wines is a boutique sparkling wine house where Jay's dream to "capture his expression of the local wine scene in a bottle" has been achieved, with great panache. They specialize in bubble—elegant, delicious bubble that formed an instant cult following both for its high quality and pretty bottle design. Making a brut, rosé, and now western Canada's first natural Ancestrale sparking wine, they offer different labels by region, allowing wine aficionados to literally taste the variance in terroir from across the Okanagan Valley.

LOCATION **4320 Gulch Road, Naramata, BC**   TWITTER **@bellawines**   FB **BellaWines**   WEB **bellawines.ca**

KAREN BARNABY ✵ THE CHEF

LIKES TO EAT CRAB IN THE SNOW.

Chef, cookbook author, columnist, cooking instructor, food photographer, speaker, whittler of cool cooking utensils (really) . . . Is there anything this woman cannot do? By the way, she is also the only female chef to be honoured with the British Columbia Restaurant and Foodservices Association Back of the House Award for Excellence.

Karen Barnaby's name has become synonymous with fine seafood in the west coast community. Her years of serving up amazing seafood and local fish-focused creations at The Fish House made her famous, and her local sourcing efforts and community focus made her a legend. Karen is an ethical person who has given countless hours to local charities and shared her passion through many a cooking class and through her many best-selling cookbooks, she has said: "There should be no snobbery in food, only a desire to eat well and share your knowledge."

Inspired by her grandmothers, Karen hit the kitchen at the tender age of eight and leapt heart and soul into the cooking world, without professional training, at age twenty. "Everything I learned, I learned on my own." From Ottawa, she found her way to Vancouver in 1991 and to The Raintree Restaurant where she focused on fresh, local, seasonal, and sustainable products. From there, it was The Fish House where she continued her practice of personally sourcing local and building strong relationships with west coast fishers like Rick Burns as well as sea farmers, foragers, artisans, and farmers. She lived and breathed this philosophy before it was cool.

Karen is passionate about protecting our beautiful waters:

"A lot of people like to pay lip service to sustainability. And a lot of people are sleepwalking through life. When it comes right down to it, price usually trumps the right thing to do. Words are cheap, and so are intentions. Take action by supporting sustainable fishing culture. Everyone deserves a living wage. Resist buying junk food or milkshakes posing as coffee and invest that money into better quality, real food. Be part of the joy that will allow our progeny and planet to have a bright future."

Chef of Product & Business Development for Albion Fisheries, Intercity Packers & Fresh Start Foods, Vancouver, BC   WEB karenbarnaby.com

⚓

RICK BURNS ⛵ THE FISHERMAN

IN THE PINK.

Rick Burns is a meticulous fisherman and provides the freshest product possible. To maintain the ultimate freshness, he flash freezes the fish at sea—but his trick to preserve the fresh-caught taste is to immediately bleed and clean the fish after they are reeled in. Many fisherman do not take the time to make this step a priority, but Rick maintains that this is the way to provide the best possible product for his customers.

Rick was bitten by the fishing bug in grade nine. Growing up, his family travelled with his dad's mining career and, lucky for him, in 1964 his dad was transferred to Ucluelet on Vancouver Island. Rick joined the rest of the boys whose families were all in the fishing business as a deckhand that summer. "It was so fun! Catching fish provides the same thrill for me today as it first did back then."

Rick now holds a northern fishing license and his season begins June 19th. He hits the high seas in his Pacific Provider boat on June 10th to make the journey up to Haida Gwaii where he will remain until September.

Rick and his wife Lynn Prestash offer direct sales to many of the west coast's finest restaurants and beyond, but they also sell to consumers (email them!).

Rick is also known as an ambassador for pink salmon, a species of salmon that are aplenty in our Pacific waters. Karen Barnaby explains, "I met Rick in 2005, he was passionate about his fish, a little quirky, and cute, all qualities that I find attractive. The Salmon Marketing board was promoting his salmon and I was asked to do a demo with it. Pinks were featured and I'll admit that I was skeptical, but his looked perfect with none of the bruises and other marks of abuse that you usually see on pinks. I took a leap of faith and started ordering Rick's pink salmon. I ordered A LOT of it and was proud to call it by name and feature it on the menu."

COMPANY Pacific Provider   LOCATION Vancouver, BC   EMAIL prestash-burns@shaw.ca

······ FEATURED INGREDIENT ······
Pacific sablefish

SABLEFISH

1 large fillet (3–4 lb)

STEAMED MUSSELS

100 mL shallots, sliced
3 garlic cloves, sliced
100 mL white wine
1 sprig basil
1 lemon, juiced
1 lb Pacific mussels

ARTICHOKE BARIGOULE

7 garlic cloves, sliced
15 mL olive oil
100 mL carrot, diced
100 mL celery, diced
200 mL shallot, sliced
400 mL white wine
1 sprig basil
1 fresh bay leaf, crushed
1 sprig chervil
15 pc baby artichoke, trimmed, halved,
    and held in acidulated water
1.2 L vegetable stock
salt and pepper
1 lemon, juiced

BASIL OIL

1 L picked basil, packed
500 mL canola oil

TO FINISH

8 medium nugget potatoes, quartered and
    cooked, a few small basil leaves, a few
    small parsley leaves, and some sea lettuce
    if you live by the sea, butter, canola oil,
    lemon, salt and pepper

PACIFIC SABLEFISH WITH ARTICHOKES & MUSSELS

Chef Barr is able to literally walk out his kitchen door directly into the sea. He picks fresh sea lettuce off the rocks in front of the Wickaninnish Inn, forages from the surrounding forests, and obviously accesses the freshest possible fish and seafood. Lutz is the dude who brings him the best catch.

SABLEFISH Remove the skin from the fillet, noting which side the skin came from. Use your fingertip to follow the bones down the fillet (about halfway) and cut the fillet across at that point. Using the tip of your knife, follow the bones down the larger half of the fillet on either side to cut the flesh away from the bones. Cut the fish into 6 equal portions, some portions may be made up of two pieces.

MUSSLES In a medium pot, combine all of the ingredients except the mussels and reduce by half. Add the mussels and cover the pot. Steam until all of the shells have opened. Strain the nectar and reserve. Remove the mussels from their shells and reserve just enough nectar to cover them.

ARTICHOKE BARIGOULE In a wide rondeau (a wide, heavy-bottomed pot with straight sides and two loop handles), sweat the garlic in the olive oil. Once translucent, add the carrot, celery, shallot, and salt and continue to sweat being careful not to get any colour. Add the white wine and reduce by half. Add the herbs and cover the vegetables with a layer of cheesecloth. Add the artichokes and the vegetable stock. Season with salt and pepper and bring to a simmer. Add the lemon juice, adjust seasoning and continue to simmer with a cartouche (a piece of round parchment of grease-proof paper that covers the surface of a stew, soup, stock, or sauce to reduce evaporation) to cover until the artichokes are tender. Using the cheesecloth, remove the artichokes and cool on a tray. Strain the Barigoule broth and reserve for sauce.

BASIL OIL Blend ingredients and heat in a pot to 50°C. Strain into a bowl set over ice and re-strain through a coffee filter.

Season the sablefish with salt on both sides and leave to temper for 10 minutes. Mix the reserved Barigoule broth and mussel nectar in a ratio of 2 parts Barigoule to 1 part mussel nectar. Adjust seasoning with lemon, salt and pepper. Place 750 mL of the broth in a pot and begin to heat. Heat a large frying pan (or two medium frying pans) until very hot. Add some canola oil and once the oil is smoking, dab any moisture off the sablefish and place in the frying pan, skin side up. Sear until golden in colour, this will take a minute or two. Flip the fish over, pour off any excess oil, and add some butter, lemon juice, and a splash of water. Remove from the heat and baste the fish with the melted butter until a cake tester or thin knife passes through the flesh without resistance. Meanwhile, in another pan, glaze the artichokes, mussels, and potatoes with a splash of water and some butter. Season with salt and pepper. Place the fish portions in the middle of 6 large dinner bowls. Arrange the mussels and vegetables in a ring around the fish. Pour some broth into each dish, not enough to cover the vegetables or fish. Float some basil oil in the broth of each bowl and garnish with the picked herbs (and sea lettuce if you have).

LUTZ ZILLIKEN ⛵ THE FISHERMAN

LIKES TO SMOKE FISH.

Born and raised in Weiburg, Germany on a trout fish farm, Lutz moved to Canada in 1977 when his father (whom Lutz refers to as a "fishing fanatic") bought a lodge on Quesnel Lake in the BC Interior. During his time there with his father, they were also involved in helping the salmon recreate their waterways from ocean to lake by clearing the dams that beavers had built. This was a wonderful contribution to the environment.

The ocean beckoned, and he moved to Tofino in 1998 to get into commercial diving for geoduck, which was a new industry at the time. Diving morphed into commercial fishing; Lutz says his favourite gig was when he was reef fishing for live cod—he would spend his time fishing off the shore with rod and reel, keeping the fish in the tank to be delivered live to restaurants.

Everyone knows Lutz, his smile is contagious and he has a great sense of humour. He also seems to have been involved at some point in every part of Tofino life and business. From processing fish, to commercial fishing and diving, to offering a wholesale fish store, storage units, and even now an oyster bar! His personal connections to the local fishermen make him an invaluable source as a fish supplier and he is known for "supplying a gold product to the restaurants."

After our visit, Lutz was going to fire up his boat to head out fishing after an eight-year hiatus (too busy to fish!) to rekindle his romance with the sea.

FISHERMAN West Pacific Seafood/The Fish Store and Oyster Bar
LOCATION 368 Main Street, Tofino, BC

WARREN BARR ✵ THE CHEF

SERVING THE WEST COAST ON A PLATE.

Warren Barr took over the rank of executive chef at The Pointe Restaurant at the Wickaninnish Inn in 2013 after spending three years on the kitchen team. Barr follows a great legacy of amazing chefs, including Rod Butters, Andrew Springett, and Nicholas Nutting, and takes on his role with great pride and dedication, "injecting his love of all things Canadian into every meal."

Barr's philosophy and style: "I find most of my inspiration in the ingredients and in the environment I'm in. Out here on the west coast, we have all sorts of lovely seafood and wild edibles growing that it is easy to find some inspiration. My philosophy or 'point' is to embody the seasons and the west coast of Vancouver Island on the plate. Knowing where my product comes from is a huge part of my cooking, I will often try to create a dish that is a snapshot of a time and place."

The "Wick" as it is affectionately known, is a unique and enchanting place to "be." It exudes a calmness and a beauty where the architecture has almost been absorbed by its supernatural seaside surroundings, making them one. The Wick is family-owned and operated with great pride by the McDiarmid family.

Chef Barr on life at the Wick: "In Tofino, we all work hard to create a fun and exciting town to visit, but at the end of the day we all know that the visitors, and even ourselves, are here because of the wild and powerful beauty of this place. I also find quite a bit of inspiration in the environment I work in. The Wickaninnish Inn is filled with engaged and passionate people. My team in the kitchen has a lot of young cooks in it and it is important for them to be interested and constantly learning. This pushes me to be constantly moving forward and trying new things so that the whole team can be learning together."

RESTAURANT The Pointe Restaurant at The Wickaninnish Inn **LOCATION** 500 Osprey Lane, Chesterman Beach, Tofino, BC **TWITTER** @wickinnbc **FB** wickinn **WEB** wickinn.com

"My philosophy or 'point' is to embody the seasons and west coast of Vancouver Island on the plate. Knowing where my product comes from is a huge part of my cooking, I will often try to create a dish that is a snapshot of a time and place."–Chef Warren Barr

UNSWORTH VINEYARDS 🍷 THE WINE MAKER

MARJORIE'S DREAM COME TRUE.

After 40+ years working in BC's fishing industry, Tim and Colleen Turyk, who both have a deep love for the Cowichan Valley, had the opportunity to become part of the community by purchasing a vineyard and winery in 2009. They named the property for Tim's mother Marjorie—whose maiden name was Unsworth. Marjorie grew up spending summers in the Cowichan Valley and she continued that tradition with her own children.

The vineyards are also home to Unsworth Restaurant that was opened in the restored 1900s farmhouse on the property. The restaurant specializes in Vancouver Island produce and products and features farm-to-table cuisine.

What is super interesting about this restaurant is that it offers a CSR (Community Supporting Restaurant) Program! Modelled after a Community Supported Agriculture (CSA) program, it offers a membership for a fee.

LOCATION 2915 Cameron Taggart Road, Mill Bay, BC **FB** unsworth-vineyards **TWITTER** @unsworthv **WEB** unsworthvineyards.com

⛵ THE PARTY MAKER
Kevin Perra
Bowen Island, BC

☸ THE CRAB BOIL MAKER
Brent Beasley
Vancouver, BC

······· FEATURED INGREDIENT ·······················
Dungeness crab

CRAB BOIL

1–2 pkg Louisiana brand Crawfish,
    Shrimp, and Crab boil spice mix
12 Dungeness crabs, cleaned (Do it yourself
    or ask your fishmonger to clean them
    right before you pick them up)
12 cobs of corn, shucked
5 lb baby red or white potatoes
    (about 4–5 per person)
12 mild Italian sausages (partially pre-cooked)
6 lemons, halved
6 onions, peeled and halved

POTATO DIPPING SAUCE

2 cups of mayonnaise
2 tsp chipotles in adobo sauce (or more to
    taste!), finely chopped or puréed

TO SERVE

3–4 fresh French baguettes
melted butter

A WEST COAST CRAB BOIL

For me, nothing celebrates west coast life better than a seafood boil in the sand. My friend Kevin Perra has a house on Bowen Island and our friend Brent Beasley is the captain of our many crab boil parties. Although it may look difficult, this is really quite an easy and impressive dinner party to throw. I purchased a huge pot and gas burner from an Italian restaurant supply store. It is actually a gigantic pasta pot with a built-in strainer that makes it ideal for a seafood boil. A crab boil can be executed for as few or as many guests as you like. I've used 12 as a start, but adjust to your group size.

SET UP First, make sure you have G & Ts to enjoy during set up! Rent a long, fold-up table and chairs to set up in the sand as close to the shore has possible (don't forget to check the tide schedule). The rest of the table setting is easy because the delicious contents of the entire pot are dumped right onto the table—you don't need plates or cutlery for this affair. Plastic tablecloths are ideal, but newspaper works too.

Make the Potato Dipping Sauce, and set aside. I like to serve a variety of flavoured butters by stirring lemon zest, chopped basil leaves, chili sauce or just good old minced garlic into softened butter earlier in the day. Then you can just melt it before serving. You will also need crab picks and crab crackers for each guest. I also like to offer rolled up damp, lemon-scented facecloths as an alternative to napkins so that guests can scrub their buttery fingers and lips with gusto. Use plastic sand pails from the dollar store to hold discarded crab shells. (At the end of the feast, the crab shells are flung back into the ocean as a gesture of our gratitude.)

CRAB BOIL Bring your big pot of water to the boil. Use enough water to come up at least half way to the top, keeping in mind you'll be adding a lot of ingredients. Add the Louisiana spice mix, lemons and onions, and let simmer for 10 minutes. Drop the potatoes in and cook for 5 minutes. Do a fork test for tenderness; they should be just partially cooked. Add the sausage and then bring back to a boil. Add the crab and boil for 6 minutes. Then add the cobs of corn and boil for another 3 minutes. This makes it a total of 9 minutes for the crab at a boil (this is expert advice from the Crab King George Blair), and then turn off the heat.

Strain your feast and then spread 'er on the table—no forks and knives. This is hands-on fun! Serve with baguettes, melted flavoured butter, and the potato dipping sauce (both in ramekins or little bowls). And lots of bubbly. Have a ball!

🍷 **THE DRINK MAKER**
Kate Hill
Vancouver, BC

✳ **THE FARMER**
Hopcott Farms
Pitt Meadows, BC

···· **FEATURED INGREDIENT** ····
Hopcott cranberries

KOMBUCHA

3 litres of filtered water

5 organic black tea bags

1 cup organic cane sugar

1 scoby (acronym: symbiotic culture of bacteria and yeast) It can be purchased from a health food store or online—even better, get one from a friend who is making some (thanks, Zilya!)

1 cup of local Hopcott cranberries (frozen or fresh)

OR

Buy plain kombucha from your natural food store

CRANBERRY KOMBUCHA

My book designer, Kate Hill, also happens to be a fabulous cook and a holistic health coach! For those who do not want to imbibe wine or cocktails at the beach party, she has created this delicious and healthy drink featuring local Hopcott cranberries.

To make from scratch, kombucha takes a week to brew at home, so it's up to you if you want to buy it or brew it. Both versions taste amazing but, as with all cooking, it is strangely satisfying to make it from scratch.

In a clean glass container that can hold over 3 litres, pour in the boiling water along with the tea bags and the cane sugar. Let sit for 10 minutes until the cane sugar has dissolved and then remove the tea bags. Allow time to cool, then place the scoby on top and cover with a tea towel so the bugs don't get in! Place the jar in a dark place for seven days and wait for it to do its magic! When the time is up, with sterile hands, remove the scoby from the kombucha and transfer it to a clean bowl to sit. Blend one cup of cranberries in blender with 2 cups of filtered water, and then add the mixture to the kombucha in a glass sterile jar that seals. I love to use large mason jars; they look great and are super practical for storage.

Leave the kombucha jar on your kitchen counter for 1 to 2 days; this will further the fermentation process and create that lovely effervescent quality. Store in the fridge for a few weeks to enjoy.

Shortcut way to make this delicious cranberry kombucha cocktail: Purchase your favourite brand of plain kombucha and pour into a large mason jar with cranberry blend (ratio 1 cup of kombucha to ¼ cup of cranberry blend).

TO SERVE Garnish with a few whole cranberries or other fruit and, over ice, enjoy this beautiful, healthy drink that people have made for centuries. Go online to read more about the many health benefits of kombucha and the interesting fermentation process.

Bob Hopcott. See more on page 140.

THE COOK
Tammy Renard
Pemberton, BC

THE FISHERMAN
The Blair Family
Birch Bay, BC

THE WINE MAKER
50th Parallel Estate Winery
Lake Country, BC

FEATURED INGREDIENT
Leftover Dungeness crab

1 red pepper, finely chopped

1 small onion, finely chopped

1 celery stalk, finely chopped

2 Tbsp fresh parsley, finely chopped

1½ cups fine bread crumbs

2 eggs, beaten

2 tsp Worcestershire sauce

1 Tbsp lemon Juice

½ tsp granulated garlic

shot of Tabasco sauce

salt and pepper

olive oil

1 cup Dungeness crabmeat

TAMMY'S BIRCH BAY CRAB CAKES

Part of my love story with the sea includes one of my oldest and dearest friends, Tammy (Blair) Renard. We met in Kelowna when she and her family (George, Sandy, and her brother David) were visiting their cousins who lived on a farm up the road from us. We were about 10 years old and became fast friends. This friendship allowed me wonderful visits to the big city to visit them during the summer holidays and they became my Vancouver family. The Blairs spend most of their time as close to the ocean as possible, and they are renowned crabbers. Each year they have a crab-a-thon and feast like kings on these amazing West Coast shellfish. The leftover crabs are picked clean and set aside to make delicious dishes like Tammy's recipe for crab cakes. Although Tammy now lives in Pemberton, her freezer is always full of vacuum-packed, fresh-picked crab from their summer visits to Birch Bay where her parents keep a second home.

Combine all ingredients together in a large bowl except for the crabmeat. Shred crabmeat into small pieces and then mix into ingredients. (Do not overmix or crabmeat will become gummy.) Form into small patties and add to frying pan with hot oil. Cook approximately 2–3 minutes each side or until golden and crispy. Add more oil to the pan as needed. Serve to your favourite people warm or cold with a Horseradish Caesar cocktail.

Tammy and Duke

The Crabbing Gang
LEFT TO RIGHT: David, George, Trevor and Tammy (Sandy, not shown, was taking photo)

THE FARMER
Bob Hopcott
Pitt Meadows, BC

THE CHEF
Dana Reinhardt
Port Coquitlam, BC

THE WINE MAKER
TIME Estate Winery
Oliver, BC

········ FEATURED INGREDIENT ········
Hopcott Farms short ribs

SHORT RIBS

4 Tbsp + 4 Tbsp canola oil

10 lbs beef short ribs, trimmed of excess fat

¼ cup tomato paste

3 cups red wine

4 cups veal stock or chicken stock

2–14 oz cans white beans, strained

MIREPOIX

2 carrots, large chop

2 onions, peeled and halved

3 celery ribs, large chop

10 cloves garlic

SPICE SACHET

1 Tbsp allspice

1 Tbsp coriander seeds

1 bay leaf

1 Tbsp cumin seeds

1 Tbsp pink peppercorns

½ cinnamon stick

3 cloves

3 sprigs fresh thyme

1 large square of cheesecloth and twine

CREAMY POLENTA

1½ cups coarse polenta

¼ cup unsalted butter

½ cup Parmesan cheese, grated

BRAISED BEEF SHORT RIBS
WITH WHITE BEAN RAGU

Slow-cooked short ribs are a favourite comfort food, and when you use local Hopcott beef ribs and add this delicious white bean ragù, the comfort food becomes a five-star meal. Chef Dana's Italian spin on the dish is testimony to her passion for Tuscan flavours. This is a slow food dish that demonstrates how relaxing it is to braise meats hours before serving. The rich, hearty flavours will make you want to sit down and share a long, relaxing dinner at the table with friends. **SERVES 8 PREP TIME: 45 MINUTES COOKING TIME: 4 HOURS**

Bring 6 cups of salted water to a boil in a large pot. Whisking constantly, gradually add the polenta and reduce the heat to med/low. Cook, whisking often, until polenta is tender and creamy about 25 minutes. Add the butter and Parmesan and whisk in. Season to taste with salt.

In a large skillet, heat the first 4 Tablespoons of canola oil over medium/high heat. Season ribs well with salt and pepper. Sear both sides of the short ribs until nicely browned. Place the ribs in a large ovenproof baking dish. Heat the remaining canola oil and sauté the carrots, celery, and onions until golden brown. Meanwhile bring the veal stock to a simmer. Add the browned vegetables to the ribs. In the skillet, add the red wine and bring to a simmer. Add the tomato paste and mix well. Add red wine mixture to the ribs and cover with the simmering stock Add the spice sachet and cover with tinfoil. Poke a few small holes in the foil and braise at 325°F for 4 hours, until ribs are very tender. Separate the ribs from the sauce and strain the sauce through a fine mesh strainer. Skim the fat from the top of the sauce and set aside. Pull apart the ribs from the bones and mix with the sauce and the beans. Season to taste with salt and pepper and serve over creamy polenta. *Mangia e bevi!*

········ DRINK PAIRING ········

2012 TIME Red Meritage
A traditional blend of 60% Merlot, 29% Cabernet Sauvignon, and 11% Cabernet Franc, this wine will continue to develop and age beautifully in the bottle until 2020. Classic aromas envelop the glass with red berries, black cherries, and peppery nuances. Fragrant characters of rose petal and sage mingle with the darker fruit elements. This wine is rich and structured, with excellent depth and silky well-integrated tannins.

BOB HOPCOTT ✴ THE FARMER

A FAMILY FARM BY THE SEA.

The Hopcott family is a third-generation family farm owned and operated in Pitt Meadows. They do things the old-fashioned way. They work together as a family, have strong ethics and philosophies, and respect their land and their animals. Dad and Mom, Bob and Debbie, are both still involved in the daily operations of the farm and store, working closely alongside their three kids in various capacities. Son Brad takes care of the cattle, Travis focuses on the produce and cranberry operations, and Jennifer manages the butcher shop and store.

The Hopcott family is trusted and respected for providing "hormone and antibiotic-free" meats, local produce, no-spray berries, and a strong commitment to ethical farming practices. "It means to treat our animals with respect, from the way we handle them to what we feed them. We care about raising happy livestock that don't suffer from stress in any way."

The family farming business began as a dairy farm in 1934 eventually evolving into the cattle raising business in 1957. There is a farm store on site that has grown considerably over the years. The store offers all of their products as well as other locally raised animals, vegetables, and products created by local artisans. "Having a storefront allows us to create a direct and emotional connection with our customers. They love knowing where their food comes from and I don't feel that this is a trend but, rather, a food philosophy of 'know your farmer, know your food.'"

In 1996 they took a leap into another new industry—cranberries—by converting 70 acres of cornfields into cranberry bogs. "Without question, growing and harvesting cranberries is a labour of love. While cranberries are a relatively hearty fruit, they require a concerted effort. Once ripe, they are harvested by flooding the field, and workers require hip-waders to collect the berries that float to the surface," says Bob Hopcott.

FARM Hopcott Premium Meats FB HopcottFarms TWITTER @hopcottfarms
LOCATION 18385 Old Dewdney Trunk Road, Pitt Meadows, BC WEB hopcottmeats.ca

DANA REINHARDT ✳ THE CHEF

FOOD MAESTRO.

A true Vancouverite, Dana Reinhardt spun cotton candy and sold corn dogs at the local PNE (Pacific National Exhibition) as a kid. With a family in the wine import business, she was raised in a world of food, wine, and travel—an amazing formula that has translated into her own career.

After formally training as a chef at DuBrulle Culinary School, Dana cut her teeth in one of the first Okanagan winery restaurants, The Cellar Door, at Sumac Ridge Winery in Summerland. There she honed her skills on farm-to-table cooking and took that education a step further by moving to London, England to work at the legendary River Café! She returned to Vancouver and opened up CRU, a tiny eatery focused on small plates and fine wines that became a legend in its own right. "Cooking in Vancouver is fabulous for a chef. We have an enormous bounty of local ingredients paired with a large variety of cultures. It's like being a painter and being able to use the entire spectrum of colours, not just one culture or tradition," she beautifully explains.

Dana now is a food and hospitality consultant at her own business, SOL Kitchen, and has recently realized a dream to teach cooking classes on site at a beautiful biodynamic, organic farm in Tuscany. There she will lead students through hands-on farm-to-table and foraging-to-table cooking, also incorporating visits to local artisans and farmers to complete the true philosophy of living from the land.

"Italians love to eat and respect the rituals of sitting down and honouring the cook with their presence. Meals are important times to connect and savour what is in season; to talk, laugh, and take a respite from the day. And they do it every day around almost every meal."

COMPANY SOL Kitchen   LOCATION 2452 Begbie Terrace, Port Coquitlam, BC
TWITTER @cookindana   FB cookindana   WEB sol-kitchen.net

"Know your farmer, know your food."

TIME ESTATE WINERY 🍷 THE WINE MAKER

THE TIME HAS COME!

Harry McWatters, known as the godfather of the Okanagan wine industry, and his family launched the new TIME label in 2014 and are about to open a new winery in Oliver. He explains, "We started this path 36 years ago and have been growing grapes for more than two decades at our Sundial Vineyard on the Black Sage Bench. Our vines receive more hours of sunshine than any other viticulture region. This project has re-energized me for what TIME will bring over the next 20 years."

LOCATION Oliver, BC   TWITTER @timewinery   FB timewinery   WEB timewinery.com

THE BUTCHER
The Masi Brothers
Vancouver, BC

THE CHEF
Andrey Durbach
Vancouver, BC

THE WINE MAKER
Howard Soon
Kelowna, BC

FEATURED INGREDIENT
Columbus Meat Market pancetta

500 g flat pancetta, diced
60 mL olive oil
1 large onion, diced
5 cloves garlic, sliced very thin
1 celery rib, diced
1 fresh green chili, minced, with seeds
1 tsp whole fennel seeds
200 mL red wine
1 796 mL tin San Marzano tomatoes
8 basil leaves, chopped
¼ bunch flat parsley, chopped
1 Tbsp black pepper, coarsely ground
125 g Bucatini pasta (or spaghetti) per person
Pecorino cheese, freshly grated to finish

BUCATINI AMATRICIANA

This dish is named for the town of Amatrice, about an hour east of Rome, and is one of my favourite pasta dishes! Andrey's recipe features the house-made pancetta at Columbus Meat Market, but if you are not near the East Vancouver Renfrew Street hood, source your best local butcher alternative. Vancouver has many Old World, Italian butcher shops to graze upon.

Render pancetta with the olive oil in a saucepot over medium heat until golden brown and lightly crisped. Remove pancetta from the pot and drain on a paper towel. In the rendered pancetta fat, gently fry the onion, garlic, celery, green chili, and fennel seed until vegetables are translucent and well softened.

Add pancetta back to vegetables and pour in the red wine. Cook until wine has almost evaporated

Crush tomatoes by hand and add to the pot, along with all the tomato juice. Add basil, parsley, and pepper, bring to a boil, and then turn down to low heat and simmer slowly for 45 minutes. Season to taste with salt.

Cook pasta al dente, and toss with Amatriciana sauce.

Finish with a generous sprinkle of grated Pecorino cheese.

Cin Cin!

DRINK PAIRING

2011 Sandhill Small Lots Barbera
"Our Barbera planting is at the base of the cliff at the southern tip of our estate vineyard. The accumulated heat offered by the cliff resulted in fully ripe grapes with moderate acidity. Careful attention by our vineyard manager to limit yield, brings full, ripe flavours and smooth tannins. This vineyard captures the true expression of Canada's only Barbera."

LEFT TO RIGHT: Masi brothers Vince, Vito, Giancarlo, Chef Andrey, and Eugenio

THE MASI MEN 🦀 THE BUTCHERS

FAMILY TRADITION.

Columbus Meat Market has been located on Renfrew Street in East Vancouver for over 50 years. It is an Old World, neighbourhood butcher; the meats processed and sold here are free from antibiotics and hormones.

Originally owned by Armando Belmonde, the three Masi brothers, all butchers, purchased the business in 1991 and continued Belmonde's tradition of servicing the Italian-rich neighbourhood surrounding the shop.

The Masi brothers Eugenio, Vito, and Giancarlo were born in Italy where they come from a long line of butchers that take their craft very seriously. Catering to the needs of their customers and many chefs who demand the highest-quality cuts, the brothers also create sausage and smoked charcuterie like the pancetta that Chef Durbach loves. "I really enjoy working with the butchers at Columbus Meats," he says, "It's as close as you come to a traditional European craft butcher shop. They cut everything by hand, make sausage, salumi, and bacon in small batches, and always have fresh rabbits and veal from their friends' farms. It's an old-fashioned, throwback of a place, dedicated to quality, which has quietly gone about its business of serving the community for decades, and you always get what you pay for!"

BUTCHER Columbus Meat Market   LOCATION 1665 Renfrew Street, Vancouver, BC
WEB columbusmeatmarket.com

ANDREY DURBACH ⁜ THE CHEF

THE NEIGHBOURHOOD RESTAURANT GUY.

Born and raised in Vancouver, Andrey Durbach joined the restaurant scene at the tender age of 16 as a dishwasher. "I knew from the time I was in my late teens that I wanted to be a chef . . . I loved the atmosphere from the first moment. The energy of the buzzing busy kitchen and the need to excel under immense pressure was very compelling to my young self."

The only time Durbach left the kitchens in his long-lived career, was to take a hiatus to get a degree in theatre at UBC. From there he dove straight back into the culinary world and attended the Culinary Institute of America in New York in 1990.

Back in Vancouver, which led Andrey began gathering experience in various establishments, which lead him to open his first restaurant, Etoile. It also garnered him the honour of being included in *Gourmet* magazine's Top Tables list in 1996.

"Being by the sea, in a port city, means that one has access to products and people from all over the world. I love the diversity of foods, cultures, and cuisines on offer in our city by the sea."

Andrey partnered with Chris Stewart over ten years ago and together they have opened many restaurants focusing on the same philosophy: "basic elements and fresh, high-quality ingredients to create cuisine that is simple and yet deeply satisfying." Currently the two run La Buca, Pied-à-Terre, The Sardine Can, and, most recently, The Abbey, a progressive tavern in Crosstown.

Andrey is also the co-author, with Vancouver artist Robert Chaplin, of the playful children's cookbook *Delicious Chicken Soup*.

RESTAURANT La Buca (+ The Sardine Can, Pied a Terre, The Abbey) TWITTER @labuca /La-Buca-Restaurant
LOCATON La Buca-4025 MacDonald Street, Vancouver, BC WEB labuca.ca

SANDHILL WINES 🍷 THE WINE MAKER

CANADA'S SUPERSTAR WINE MAKER.

Howard Soon is a celebrity in the Canadian wine world and is a true pioneer in the industry. He is kind man, well loved and respected for his craft. Howard has also been generous in sharing his vast knowledge in wine making and viticulture and has mentored and nurtured many talents over the years.

Howard joined Sandhill in 1997 and has created a special portfolio of small lot wines that represent his best wine-making efforts and was the first wine maker in BC to release a series of single vineyard wines. "Our Small Lots Program provides a glimpse into our wine-making future, capturing the essence of small batches of promising new varietals."

Recently, Howard became the first wine maker in history to receive all three top honours for Sandhill Wines at the 2009 Wine Access Canadian Wine Awards, winning Best Red Wine of the Year, Best White Wine of the Year, and Winery of the Year.

LOCATION 1125 Richter Street, Kelowna, BC FB sandhillwines TWITTER @sandhillwines WEB sandhillwines.ca

THE FARMER
Sandra Zambrano
Abbotsford, BC

THE CHEF
Faizal Kassam
Vancouver, BC

THE WINE MAKER
Hester Creek Estate Winery
Oliver, BC

FEATURED INGREDIENT

Campagna Farm bone-in rib steak

STEAK

1 32 oz bone-in rib steak

kosher salt

black pepper

HORSERADISH CRÈME FRAÎCHE

Yields 250 mL

1 Tbsp crème fraîche

splash of red wine vinegar

1 Tbsp fresh horseradish, finely grated

salt to taste

RED WINE LENTILS

Splash of extra virgin olive oil

1 red onion, finely chopped

1 celery heart, finely chopped

1 medium carrot, finely chopped

3 cloves of garlic, finely chopped

250 g Umbrian lentils

1 L chicken stock, kept hot, 150 mL reserved

500 mL red wine, preferably something
    good and robust, 100 mL reserved,
    the rest kept hot

Splash of red wine vinegar

GRILLED BONE-IN RIB STEAK
WITH HORSERADISH CRÈME FRAÎCHE

This hearty yet elegant meal is served best on a chilly west coast day with a big glass of BC red wine. Faizal uses beef provided by the restaurant's exclusive Campagna Ranch, which is not available to the public; however, do choose the best-quality locally farm-raised beef that you can find, like Hopcott Meats or Pemberton Meadows Beef. The horseradish crème fraîche adds a luxurious touch to the dish, and the red wine lentils are the perfect side. **2–3 SERVINGS**

STEAK Allow steak to sit at room temperature for 30 minutes before cooking (this will ensure it cooks evenly). Preheat the oven to 450°F. Preheat your grill to high heat. Generously season the steak with salt and pepper. Mark the steak on the grill (about 1 minute on each side). Place on a pie pan and cook in the oven for 5 minutes per side (flipping halfway). Let the steak rest for 10 minutes before slicing. Serve with horseradish crème fraîche.

HORSERADISH CRÈME FRAÎCHE Combine all ingredients in a bowl, and season to taste.

RED WINE LENTILS This is a beautiful way to express the elegance of the lentil. The red wine adds a gorgeous richness and colour that pairs beautifully with the steak. Yields 4 servings. In heavy-bottomed saucepan over medium heat, add a little oil. Add the onions, celery, carrots, garlic, and a good pinch of salt. Turn down the heat and cook until soft, about 10–15 minutes. Add the lentils to the vegetables and slowly add a little bit of stock and a little bit of the red wine. Stirring continuously, keep alternating between the stock and red wine until the lentils are soft but still have a bit of texture, about 20 minutes. Taste and season with salt and add a splash of red wine vinegar.

DRINK PAIRING

2012 Hester Creek Estate Winery Reserve Cabernet Franc
This single-varietal Cabernet Franc begins with complex aromas of cherry, raspberry, and toasty vanilla, followed by vibrant flavours of cherry and bramble fruits with a lingering finish of spice and chocolate.

LEFT TO RIGHT: Sandra and Faizal

FAIZAL KASSAM ✴ THE CHEF

RESTAURANT GROWS ITS OWN COWS.

Born and raised on Vancouver's North Shore, Faizal was inspired to become a chef at a young age. Growing up, his mother and grandmother created delicious, flavourful meals at home that enticed him into the sensory world of cookery.

Faizal's menu at Cibo Trattoria features splendid, rustic Italian cuisine. Throughout his work history, with time spent under the tutelage of the formidable David Hawksworth at Hawksworth Restaurant, he was able to fully exercise his philosophy of sourcing local ingredients to create true west coast cuisine. Faizal says that, "For me, the greatest thing about cooking by the sea is that all of the ingredients are incredibly fresh. Being close to the ocean also means we're able to use ingredients that don't typically have a long shelf life, which I see as a big advantage."

Now in the position of executive chef, Faizal has access to an amazing lineup of producers to design his menu around. Most interestingly, the ranch where he sources his beef is actually owned by the owner of the hotel. He explains, "Cibo is actually the owner of Campagna Farm, which is located in Abbotsford, BC and run by a husband and wife team of veterinarians who responsibly raise cattle for our menu. I really like the exclusiveness of the beef, as we're the only restaurant that serves it. The quality of their product is beyond compare in terms of flavour and texture."

RESTAURANT Cibo Trattoria   LOCATION Moda Hotel, 900 Seymour Street, Vancouver, BC
TWITTER @CiboTrattoria   FB CiboTrattoriaUvaWineBar   WEB cibotrattoria.com

SANDRA ZAMBRANO ✴ THE FARMER

WHERE THE COWS ARE SERVED WINE WITH THEIR HAY.

Cibo's owner, Gerry Nichele, who also owns the Moda Hotel, is passionate about his restaurant's cuisine and he takes the farm-to-table philosophy very seriously—so seriously that he bought his own 280-acre farm to raise his own cattle for the menu. Operated by Sandra and Leonardo Zambrano, a husband-and-wife team of veterinarians from Colombia, the herd is thoughtfully raised and fed a proprietary blend of all-natural hay and grain. These lucky cows are served red wine for a minimum of 30 days during their finishing process, which adds to the flavour and tenderness of the beef.

The Zambranos came to Canada to start a new life and raise their family. Sandra was raised on a cattle ranch in Colombia where her father instilled in her the importance of gentle animal treatment. Sandra explains, "For me, it is very important to provide them with lots of love and care. When you provide a safe, clean, no-stress environment, and high-quality food for the animals, the results are the best. We have happy cows, happy farmers, and happy consumers for sure."

FARM Campagna Farm   LOCATION Abbotsford, BC   WEB cibotrattoria.com

HESTER CREEK ESTATE WINERY ♀ THE WINE MAKER

FROM THE EARTH.

Owner Curt Garland purchased the beautiful Hester Creek Estate Winery in 2004. Two years later he signed on wine maker Rob Summers, who has created a rich wine portfolio that has celebrated much success. The winery property offers luxurious villas for rent and a gorgeous restaurant called Terrafina, where guests can while away the hours surrounded by vineyards under the Oliver sun. The oldest vines on the property were planted in 1968.

Rob Summers

LOCATION 877 Rd 8, Oliver, BC   TWITTER @HesterCreek   FB HesterCreek   WEB hestercreek.com

THE FARMER
The Falk Family
Chilliwack, BC

THE MATCHMAKER
Jason and Margot Pleym
Vancouver, BC

THE CHEF
Trevor Bird
Vancouver, BC

THE WINE MAKER
Anarchist Mountain Vineyard
Osoyoos, BC

········· FEATURED INGREDIENT ·········
Fraser Valley duck

1 whole duck
3 lbs small roasting potatoes
1 cup salt
12 small carrots, washed
6 golden beets
splash red wine vinegar
10 fiddleheads
6–8 button mushrooms, quartered
splash sherry vinegar
extra virgin olive oil
salt and pepper

GLAZE
1 cup sherry vinegar
1 cup local honey
1 head star anise
1 stick cinnamon

WHOLE ROASTED DUCK

"At Fable we do a lot of family-style cooking, and one of our most popular dishes is whole duck. With the long slow roast and heavy basting of the duck, it makes for a nice sticky glaze that will impress."—Chef Bird **SERVES 4**

DUCK Preheat oven to 250°F, or 225°F in a convection oven. Rinse the duck well with water, pat dry and season with salt and pepper. Mix together honey and sherry vinegar and stir in cinnamon stick and star anise, set aside. After 3 hours of cooking, start to brush the duck with the glaze every 30 minutes. Check the duck after 5 hours; the leg will pull away from the body very easily like a confit when ready. If not yet at that stage, return to the oven for 1 more hour.

While the duck is roasting, boil the potatoes for approximately 20 minutes in heavily salted water (1 cup of salt in a large saucepan) until tender. Remove to cool.

In another saucepan, blanche the carrots in boiling water for 3 minutes. Remove to a cold water bath to cool. Fill another saucepan with cold water, add the beets and splash of red wine vinegar, then bring to a boil and simmer for 45 minutes until tender. Cool and then peel.

Bring a pot of heavily salted water to a boil. Blanch fiddleheads for 2 minutes and then shock in an ice bath. Toss all of the vegetables together in extra virgin olive oil and season well with salt. For the last hour of the duck roasting, place the vegetables around the duck to finish roasting. Right before serving, toss mushrooms in a little extra virgin olive oil and roast them in a shallow pan on very high heat, season with salt, finish with a splash of sherry vinegar. Remove from oven and let cool for 30 minutes; brush the vegetables and the duck with the honey and sherry mixture, serve family-style on a platter surrounded by the vegetable topped with mushrooms. The whole bird falls apart so just grab some forks and dig in!

········· DRINK PAIRING ·········

2012 Anarchist Mountain Wild Fire Pinot Noir
"As a wine maker, Andrew has had the advantage of being coached by Chris Carson from Meyer Family and Matt Holmes from Liquidity. It shows in this pretty and well-made wine. Aromas of cherry and strawberry are echoed on the palate, with delicate and lingering fruit flavours. Silky tannins give the wine good weight and a svelte texture. 91 points"—John Schreiner

Jason

JASON AND MARGOT PLEYM ✳ THE FARMER/CONSUMER MATCHMAKERS

MEAT AND GREET.

Two Rivers Specialty Meats is a unique purveyor. They are a distributor with a conscience and specialize in the best-quality locally sourced meats that are free of antibiotics, hormones, and chemical feed additives. For this reason, they have become indispensable to chefs who are focused on direct sourcing their products.

You would never connect romance with a meat supply business, however; in this case, there is a wonderfully romantic tale to tell about the Two Rivers name and of the young couple that own it.

Once upon a time in 2007, a couple of young newlyweds who were glamorously living in an old school bus beside the river in Golden, BC, had an epiphany to join their skill sets and values and start a distribution company that would be Two Rivers Specialty Meats. Further romance . . . the name was in memory of their Pemberton farm wedding in 2006,

where famous country singer Barney Bentall serenaded them with the song "Where Two Rivers Meet" (Get it? *Meat*). The two rivers symbolized their union but also represented the two rivers, the Lillooet River and Ryan Creek that run through Pemberton.

So happily ever after, the Pleyms now have a young family and a busy business that is strengthening the relationships between the producer and consumer by sharing their stories, as well as offering their customers peace of mind knowing and trusting that the farmed animals were ethically and sustainably raised.

Chef Trevor Bird uses Two Rivers to supply ducks, like the one he used in this recipe.

COMPANY Two Rivers Specialty Meats   LOCATION 180 Donaghy Avenue, North Vancouver, BC
FB TwoRiversSpecialtyMeats   TWITTER @TwoRiversMeats   WEB tworiversmeats.ca

ANARCHIST MOUNTAIN VINEYARD ♛ THE WINE MAKER

RENEGADES MAKING WINE IN THE MOUNTAINS OF OSOYOOS.

Andrew Meyer Stone and Terry Meyer Stone dove into vineyard life almost directly from life in the city. "We lived at Meyer Family Vineyard in Okanagan Falls working with my brother JAK at his winery for a year. He's the reason we ended up out here so I'm grateful for that!" Terry smiles.

Neither knew much about wine except that they loved to drink it and then they fell in love with a vineyard atop Anarchist Mountain in Osoyoos. Rumour was that the grapes on the property were coveted by many of the Okanagan's top wine makers so they continued to grow and sell. One day they decided, wouldn't it be fun to have our own label? And thus, Anarchist Mountain Vineyard Chardonnay and Pinot Noir were born.

*They are also the inspiration winery for the Garagiste North-Small Guys Wine Festivals-featuring the under 2000 case producers. www.garagistenorth.com

LEFT TO RIGHT: Terry and Andrew

TWITTER @anarchywines   FB anarchist-vineyard   WEB anarchistvineyard.com + garagistenorth.com

LEFT TO RIGHT: Paul and Jason

THE FALK FAMILY ✳ THE FARMER

LIFE IS DUCKY!

The Falk family has been running farm operations here for over 40 years and three generations. Growing a wide variety of poultry, they have certified organic chicken, Taiwan chicken, squab, turkey as well as their Peking ducks and geese. Their birds are humanely raised in open-air barns with no antibiotics used. Ninety percent of their market is from the Asian community, where Peking duck is a favourite cuisine.

The farm store opened in 2014 and its instant success is a wonderful sign that consumers want to shop locally and from farm gate. Paul Dick is the one in the family that handles marketing and

he says that "it is important for customers to see that the animals are humanely raised." The store is chock-full of their own wide array of poultry and products, including a delicious duck pepperoni (duckeroni) as well as many other locally sourced products. Love this: the bread is baked by a passionate local fourteen-year-old boy whose mom and grandmother deliver his beautiful European-style breads to the store.

FARM Fraser Valley Specialty Poultry (Fraser Valley Duck & Goose)
LOCATION 4540 Simmons Rd. Chilliwack, BC FB fraservalleypoultry WEB fvdg.com

TREVOR BIRD ✹ THE CHEF

BIRD IS THE WORD.

I love the name of this restaurant—who doesn't love a fable? However, when the name represents the clever combination of farm-to-table, it makes me love it even more.

Chef Trevor Bird, while starring in *Top Chef Canada* season two, came up with the Fable name, and the creative concept unfolded from there. It would be a restaurant that focused on good, from-scratch food created from local products.

"I was in Tofino and I told myself I would make my way east till I found a place I liked. I didn't make it past Vancouver," Bird says. Fable launched into the open arms of the Kitsilano hood in 2012 and since then, Bird is the word.

What inspires Trevor's cuisine: "Seasons and everything in life. Inspiration comes from the most unlikely places or conversations. As a chef everything we look at comes back to food—colours, shapes, textures. When we look at the world, we always think 'how can I mimic that colour, texture, shape in edible form?'"

Trevor's philosophy to source local, brought him to Two Rivers Specialty Meats, where he enjoys a great relationship with their producers. "Two Rivers is a great middle man; they share the philosophies we have at Fable and are always willing to share new products and help connect us with new farmers."

And so the chef, the ducks, and Two Rivers continue working together, happily feeding their neighbourhood.

RESTAURANT FABLE Kitchen   LOCATION 1944 West 4th Avenue, Vancouver, BC
FB fablekitchen   TWITTER @fablekitchen   WEB fablekitchen.ca

····· FEATURED INGREDIENT ·····
Lostock Farm squab

PASTRAMI BRINE

1 L water
10 g brown sugar
72 g kosher salt
7 g peppercorn
5 g fresh thyme
3 g fresh bay leaf
6 g cloves
4 g garlic cloves
2 g juniper berries

POULTRY CURE

4 Tbsp coarse salt (pickling salt)
1 Tbsp sugar
1 orange rind
1 cinnamon stick
1 star anise
1 tsp coriander
1 tsp black peppercorns

SQUAB

3 whole squabs
duck fat, enough to cover the squabs

POULTRY GLACE

1 large onion, diced
1 celery rib, diced
1 carrot, diced
1 Tbsp tomato paste
100 mL red wine
3 L chicken stock
1 Tbsp butter, cold *smoker needed

SQUASH PUREE

300 g butternut squash (approx 1)
15 g butter
1 shallot, minced
15 g heavy cream
nutmeg
salt and pepper

CHANTERELLES

40 chanterelle mushrooms, button size

LOSTOCK FARM SQUAB
WITH CHANTERELLE MUSHROOMS

Chef Jaeger is all about the game bird and this elegant dish is an example of his celebrated, sophisticated style of food preparation. It is almost too pretty to eat! (almost . . .) **SERVES 6**

PASTRAMI BRINE Bring all ingredients to a boil, chill. Keep refrigerated until needed.

POULTRY CURE Mix all ingredients together. Set aside.

SQUAB Remove legs from body, remove breasts and trim excess fat and sinew. Remove excess fat from carcass.

Liberally season legs with poultry cure. Leave for 24 hrs, rinse well. Pat dry. Arrange legs in a roasting dish and cover in duck fat. Cook (confit) for 4 hrs at 270°F.

Brine breasts for 1 hour in pastrami brine. Cold smoke for 10 minutes.

Roast squab carcasses in 425°F oven until evenly browned. Remove from pan; add onion, celery, and carrot. Roast vegetables until brown. Add 1 Tbsp tomato paste, stir and roast for 5 more minutes. Deglaze pan with red wine, return squab bones, cover with chicken stock and simmer for 2–3 hours. Strain through a fine mesh sieve and reduce until it reaches a sauce consistency.

SQUASH PURÉE Begin by peeling, seeding, and coring the squash, removing any green fibrous portions. Next break down the squash into a large dice. Add flesh to a sauce pan along with butter, shallot, and seasoning. Add enough water to come halfway up the squash, cover and simmer until very tender. Blend in a high-speed blender, incorporate cream while running; strain and season to taste.

CHANTERELLES Begin by lightly brushing the mushrooms of any visible dirt/impurities (stem may be scraped if desired). Heat a pan with a small amount of neutral oil. Sauté the mushrooms on medium high heat to attain initial colour, once browned reduce heat slightly and add a small amount of butter. Season liberally with salt and pepper. Once tender, mushrooms can be finished with a small amount of poultry glace and chopped fine herbs.

TO SERVE Return legs skin-side down in oven until crisp. Roast breast skin-side down 6–8 minutes, flip over, and allow heat to penetrate; core temperature should reach 52°C. Allow to rest. Rechaud breast, skin-side down in duck fat until re-crisped, about 2 minutes. Reheat sauce, and add 1 sprig of thyme for 1 minute. Remove from heat, and whisk in 1 Tbsp of cold butter, one small cube at a time. Serve with squash purée and chanterelles.

LEFT TO RIGHT: Bob and Linden, Stephanie and Scott, and Gus

David Paterson

TANTALUS VINEYARDS ♀ THE WINE MAKER

PINOT NOIRISTS.

It was love at first vintage for wine critics in 2005 after tasting the inaugural release of the 2005 Tantalus Riesling. From that moment on they became the benchmark for fine Canadian Riesling. Proprietor Eric Savics built a stunning winery on a property blessed with wide views of Kelowna and Lake Okanagan. The property was "first planted to table grapes in 1927 and today is known as the oldest continuously producing vineyard in British Columbia." Tantalus is also British Columbia's first LEED-certified winery. Wine maker David Paterson has created a beautiful portfolio of wines that includes an award-winning Pinot Noir.

LOCATION 1670 Dehart Road, Kelowna, BC   TWITTER @tantaluswine   FB tantalusvineyards   WEB tantalus.ca

BOB AND LINDEN HULL ✶ THE FARMER

SPEAKS PIGEON.

As you wind your way through the beautiful country roads of Abbotsford, you will come upon an idyllic ten-acre farmscape that is Lostock Farms. A rich piece of land with Page Creek running through the corner, the soil and weather conditions here are some of the best in the Fraser Valley. Bob and Linden chose a life of farming five years ago. "We wanted to raise our kids on property and be able to work together," Bob explains. "I grew up on a farm, but this was all new for Linden."

The farm is named for a town named Lostock (pronounced Lost-ock) near Bolton, England, where Linden lived until she moved to Canada to marry Bob.

On the farm they raise squab, rabbit, and Taiwanese chicken. The squab is what Chef Jaeger utilizes at his famous Vancouver restaurant, The Pear Tree (. . . and a squuuu-ab in a pear tree). Scott and Stephanie Jaeger were one of Lostock's first customers, and their products are now used all over Greater Vancouver by discerning restaurants.

The animals at Lostock are raised ethically and humanely. Bob explains that "Linden and I wanted to raise animals that we would want to feed our own family. We do some things a little different, such as adding Chinese herbs and roots to our pigeon's feed. No antibiotics. They are healthier and tastier."

FARM Lostock Farms   LOCATION Abbotsford, BC   FB Lostock-Farms
TWITTER @lostockfarms   WEB lostockfarms.ca

⚓

SCOTT JAEGER ☸ THE CHEF

CHEF ON TOP OF HIS GAME.

Chef Scott Jaeger and his wife and partner Stephanie opened The Pear Tree in an unassuming Burnaby location in 1998. What seemed like an off-the-beaten-track site turned out to be a brilliant move and offered a much-needed culinary booster shot for the area. The restaurant became an instant favourite for locals and gourmands alike. Scott's menu focuses on seasonal local, organic, and sustainable ingredients and his brilliant, creative cuisine is both cutting-edge and classic. His philosophy of supporting local farmers is well known and he elaborates, "Sourcing local to me is about the connection, getting to know the farmer, the area the product comes from and the passion that is put into each product."

The relationship between the Jaegers and the Hulls is a clear example of what the concept of this cookbook is all about: real relationships based on trust and respect. Chef Jaeger explains, "When you speak to Bob at Lostock Farms you get a sense of calm. He does not brag about his birds or preach the right or wrong way to do things. Usually the first point of the conversation is about the health of the birds and what they are eating, or how the weather is affecting the farm. From the moment the birds are on the cutting board, you know it is a world-class product." And you also know that your investment into a farm product is going directly back into that family farm and that message to consumers is massive.

In 2005 Chef Jaeger competed for the chance to represent Canada in the prestigious Bocuse D'Or Culinary Competition in Lyon, France. He won the honour and began preparing for the 2007 competition against 24 other countries. In January of 2007, Chef Jaeger and his team went to Lyon, bringing home a seventh-place honour.

RESTAURANT The Pear Tree Restaurant   LOCATION 4120 East Hastings St, Burnaby, BC
FB The-Pear-Tree-Restaurant   WEB peartreerestaurant.net

THE FISHERMAN
Alec Fraumeni
Victoria, BC

THE CHEF
Peter Zambri
Victoria, BC

THE WINE MAKER
Blue Grouse Winery
Duncan, BC

········ **FEATURED INGREDIENT** ········
Finest At Sea spot prawns

6 Tbsp unsalted butter

6 Tbsp extra virgin olive oil

10 cloves garlic, cut into thick pieces
  *important: thickly sliced garlic will
  go brown but not burn

½ tsp chili flakes

1 jalapeño pepper, cut into medium thick rings

sea salt and pepper

16 large, fresh, unpeeled spot prawns with
  heads on (very important to be fresh, not
  peeled, and head on as this is where the
  sauce's flavor comes from!)

4 Tbsp fresh parsley, chopped

1–500 g package of good spaghetti

4 Tbsp breadcrumbs

4 Tbsp Parmigiano cheese, grated

SPAGHETTI AGLIO E OLIO WITH PEPPERONCINO & SPOT PRAWNS

This delicious pasta dish celebrates our west coast's seafood darling, spot prawns. These sweet local prawns are a reasonably new rockstar on the culinary scene, due almost exclusively to the Spot Prawn Festival spearheaded by fisherman Steve Johansen and chef Rob Clark almost a decade ago. The spicy, fun nature of this dish reflects the personality of its creator, Peter Zambri! **SERVES 4**

Bring a large pot of salted water to a boil for the pasta.

Choose a heavy-bottomed pan that will snugly fit all of the spot prawns so they are not piled on top of each other. Gently melt the butter and oil. Put the garlic, chili flakes, and pepper rings in the oil and lightly season with salt and pepper. Now arrange the spot prawns in the pan and generously season the top with more salt, pepper, and the chopped parsley. Note: you will only be flipping the spot prawns once.

Drop your pasta into the pot and cook according to the time on the package. When there is 7 minutes left, start the prawns on high heat. When the garlic starts to turn golden, the peppers are softening, and the spot prawns are starting to turn red, it is time to turn them one by one onto the uncooked side. Lower the heat to half and gently finish the prawns.

By this time the spaghetti should be al dente and perfect. Try a noodle to ensure it is cooked properly.

Set out four nice hot bowls and sprinkle the breadcrumbs and grated cheese in the bottom of the bowls. Quickly portion out four plates of drained hot spaghetti and put four hot spot prawns on each bowl of hot pasta. Equally divide the reserved oil, butter, peppers, and garlic over the prawns and into the pasta. Enjoy!

········ **DRINK PAIRING** ········

2013 Blue Grouse Winery Ortega
A cross between Muller-Thurgau and Siegerrebe, Ortega is the region's staple grape variety. It is clear and bright with a bouquet of apple, stone fruit, and almond. A light-medium wine balanced with a refreshing acidity and flavours of tangerine, white peach, and citrus round out the palate.

Chef Peter

ALEC FRAUMENI ⛵ THE FISHERMAN

SALTWATER RUNNING THROUGH HIS VEINS.

Alec is the son of Bob Fraumeni, affectionately known as "Bobby Blackcod," owner of Finest At Sea. This is a family of true "men of the sea." Bob bought his first boat at age eleven, and son Alec has been on fishing boats for as long as he can remember. Operating since 1977, Finest At Sea offers products that are 100% wild and caught by their own fishers using only sustainable fishing practices. It has three stores, two in Vancouver and one in Victoria.

Alec explains, "I grew up in Victoria, my dad started taking me out commercial fishing at the age of eight! Spending the whole summer on the water, I had some of the most valuable life experiences I will ever have, and saw some of the most beautiful places I will ever see—it definitely made me who I am today. I love and respect the ocean just as much as my dad does because of the way he has taught me. Now, at the age of twenty, I run my own boat. Last summer was my first season as captain, fishing for tuna and salmon. After a long winter of fixing up my boat, I will be running it for prawn longline and then taking it out for tuna and salmon."

An ode to life on the sea by Alec: "Once you are three hours north of Vancouver/Victoria, it is like a completely different world that is seen by very few people—and that's the part I enjoy most. The untouched wilderness is so beautiful between here and Alaska and I hope it stays that way. It is incredible how much life the ocean can sustain, and the fact that we can responsibly supply food to our local communities makes me very grateful.

Without a doubt, I will always be a fisherman. I've been born and bred into it and I couldn't imagine a life away from the sea. I lived in Saskatchewan for a year and that was a bust. Couldn't handle being away from the sea."

COMPANY Finest At Sea   **LOCATION** 27 Erie Street, Victoria, BC   **WEB** finestatsea.com
TWITTER @finestatseavic   **FB** Finest-At-Sea-Seafood-Boutique-Victoria

PETER ZAMBRI ✳ THE CHEF

THE PASSIONATE CHEF.

Peter Zambri is a force. The guy vibrates with energy and has a contagious grin; it is no wonder Zambri's is one of Vancouver Island's favourite restaurants. You also have to love a guy that runs a restaurant with his sister. Peter and Jo(sephine) have been operating their family business since 1999. "It's taken a lot of time and dedication, but I think we have produced tens of thousands of beautiful plates—and some stinkers, to be candid. Overall, I deeply believe we have played an important part in the happiness of Victoria's city diners," says Peter.

Peter spent some of his early career worshipping at the church of locavorism, Sooke Harbour House. He recalls, "That place gave us the opportunity to spread our wings and look at cooking and food production in a whole new light. Remember, this was like twenty-five years ago; not many places were promoting local, seasonal cooking. It schooled me and opened my mind to possibilities I would have previously never thought of. We had some team there in those days. We pushed the boundaries every day and created some real masterpieces. My training, philosophies, and instructions to my current staff still go back to what I learned in my four years there."

Peter is passionate about his food, his city, and feeding people, "I think that the biggest inspiration I derive through cooking is the ability to nourish people in different ways. It's a very special gift to be able to bring together healthy ingredients, good techniques, artistry, and interesting flavour combinations to satiate someone's desire to eat. I take that very seriously. There are not many career choices that bring those elements together."

RESTAURANT Zambri's Restaurant   LOCATION 820 Yates Street, Victoria BC
TWITTER @zambrisvictoria   FB ZambrisVictoria   WEB zambris.ca

"I couldn't imagine a life
away from the sea."–Alec

BLUE GROUSE WINERY ♟ THE WINE MAKER

SUSTAINABLE WINES AND VINES.

Blue Grouse Winery in the beautiful Cowichan Valley has a long history with original vines being planted back in 1977. The new owners, the Brunner family, have invested in updates to the winery focusing on sustainable elements, including locally sourced construction materials, the use of geothermal energy, onsite water collection and treatment, as well as other features that reduce mechanical heating and cooling. The grand opening of their new facility was in the spring of 2015.

Wine maker Bailey Williamson began his career as a chef before catching the wine-making bug. Bailey also manages the vineyard allowing him the full experience as a vigneron, taking grape from vine to bottle.

LOCATION 2182 Lakeside Road Duncan, BC   FB bluegrousewines   TWITTER @bluegrousewines   WEB bluegrouse.ca

Bailey

THE FARMER AND CHEESE MAKER
Cory Spencer and
Kirsten Thorarinson
Duncan, BC

THE CHEF
Bill Jones
Duncan, BC

THE WINE MAKER
Averill Creek Vineyard
Duncan, BC

······ FEATURED INGREDIENT ·······
The Happy Goat Farm goat

GOAT

1 Happy Goat loin (about 1 lb/454 g)

1 Tbsp (15 mL) garlic

1 Tbsp (15 mL) prepared mustard

1 Tbsp (15 mL) olive oil

2 Tbsp (30 mL) mushroom powder

1 Tbsp (15 mL) grand fir needle tips, minced

1 Tbsp (15 mL) sea salt

1 Tbsp (15 mL) butter

1 lb (454 g) new potatoes

SAUCE

¼ lb (115 g) fresh asparagus, trimmed

2 Tbsp (30 mL) fresh mint, chopped

½ lemon, juice and zest

1 cup (250 mL) sour cream

1 tsp (5 mL) honey

1Tbsp (15 mL) olive oil

sea salt and pepper to taste

GOAT LOIN ROLLED IN MUSHROOM POWDER
& GRAND FIR SALT WITH NEW POTATOES &
SOUR CREAM, MINT & ASPARAGUS SAUCE

Bill Jones lives a virtually self-sufficient food lifestyle, using products grown or foraged on his Deerholme Farm and friendly forest. He also works with the neighbours to source other delicious items like goat. Happy Goat Farm (also awesome cheese makers) do sell their happy goats as well. Lamb would also work beautifully in this dish—but if you have the chance, give goat a go! It is delicious too. You can make the mushroom powder by pulsing dried mushrooms in a coffee or spice grinder. **SERVES 4**

Preheat oven to 375°F/180°C. In a container with a lid, add the goat loin and season with garlic, mustard, and olive oil. Roll in seasonings and cover with lid. Allow to marinate for at least 1 hour on the counter or place in the fridge overnight. Remove lamb from container and sprinkle with mushroom powder to coat. Combine grand fir needles and salt and sprinkle on outside of the loin.

Heat an ovenproof skillet over medium-high heat and add butter. Add the goat loin and brown well on all sides. Transfer to a hot oven and roast for 7–8 minutes or until an internal temperature of 130°F. Remove from oven and allow to rest for 10 minutes.

Meanwhile, bring a pot of salted water to a boil and cook the asparagus until tender, about 5–6 minutes. Remove with a slotted spoon (retaining the water) and place in cold water to chill. Add the potatoes to the water, bring back to a boil, and then reduce heat to a simmer. Cook potatoes for about 10 minutes or until fork tender, drain, and reserve, keeping warm. Meanwhile, drain and chop the asparagus into thin slices (reserve the tips for garnish) and place in a small mixing bowl. Add the mint, lemon juice and zest, sour cream, honey, and olive oil. Season well with salt and pepper and set aside. To serve, place the warm potatoes in the centre of the plate, slit the tops, and squeeze to expose the insides. Slice the goat and place on top, drizzle with asparagus sauce and garnish with reserved asparagus tips.

···· DRINK PAIRING ·····················

2009 Averill Creek Pinot Noir

"In the glass, the finished wine exhibits all the hallmarks of a classic Pinot Noir. It has a deep ruby colour with aromas of violets, black cherries, leather, and tobacco. The silky medium-bodied palate offers flavours of strawberry and plum with soft seductive tannins, followed by a lasting well-balanced finish. 89–90 points."—John Schreiner

Bill, Cory, Kirsten, and happy goat ladies

CORY SPENCER AND KIRSTEN THORARINSON ✳ THE FARMER AND CHEESE MAKER

KIDDING AROUND WITH HAPPY GOAT LADIES.

From city folk to farm folk, Cory Spencer and Kirsten Thorarinson left their corporate careers to follow their dream to move to the Island and live the good life. Neither had a background in agriculture, but after taking a cheese making course in 2006, Cory was inspired and began working on dairy/cheese making farms in Canada, France, and Northern England to learn the trade.

Kirsten explains, "Farm life is a big change from what I am used to . . . but a change for the better. I'm constantly surrounded by beautiful scenery, have a huge extended farm family of goats, and three cats and a dog who keep me company when I work. I definitely work a lot more now than I ever have before, but it is extremely rewarding to do something I am passionate about."

What makes their cheeses unique is that they specialize in aged, hard, raw-milk cheeses and they are truly amazing. "Our cheeses draw inspiration from many traditional European varieties that have been made for hundreds of years," Cory explains. "Kirsten and I milk on a seasonal basis, meaning that all of our goats are bred

at the same time, they all kid at the same time, and are all dried off at the same time. This schedule allows us two months of slow time during mid-November to mid-January, and gives the goat ladies a break during the last trimester of their pregnancy. One of the benefits of this model of production is that we're able to follow and capture the seasonal changes in the milk. The flavours of the milk (and thus the cheese) will change depending on what it is the goats are eating—in the early season they'll be on hay, and by mid April they'll be back on fresh pasture until late summer. By fall, our volumes drop, but we get a really rich and creamy milk (sometimes up to 6.5% butterfat/protein versus the 3.25% butterfat/protein we'd see while on pasture). These different sorts of milk lend themselves to making different sorts of cheeses and it's nice to be able to capture that."

FARM The Happy Goat Farm & Dairy and The Happy Goat Cheese Company
LOCATION 5060 McLay Rd, Duncan, BC   TWITTER @happygoatcheese
FB thehappygoatfarmanddairy   WEB thehappygoat.ca

BILL JONES ✻ THE CHEF

LIVING HAPPILY EVER IN A MAGICAL RAINFOREST BY THE SEA.

Bill Jones is a chef and a legendary pioneer in the local foraging world. Those involved the local culinary scene explain it: "Bill was foraging before foraging was cool." He has created his own culinary biosphere on Deerholme Farm and is an integral part of the Cowichan Bay/Vancouver Island intensive food/farm-minded community and voice for the forest. He has in fact carved out a unique culture of his own.

Bill Jones lists a lengthy line of enviable credentials that include being a French-trained chef, author of twelve cookbooks, and winner of two world cookbook awards; he is a respected journalist, food consultant, and teacher—both foraging and cooking classes. With several cookbooks in his repertoire, Bill shares his knowledge and discoveries through his instructive foraging insights and delicious recipes. His current bestseller, *The Deerholme Foraging Book*, is a follow-up to *The Deerholme Mushroom Book*. Both are amazing. Watch for a copy of his latest book, *The Deerholme Vegetable Cookbook*.

Cooking from his Deerholme Farm in Cowichan Bay, Bill's cuisine is both a farm-to-table and forest-to-table experience. I have walked into his kitchen to find an entire table full of gorgeous chanterelle mushrooms, just picked from his beloved rainforest out back. I love how he loves his forest, how he respects it.

Doing a foraging walkabout on the property is utterly mind-boggling. Nipping new grand fir needle tips off, picking herbs, discovering mushrooms, or chasing chickens around with his furry sidekick Oliver, Bill Jones and his wife Lynn could almost live self-sufficiently off their farm.

When I last visited, I was gifted with a jar of grand fir sea salt and a bag of chanterelles with a note that read: *A gift from the forest.*

FARM Deerholme Farm   LOCATION 4830 Stelfox Rd, Duncan, BC
FB bill.deerholme   TWITTER @deerholme   WEB deerholme.com

"We handcraft each of our cheeses in small batches using only fresh, raw milk from our own herd of dairy goats. Every step of the cheese making process is completed by hand. Aged, hard cheeses with a natural rind are our specialty."—Cory

AVERILL CREEK VINEYARD ♟ THE WINE MAKER

A PRESCRIPTION FOR THE GOOD LIFE.

Andy Johnston is a retired doctor turned wine maker who has written himself a prescription for the good life. With a stunning winery and vineyard built into the side of Mt. Prevost with views to the sea, he and his wife Wendy have created a sanctuary.

Andy's repertoire of fine wines continues to garner acclaim, especially his Pinot Noir of which he is very proud. Wines created here are all 100% estate grown, proving that the grape growing conditions on the island are very agreeable.

LOCATION 6552 North Rd, Duncan, BC   FB AverillCreekVineyard   TWITTER @AverillCreek   WEB averillcreek.ca

Andy

⛵ **THE FISHMONGER**
Robert Clark
Vancouver, BC

☸ **THE CHEF**
Caren McSherry
Vancouver, BC

🍷 **THE WINE MAKER**
Painted Rock Estate Winery
Penticton, BC

····· FEATURED INGREDIENT ·····················

The Fish Counter seafood

¼ cup olive oil

2 medium yellow onions, diced

3 garlic cloves, minced

2 cups plum tomatoes, chopped

1 cup white wine

1 green pepper, diced

1 bunch fresh parsley, chopped

sea salt

freshly ground pepper

piri-piri sauce to taste or Tabasco

24 Manila or littleneck clams in shells

24 mussels in shells

12 wild prawns in shells

¼ cup brandy

1 chorizo sausage, sliced

6 cups cooked rice

CATAPLANA

"A cataplana is indispensible to a Portuguese kitchen. This clam-shaped copper steamer is not only the cooking vessel but also the serving dish. When opened at the table it dramatically releases the fabulous aroma of what's inside. A large pot with a tight lid can be substituted. The traditional version of cataplana does not include mussels or prawns, but living on the west coast inspired me to add them for local flavour."—Caren
"I HAD to buy one from Gourmet Warehouse after seeing this recipe!"—Jennifer
SERVES 6–8

In a cataplana dish, heat the olive oil, add the onion and garlic, soften but do not brown. Add the tomatoes, wine, green pepper, parsley, salt, pepper, and piri piri sauce to taste.

Bring to a boil, stirring frequently. Add the shellfish and brandy, cover and cook for about 5 minutes. Discard any unopened shells. Meanwhile, fry the chopped chorizo until crisp. Set aside.

Serve cataplana over rice with the chorizo as garnish.

···· **DRINK PAIRING** ·······················

2014 Painted Rock Winery Chardonnay
"This wonderfully balanced, full-bodied Chardonnay showcases tropical fruit flavours with a zingy acidity, all wrapped up with just a kiss of oak to round off the flavours. A mineral structure is a welcome component to this wine, coupling with citrus notes to make it very food friendly. It is an excellent accompaniment to various seafoods and creamy pasta dishes."—Mireille Sauvé, The Wine Umbrella

ROBERT CLARK ✳ THE FISHMONGER

THE MAN FROM ATLANTIS.

From five-star chef to sustainable fishmonger, this dude knows everything there is about the sea. Rob's change of careers was more like an evolution, a destiny. After acting as executive chef of the acclaimed C Restaurant in False Creek for fifteen years, Rob decided to pursue another dream. At C, he specialized in beautiful seafood dishes and sourcing the best possible products, focusing on local products. Rob's passion for sustainable seafood and healthy oceans made him a guru on the subject. He helped to grandfather the sustainable seafood movement in Canada and he is the proud recipient of the Murray A. Newman Award for his conservation efforts.

Rob decided that he could make a difference on the retail side of the seafood world and thus The Fish Counter opened with much hurrah on hip Main Street in 2014. Offering a fishmonger's array of sustainable bounty to local shoppers in one half of the shop, the other half is a fish-fry paradise with stools and counters and delicious takeaways and gourmet items. Of course, Rob's partner would also be a major dude in the ocean world, Mike McDermid is a marine biologist, conservationist, and sustainable seafood expert and he worked with Vancouver Aquarium and proudly spearheaded the Ocean Wise program! Go, fish guys!

Another legendary fish story (this one is true though): Rob and fisherman friend Steve Johansen, from his Granville Island based fishing company Organic Ocean (more on Steve on page 125), were out fishing together one day when Steve pulled up some prawns that Rob had never seen before. Steve explained that these were spot prawns that were almost all exported to Asia and had never been exposed to the local market. Rob ripped off the head of one and popped it in his mouth. Okay, maybe I made that up, but it *is* true that after he tasted one, Rob was hooked, and the two embarked on a mission to change the spot prawn into a local food celebrity. That day, the idea for the Spot Prawn Festival was conceived and spot prawn mania erupted.

SHOP The Fish Counter   LOCATION 3825 Main Street, Vancouver, BC
TWITTER @thefishcounter   FB the-fish-counter   WEB thefishcounter.com

CAREN McSHERRY ✳ THE CHEF

BUILT A HOUSE OF FUN FOR FOODIES.

I remember when I first visited Gourmet Warehouse after it opened in 1998. It was like Xanadu for foodies with every dreamy foodie ingredient, magazine, book, and cooking utensil that you read about in faraway places or couldn't afford! All housed in one awesome little 700-square-foot haven down an alley in what was the sketchy part of East Van. It was heaven. Gourmet Warehouse's new location is 19,000 square feet and still stuffed to the rafters with glorious and sundry items.

Caren has studied the culinary arts around the world, including training at the distinguished Cordon Bleu in London, England, The Oriental Hotel, Bangkok, and the Culinary Institute of America; New York.

She has touched every area of the food scene in Vancouver: from her legendary store to writing cookbooks and teaching cooking classes to having a radio show and becoming a television host—everything. The wide array of cooking classes offered at Gourmet Warehouse is constantly evolving, offering a huge variety of inspiring and delicious instruction to passionate cooks. Caren's Cooking School is actually the longest-running private cooking school in Canada!

Co-founder of the BC Chapter of philanthropic organization Les Dames d'Escoffier, Caren is and has been involved in countless other charity programs. She is also a former inductee into the BC Restaurant Hall of Fame.

SHOP Gourmet Warehouse   LOCATION 1340 E Hastings Street, Vancouver, BC
TWITTER @gourmetwhouse   FB the-gourmet-warehouse   WEB gourmetwarehouse.ca

> "Chef Rob Clark is responsible for making local spot prawns the new rock stars of the local shellfish world."

PAINTED ROCK ESTATE WINERY 🍷 THE WINE MAKER

WRITTEN IN STONE.

This sixty-acre winery is perched on a bluff overlooking Skaha Lake in Penticton. It was once a huge apricot orchard, now the vineyards here are producing top-quality grapes that have resulted in award-winning wines. The winery name was chosen after a discovery of ancient pictographs on rocks found on the property and noted by First Nations to have special meaning. "Our winemaking team is headed by proprietor John Skinner in close collaboration with Bordeaux-based consultant Alain Sutre, who defines winemaking protocol, advises on viticulture, integrates vineyard and winery, blends, and teaches." The winery is owned by John and Lauren Skinner.

John, Lauren, and family

LOCATION 400 Smythe Drive, Penticton, BC   TWITTER @paintedrockwine   FB paintedrock   WEB paintedrock.ca

DESSERTS

SMOKEY TEA CARAMEL TRUFFLE   174

HUCKLEBERRY CRÈME BRÛLÉE   178

GRAND MARNIER
CHOCOLATE MOUSSE
WITH HONEY CARAMELIZED HAZELNUTS
& LOCAL SEASONAL FRUIT   **182**

GORGONZOLA GOUGÈRE WITH FROMAGE FRAIS
& CRABAPPLE LAVENDER GIN PRESERVE   186

CRUNCHY HAZELNUT NAPOLEON   190

**EMPRESS HONEY & SALT SPRING ISLAND
GOAT CHEESECAKE**   194

STICKY PECAN DATE & QUINCE CAKE
WITH BUTTERSCOTCH SAUCE & CREAM   **198**

🐙 THE CHOCOLATE MAKER
Crystal Duck
Victoria, BC

☕ THE TEA MAKER
Daniela Cubelic
Victoria, BC

········· FEATURED INGREDIENT ·········
Silk Road Lapsang Souchong tea

CARAMEL SAUCE

455 g sugar

lemon juice

55 g unsalted butter

350 mL whipping cream

GANACHE FIRST LAYER

6.5 oz high quality milk chocolate, chopped

¼ cup whipping cream

250 g caramel sauce

GANACHE SECOND LAYER

8.5 oz high-quality dark chocolate
    (66% to 70%), chopped

2 tsp Silk Road Lapsang Souchong tea
    (authentic pine-smoked black tea)

1¼ cup whipping cream

10 oz chocolate (for tempering and dipping)

SMOKEY TEA CARAMEL TRUFFLE

"There are two types of ganache and a caramel sauce for this recipe. It might seem a bit daunting but it's actually quite simple to make. I love this recipe because the pine-smoked tea creates a perfect balance of savoury with the caramel and chocolate, but it also reminds me of the west coast. That smokey taste is reminiscent of a campfire."—Daniela

CARAMEL SAUCE In a saucepan over medium-low heat, stir the sugar with a bit of water and a few drops of lemon juice until it is combined and the sugar is wet. Run a wet brush along the sides of the pot and leave it without stirring until it is a deep amber colour, swirling it around a bit if it is cooking unevenly. Remove pan from the stove and stir in the butter first and then slowly add the cream, it will bubble a bit so stand back. If there are hard bits on the bottom, return it to the heat until smooth. This makes more than you will need for the recipe, but it's so yummy, I am sure you will find many other uses for it.

GANACHE Line an 10 × 8 inch pan with plastic wrap. Place chocolate into a large glass bowl. In a saucepan, heat the whipping cream and caramel until it begins to simmer and then pour it over the chocolate in the bowl. Let it sit for a few seconds and then using an immersion blender (stick blender) mix until chocolate has melted and combined. Using a spatula, scrape the blend into the lined pan and smooth into an even layer. Chill for about an hour or so (candy thermometer recommended).

SECOND LAYER Place chocolate in a large glass bowl. In a saucepan over medium-high heat, combine tea and whipping cream and let it sit to steep together. Reheat and then pour through a strainer lined with cheesecloth over the chocolate and then, like the first layer, stir and blend with the immersion blender until smooth. Pour over the first layer of ganache and let sit until it reaches room temperature and then move to the refrigerator to chill until firm. When the ganache is firm, temper chocolate. What is tempering? Tempering chocolate is an essential step for making smooth, glossy, evenly colored coating for your dipped chocolates.

HOW TO TEMPER CHOCOLATE Set aside one-quarter of the total amount of the chocolate to be tempered (2.5 oz in this case). To melt the other three-quarters of the chocolate, Crystal suggests using a microwave because it's quick and there's no chance of water getting anywhere, which, she says, "is death to the chocolate" when tempering. So heat it up in small increments, being very careful not to burn it. When it's melted and at 110°F (using thermometer), add the one-quarter amount that was set aside and stir it down to 90°F. Let chocolates cool and harden, then attack! Using a hot knife, cut the ganache into squares and then dip into tempered chocolate. While dipping, maintain the chocolate temperature at 90°F.

········· DRINK PAIRING ·········

SUMMER SHANGRI-LA "The tea pairing is a blend I make, called Summer Shangri-la. It is a black tea infused with ripe peaches, lavender, and vanilla bean. I like to serve it straight up (no sugar, honey, or milk). Begin by taking a nibble of the chocolate truffle and letting it melt in your mouth. Next take a sip of tea and be amazed at how the flavours open up. The sweetness of the truffle naturally sweetens the tea in your mouth, and the tea clarifies"—Daniela

LEFT TO RIGHT: Crystal and Daniela

CRYSTAL DUCK 🐙 THE CHOCOLATE MAKER

CHOCOHOLIC LANDS DREAM JOB. ALSO MAKES ASTONISHING GINGERBREAD HOUSES.

Crystal is a self-taught chocolate maker. Originally from Ontario, she has been working at Spinnakers for fifteeen years—twelve in the bakery and ten specializing in making chocolate truffles. "I've always loved chocolate, but I realized from an early age that not all chocolate is created equal. It didn't actually occur to me that someone could make a living doing this!"

Truffle maker: a creamy, dreamy, delicious job handle it is. Crystal currently has a repertoire of twenty-one different types of truffles, which includes some made with Daniela's gorgeous Silk Road Tea.

When Crystal first moved to Vancouver Island she was "a bit oblivious to the local food movement until I started to go around to local farmers' markets. I realized how much could be grown on the island and what an important role farmers have here. It's hard not to be inspired every day."

Legends in the craft beer world, Spinnakers has been making craft beer since 1984—they are the original brew makers on the island. Now with a restaurant, store, and guesthouse, they have become a destination in Victoria. "Spinnakers was twenty years ahead of the local, seasonal, sustainable trend. Working with the community and using local ingredients is a part of our underlying philosophy and showcasing food grown close to home is what we love. Our community partners and staff are dedicated to sourcing the best of Vancouver Island and we put the best into everything we do."

COMPANY Spinnakers Gastro Brewpub & Guesthouses
LOCATION 308 Catherine Street, Victoria, BC   FB Spinnakers Gastro-Brewpub
TWITTER @spinnakers   WEB spinnakers.com

⚓

DANIELA CUBELIC ☕ THE TEA MAKER

QUEEN OF TEA.

Daniela Cubelic is a tea master, trained by Chinese and Taiwanese herbalists and tea masters. Internationally recognized for her great accomplishments in tea sourcing and creation, she has also developed a line of personal skin and bodycare products and operates a spa that features tea as an ingredient. An impressive entrepreneur, Daniela opened her Silk Road Tea shop in Victoria's historic Chinatown in 1992 at the tender age of twenty-two.

Daniela explains how her tea life began: "I fell in love with tea at an early age. My grandmother was a big tea drinker and favoured what she called 'Russian style' tea, which was black tea with lemon, as well as herbal infusions such as chamomile and rosehips. As a teenager, my best friend was Chinese, and I became fascinated with Asian tea traditions, and began taking up tea as a hobby, eventually studying with Chinese and Taiwanese tea masters. I was fascinated by the rituals, health benefits, and the fact that high-quality, fresh tea could be as complex as wine in terms of methods of manufacture as well as a wide variety of exquisite tastes."

Daniela sources her ingredients from farms around the globe, making sure that leaves are harvested by hand by ethically treated tea workers. She also incorporates as many local ingredients as possible through some First Nations connections as well as from local gardens. Daniela says that "Berry Victoria is a pilot project I've been working on, which involves growing tea locally; it's made with native berries and locally grown black tea leaves. There is a tea I created a long time ago called 'Seamist,' which is made with west coast peppermint, seaweed, and lemongrass. I designed it to be reminiscent of the beautiful fresh sea air on the island, and customers agree. We have quite a few customers who moved away from Victoria but regularly have it shipped to them to remind them of this place."

COMPANY Silk Road Tea–Retail Store & Spa
LOCATION Chinatown, 1624 Government Street, Victoria, BC   FB SilkRoadVictoria
TWITTER @silkroadtea   WEB silkroadteastore.com

THE FORAGER
Eunice Adams
Vancouver, BC

THE RESTAURANT
Inez Cook
Vancouver, BC

THE WINE MAKER
Nk'Mip Cellars
Osoyoos, BC

······ FEATURED INGREDIENT ···················
  Wild huckleberries

3 cups whipping cream

8 egg yolks

⅓ cup sugar

1 tsp vanilla

1 scant cup huckleberries—enough to create a
    layer on the bottom of the ramekins

½ cup sugar

HUCKLEBERRY CRÈME BRÛLÉE

Isn't huckleberry just the cutest name? This famous recipe gets a delightful new twist by adding the unique flavour of these prized berries. Any wild berries can be substituted in this dish. Saskatoon berries are a similar size and would also be delightful. **SERVES 8**

Gradually heat the whipping cream in a medium saucepan on medium-high heat and bring to a boil. Remove from heat, cover, and allow to sit for 15 minutes.

In a separate medium bowl, whisk together the egg yolks and the sugar until they start to lighten in colour. Add the whipping cream a little at a time, stirring continually. Whisk in vanilla.

Place 8 ramekins in a roasting pan or casserole dish. Add moisture-free huckleberries to form a single layer on the bottom of each of 8 ramekins, then pour the blended cream evenly over the berries, dividing equally among the ramekins. Create a water bath by pouring in enough hot water (from the tap is fine) into the roasting tin to come about 1.5 cm up the sides of the ramekins. Bake at 350°F for 30 minutes or until set.

Remove the ramekins from the oven and refrigerate for at least two hours, but preferably overnight. When you are ready to torch them, divide the half-cup cup of white sugar evenly over the tops of the custard and torch to form the famous crispy top.

Garnish with huckleberries and a mint leaf.

···· **DRINK PAIRING** ··

2013 Qwam Qwmt Riesling Icewine
Intense honey and tropical fruit nose, with baked apple and crème brûlée flavours on the palate. This inviting dessert wine displays harmonious layers of honey, baked apple, sweet citrus, and apricot. A liquid silk texture leaves a soft finish on the palate making it a sexy date for the creamy crème brûlée recipe!

EUNICE ADAMS 🐦 THE FORAGER

BERRY WELL VERSED IN NATURE.

Eunice Adams grew up in Williams Lake. Raised traditionally with her local band, she was gifted with an education from her elders who shared the secrets of survival and how to live from what the land and sea provide. Foraging, now the "in" thing to do, has been a means of survival and lifestyle for First Nations people since the beginning of time.

Eunice recounts stories of she and her sisters hiking out to their secret picking spots to harvest baskets full of huckleberries and soapberries. Now living in Vancouver with her own children and grandchildren, Eunice still makes her way into the woods to harvest these treasured berries each year when they are in season.

Both the huckleberry and the soapberry have remarkable super-food properties and were used medicinally in the First Nations culture. Soapberries are very astringent tasting and, shall we say, a preferred taste. Filled with antioxidants, they are used to treat digestive issues and when whipped with sugar make an amazing, frothy mousse-like dessert beloved by the community and known as Indian ice cream. Huckleberries are said to help circulation, lower cholesterol, and were traditionally used with camus root to make a cough syrup.

Tip for foragers: the elders remind us of the ancient tradition of singing when picking berries—this will alert the berry-loving bears that you are coming.

INEZ COOK ✳ THE RESTAURANT MAKER

GIRL REUNITES WITH LOST TRIBE.

Inez Cook is an amazing woman with an amazing story. When she began following what seemed like a new career path, a whole new world opened up to her, revealing her past.

Inez and Remi Caudron—full-time flight attendants and friends—had a crazy idea to open a restaurant just prior to the 2010 Olympics in Vancouver. It would be a First Nations-style restaurant featuring gourmet cuisine using traditional ingredients. Through media attention during the restaurant opening, word got out that one of the owners (Inez) was of Nuxalk (Bella Coola) heritage, causing some interest from members of the Nuxalk Nation who had not heard of her because of her adopted family's last name (Cook). "One woman later admitted that she came in to check, and realized it might be true and began asking me questions. I knew my biological mother's name, so I told her. She was on the phone while I was off getting her a cup of tea, and by the time I got back to her table, she was standing with her arms extended, saying, 'Let me be the first one to welcome you home; we are family.'"

From there, a beautiful story unravelled for Inez that included a reunion with her people by the sea. "On 11/11/11, I went to Bella Coola for the first time and was in a three-day potlatch, received my button blanket and my traditional name, 'Snitsmana,' 'protector of the sacred dance' and 'lively.' It was the most amazing feeling. I am fortunate to have two families now."

The Bistro supports local producers and the menu is as BC-centric as possible. Inez jokes, "The First Nations people have always lived on the 100-mile diet!" Foraging and hunting are part of their culture and they are reminding us to listen and learn.

"We have the utmost respect for our surrounding lands, which we rely so heavily on to give us our quality grapes. It is wonderful that we can give back through the resulting wines," says wine maker Randy Picton.

RESTAURANT Salmon n' Bannock Bistro   LOCATION 1128 W Broadway #7, Vancouver, BC
FB SalmonNBannockBistro   TWITTER @SnBVancouver   WEB salmonandbannock.net

NK'MIP CELLARS ♀ THE WINE MAKER

WINE IN THE DESERT.

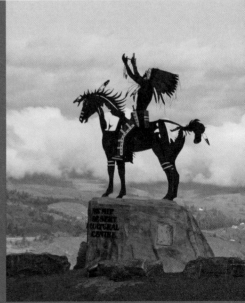

Nk'Mip Cellars (pronounced in-ka-meep) is North America's first Aboriginal winery. Led by Chef Clarence Louie and owned and operated by the Osoyoos Indian Band, the development is a glorious tribute to the history of the land and its mighty Aboriginal forefathers. The property also includes the Spirit Ridge Resort & Spa and the Nk'Mip Desert Cultural Centre, which features interpretive exhibits, nature trails, guided tours, educational programs, and cultural activities. Situated at the northernmost tip of the great Sonoran Desert, Osoyoos is well-known for its long, hot summer days, cool nights, mild winters, and minimal rainfall. All of these factors contribute to the excellent terroir that has made it a world-class grape-growing region.

LOCATION 1400 Rancher Creek Road, Osoyoos, BC   FB NkMipCellarsWinery   TWITTER @nkmipcellars   WEB nkmipcellars.com

1.5 lbs semi sweet Callebaut chocolate—
    chips, pistoles, or chunks

½ cup espresso, brewed

½ cup Grand Marnier Liqueur

1 cup whipping cream, cold

4 egg yolks

¼ cup sugar

8 egg whites, room temperature

Pinch salt

1 cup organic Fraser Valley hazelnuts,
    caramelized (recipe below)

*Optional—1 cup crème fraîche to garnish if
    desired and seasonal fruit ie. raspberries.

CARAMELIZED HAZELNUTS

1½ cup organic Fraser Valley hazelnuts

¼ cup sugar

¼ cup Mellifera honey

GRAND MARNIER
CHOCOLATE MOUSSE
WITH HONEY CARAMELIZED HAZELNUTS & LOCAL SEASONAL FRUIT

In a luxurious fusion of Paris and the west coast, Chef Ann combines a decadent chocolate mousse with a kiss of French liqueur, smuggling a treasure of local honey and hazelnuts within.

CHOCOLATE Melt the chocolate in a heavy medium-size saucepan over very low heat, stirring constantly. Stir in the espresso and then the liqueur. Let cool to room temperature.

The next step can be made in a Kitchen Aid mixer or by hand. Add the egg yolks one at a time, beating thoroughly after each addition. Whip the cream in an electric mixer until thickened, gradually adding the sugar, and continue beating until stiff. Beat the egg whites with the salt in another mixer until stiff.

Gently fold the cream and egg whites together. Stir about one-third of the cream mixture into the chocolate mixture and fold together. Then add the remaining cream mixture to the chocolate and gently continue to fold together. Add the caramelized hazelnuts and mix gently. Pour mixture into 8 individual dessert ramekins, cups, or martini glasses and place in fridge for 2 hours to set. Garnish with local seasonal fruits.

HAZELNUTS Toast hazelnuts on parchment-lined baking sheet at 350°F for 7–10 minutes until golden. Remove from oven and rub the nuts against each other in a kitchen towel to remove the skins.

Slowly heat the sugar and honey in a non-stick sauté pan until liquefied and well mixed. Remove from heat and add the hazelnuts using metal tongs rubbed with a little butter to prevent sticking. Toss until hazelnuts are completely coated with sugar/honey mixture and pan is dry. Place foil on baking sheets and brush lightly with butter. Spoon hazelnuts onto tray and place in 325°F oven until golden—approximately 10 minutes. Nuts can burn easily, so keep a close watch on them. Fold into your chocolate mousse or store in an airtight container. Save some for garnish and to nibble on.

······ DRINK PAIRING ······

La Frenz NV Liqueur Muscat
This wine is produced in a traditional solera system, meaning the average age of the blend is getting progressively older. Every year's release has a percentage of the first vintage from 1999. It has beautiful flavours of caramelized brown sugar, cinnamon, and Muscat fruit with that lovely sweet, power, and complexity that can only come from time.

LEFT TO RIGHT: Melissa and Ann

LA FRENZ WINERY ☙ THE WINE MAKER

THE ART OF VITICULTURE.

Hugely celebrated in the wine world, Jeff Martin and his La Frenz wines are multi-award winners and continue to raise the bar in both winemaking and a meticulous, cutting-edge vineyard practice.

Jeff moved his wife, Niva, and their two daughters to the Okanagan Valley from Australia to start a new chapter in their wine life in 1994. Now with four vineyards in production, Jeff has almost built his own ecosystem within his vineyards. Working in partnership with nature, Jeff uses Old World farming techniques to manage his land. Chickens (who later become an autumn feast) are put to work in moveable coops that help with pest control and fertilizing. Cows and some sheep are involved to fertilize the land or help with mowing. Jeff feels that "it is the full environment—the terroir—not just winemaking techniques and types of yeast or barrels that potentially most influences the quality and unique expression of our wines." On the side, Jeff is an internationally renowned canine judge and travels the world judging conformation and German-based pointing dog testing.

LOCATION 1525 Randolph Road, Penticton, BC   TWITTER @lafrenzwinery   FB lafrenzwinery   WEB lafrenzwinery.com

MELISSA CARTWRIGHT 🐙 THE HONEY MAKER

BEE-ING IN THE BIG CITY.

Melissa Cartwright is beautiful, young, cool, and an urban bee-keeper. She tends her hives behind a local coffee shop in Vancouver atop a chicken coop. Her former career as a shoe designer at John Fluevog shoes adds to her mystique. She explains her job shift, "Working full time in the shoe industry left my brain wanting something new to chew on. I picked up a book one weekend on bees and was hooked as I read and learned. About a year later I left my job without a plan. The bees started to take up a bigger amount of my time and it naturally grew. At first I sold honey in simple jars, then I had some help with my branding over one winter and launched Mellifera Bees the next summer!"

As we are all aware, the health of the bee population is crucial to the health of the world. The urban beekeeping movement seems to be an answer for how to deal with certain issues, like pesticides. "We keep hearing stories of colony collapse and what that means for the bees and all the creatures that rely on their pollinating efforts," Melissa explains. "In the last year, more and more research is pointing toward the overuse of chemicals on commercial crops and the direct effect that has on bees. City bees aren't exposed to those deadly pesticides, and are kept in the same location (pollinating bees can be driven quite far to pollination contracts), which I think is less stressful for them. They are also cared for by beekeepers with fewer hives resulting in a set of management practices that offer more time to observe and use preventative methods of care."

On bee-ing with bees: "The best part of being a beekeeper is seeing and caring for the bees. The honey is pretty great too! The bees can make me feel so calm at times, while at others leave me completely frazzled, especially in late summer when they are strong in number and have a lot of honey to protect."

COMPANY Mellifera Bees LOCATION 401 Industrial Ave, Vancouver, BC
FB MelliferaBees TWITTER @melliferabees WEB melliferabees.com

⚓

ANN KIRSEBOM ☸ THE CHEF

VIVE LE CHOCOLAT!

This multi-talented chef and caterer first developed a hugely successful retail line of gourmet sauces for cooking. Her most recent line, Paris in a Chocolate, comes through a partnership with France's Grand Marnier family. With her magic touch, Chef Ann created chocolate truffles infused with this luxurious liqueur as well as a Grand Marnier-spiked chocolate sauce. Each chocolate is an actual replica of the authentic Marnier Lapostolle family seal, which adorns the red moire ribbon on the iconic Grand Marnier Cordon Rouge bottle and is très chic!

The story of her partnership with Grand Marnier is so very exciting. Chef Ann now spends half of her time in Paris (le sigh). Here is how it came to be:

"Grand Marnier actually approached me as they were aware I had created a line of gourmet products, all containing alcohol. I originally created several ideas for savoury products using my favourite liqueur and eventually a chocolate sauce using the Grand Marnier and a Callebaut chocolate with organic honey. They gave me a 4-litre plastic dummy bottle to take to my events that featured products with Grand Marnier and eventually the seal fell off—the iconic red ribbon—and voila, the idea of a chocolate replica of their family seal was born. I had an inexpensive vacuum mould made here so I could test my idea and eventually, after hundreds of ganache recipes, produced a box to present to them in Paris. They never expected the chocolate to be red! They gave me the approval and I jumped on a train en route to Chocolate World in Belgium to begin the process of having polycarbonate moulds made. We then launched it at the Canadian Pavilion at the SIAL Show in Paris and at the SIRHA Show in Lyon. With my Euro passport it makes my plan to open an office in Paris much simpler and eventually to live there!" Bonne chance, mon amie!

LOCATION Box 91861, West Vancouver, BC
FB Chef-Ann-Kirsebom TWITTER @ChefAnnKirsebom WEB chefanns.com

⁎ **THE FARMER**
Roslyn Ritchie-Derrien
Langley, BC

⚓ **THE CHEF**
Lee Murphy
Langley, BC

🍷 **THE WINE MAKER**
Vista D'oro
Langley, BC

········· **FEATURED INGREDIENT** ·················
Lavender Eight lavender

GOUGÈRE

½ cup beer (stout or porter is best)

½ cup milk

100 g unsalted butter

½ tsp kosher salt

1 cup all-purpose flour

4–5 eggs

300 g Gorgonzola cheese, crumbled

LAVENDER FROMAGE FRAIS

250 g fromage frais (a soft, unaged, creamy
    fresh cheese made from whole or
    skimmed milk and cream)

2 Tbsp lavender sugar (if you can't find it,
    make it! Add 1½ cups sugar and 1 Tbsp
    culinary lavender to a food processor
    and whizz until finely choppped)

1 lemon, zest and juice

1 jar Crabapple Lavender Gin Preserve

GORGONZOLA GOUGÈRE WITH FROMAGE FRAIS
& CRABAPPLE LAVENDER GIN PRESERVE

Lee's Crabapple Lavender Gin preserve is one of her newest creations. It sparkles with a beautiful colour and a flavour profile—so different from anything else in the line. These delicious bites would work as a starter or dessert and would be special served along with the cheese course. The easiest way to describe gougères is to call them cheese puffs and once you make them at home, you will be hooked.

Preheat oven to 425°F. Bring beer, milk, butter, and salt to boil in medium saucepan. Dump flour into boiling mixture all at once, and stir constantly with wooden spoon over medium to low heat to dry out until mixture leaves a coating on the bottom of pan. Transfer mixture to stand mixer; on low add eggs one at a time, making sure to incorporate each before adding another. After the fourth egg, if mixture seems too dry and stiff, add a fifth egg. Add the Gorgonzola cheese and mix, just enough to combine.

Transfer warm mixture to a piping bag, pipe about one tablespoon of dough per gougère onto parchment-lined baking sheets, spacing them about five cm apart. Bake until golden.

Cool and slice halfway through.

MAKE WHIPPED LAVENDER FROMAGE FRAIS Combine all ingredients in stand mixer and whisk until combined. Keep refrigerated until ready to use.

TO FINISH Fill one piping bag with fromage frais and another with preserves. Pipe lavender fromage frais into gougère and follow with crabapple preserves. Voila!

········ **DRINK PAIRING** ························

2007 Vista D'oro
The ONE that started it all! The flagship of Vista D'oro, this fortified walnut wine is a blend of North Okanagan Marechal Foch, Central Okanagan Merlot and Cabernet Franc, Fraser Valley Green Walnuts and Okanagan Brandy. 13 months in French and American oak. This artisanal fortified port-style wine is hand made in small batches.

ROSLYN RITCHIE-DERRIEN ✳ THE FARMER

PURPLE HAZE.

Roslyn Ritchie-Derrien moved from White Rock to Langley about 20 years ago to realize her dream of owning a farm. And what a farm it is! The stunning twenty-acre property is home to pigs, chickens, horses, miniature horses, and a 17,000-square-foot home known as Copperstone, which has been the set for many Hollywood films and even a Superbowl commercial.

Roslyn didn't grow up in the farming industry but has always been a "country girl at heart" and wanted to live the lifestyle. An impeccable gardener, she also manages the landscaping on the property. Now that she has raised her family, she continues to grow the farm with lavender now becoming her main focus.

Inspired by the farms in the South of France, Roslyn did some research and discovered that the climate and soil conditions in Langley were conducive to growing this aromatic crop.

Now with her own sea of purple to gaze upon, she is soon to open up the experience to the public by offering farm tours (check website for details). Roz is also becoming a go-to for the local wedding industry providing lovely lavender sachets and bundles for sale. Her lavender products are currently only available for sale at her friend and neighbour Lee Murphy's farm, Vista D'oro.

FARM Lavender Eight   **LOCATION** 21122–12 Avenue, Langley, BC   **WEB** lavendereight.com

LEE MURPHY ✳ THE CHEF

QUEEN OF CONFITURE AND LOVER OF ALL THINGS PARIS.

Lee Murphy makes jam. Glamorous, delicious jam. Jam so unique that in 2014, Harrods of London chose to retail her line in its impossibly high-end food store.

"We took a trip to Paris in 2002, my first trip ever to Europe, where I first tasted Christine Ferber's jams—my 'aha' moment in Oprah speak," says Lee.

From that moment, Lee Murphy knew what she wanted to do: focus on developing an exquisite line of preserves created on her farm in Langley. What would become The Preservatory, a sophisticated commercial kitchen on the farm was started in her own kitchen. "It began with taking my rhubarb and vanilla preserve to the farmers' markets to sell alongside our tomato plants and herbs from the farm. The jam very quickly began outselling everything else we brought to the markets."

Following a lesson in Old World sustainability, Lee preserves by season: "Living on a farm, it's only natural to use what's ripe and ready."

"Our micro climate in the south Fraser Valley allows us to grow fruit, including tomatoes, not easily grown on the west coast—although not every year is ideal, we still take our chances. We've been adding to the orchard every year with crabapples and sour cherries being a new focus for us and I'm excited to add to our line of preserves with the increasing supply of both. Creating is what I love best, adding a few new flavours each year, while not sacrificing our older tried and trues."

FARM The Preservatory at Vista d'Oro   LOCATION 346–208 Street, Langley, BC
FB Vista-Doro-Farms-Winery   TWITTER @ Vista d'Oro Farms   WEB vistadoro.com

APPLES AND WALNUTS

Pack glass with ice, pour cider and D'oro over ice, add bitters. Stir gently and well. Garnish with an apple slice if desired.

2 oz Vista D'oro Farmhouse Cider
1 oz D'oro—fortified walnut wine
3 dashes Bittered Sling Orange and
Juniper bitters

CRISPY HAZELNUT WAFER

YIELD: 310 g

70 g white chocolate

150 g hazelnuts, roasted golden and puréed

100 g crushed ice cream wafer cones or
     cornflakes

CRUNCHY HAZELNUT MERINGUE

YIELD: 500 g

140 g hazelnuts, ground and unblanched

120 g icing sugar

180 g egg whites

juice of half a lemon

60 g granulated sugar

120 g whole hazelnuts, blanched

DARK CHOCOLATE MOUSSE

YIELD: 325 g

100 g dark chocolate, 66%

150 g cream 36% fat

75 g milk 3.25% fat

SOFT CARAMEL WITH FLEUR DE SEL

YIELD: 250 g

125 g granulated sugar

1 teaspoon of honey

125 g cream 36%

1 vanilla bean (optional)

Fleur de sel

CHOCOLATE WAFERS

2 oz dark chocolate, tempered

2 oz milk chocolate, tempered

2 oz caramel chocolate, tempered

CRUNCHY HAZELNUT NAPOLEON

Like everything Thomas Haas creates, this dish is a work of art! I loved watching Thomas make this dish; it was like observing a magic show. This recipe may take a little time to make, but I promise, the wow factor is worth it. **SERVES 8**

CRISPY HAZELNUT WAFER Melt chocolate over a double boiler or in a microwave. Combine puréed hazelnuts; stir into melted chocolate. Gently fold in wafer or cornflakes. Spread evenly onto parchment paper, ⅛" thick. Place in refrigerator until set, about 30 minutes. Cut eight three-inch diameter circles with cookie cutter. Keep in refrigerator until assembly.

CRUNCHY HAZELNUT MERINGUE Toast whole hazelnuts; chop coarsely. Preheat oven to 375°F. Sift icing sugar. In the bowl of a mixer fitted with whisk attachment, whip egg whites with lemon juice and pinch salt until soft peaks form. Gradually add granulated sugar and icing sugar and continue to whisk until firm, glossy peaks form. Fold hazelnut into meringue. Pipe sixteen, 3 inch diameter circles on parchment line baking sheet. Sprinkle ground hazelnuts evenly on top of meringue. Bake at 375°F until meringue is light golden and springy to touch; approx. 9 minutes

DARK CHOCOLATE MOUSSE Place chocolate in heatproof bowl, set over saucepan of hot, not simmering, water until partially melted (the water should not touch the bottom of the bowl), stirring occasionally. Remove bowl from saucepan and continue stirring until melted and smooth. Meanwhile, put whipping cream in medium bowl and beat just until soft peak forms; set aside. Add lukewarm milk, all at once, to melted chocolate and stir with spatula (not a whisk) until blended. Add whipping cream, all at once, and stir with spatula until blended. Place in refrigerator for about 30–40 minutes or until set. Pour into piping bag.

SOFT CARAMEL WITH FLEUR DE SEL Make golden caramel; add honey and melt. Add cream very slowly and scraped vanilla bean. Bring to a boil; cook for 2 minutes. Set aside to cool.

CHOCOLATE WAFERS Spread a thin layer of each of the tempered chocolates onto acetate or parchment paper. Let set and cut into eight, 3 inch diameter circles. Let rest for 1 hour before removing.

ASSEMBLY Place a disc of the crispy hazelnut wafer. Pipe dots of dark chocolate mousse to cover the circumference of the hazelnut wafer. Place a disc of hazelnut meringue inside the mousse. Place a generous spoonful of soft caramel in the centre of the hazelnut and sprinkle with fleur de sel. Place the disc of milk chocolate on top. Pipe dots of dark chocolate mousse to cover the circumference of the chocolate disc. Place a disc of hazelnut meringue inside the mousse. Place the disc of caramel chocolate on top. Decorate as you wish with hazelnuts and an egg-shaped quenelle of mousse.

THE EPP FAMILY ✳ THE FARMER

WELCOME TO THE NUT HOUSE!

Charlotte Epp and her late husband Kornelius purchased their beautiful, eleven-acre farm in Yarrow two years ago. Charlotte had met the previous owner, who invited her over to pick up some hazelnuts. When she first saw the property, it was love at first sight, and when they found out it was for sale, it was a done deal. "Yarrow has a wonderful sense of community; the downtown is only four blocks long—it's like a place that time forgot. Like Mayberry," Charlotte enthusiastically explains. The entire Epp family lives communally on the property: Charlotte's three children, Heidi (with her daughter), Jennifer (with husband Dan), and Chris (with wife Laura).

The farm is in a lush setting surrounded by gardens, a magical forest area, and has a creek running through it. The neighbours keep chickens and sheep that are welcomed into the hazelnut orchard to keep the grass perfectly mowed. This farm will produce hundreds of pounds of hazelnuts this fall. It seems like a lot of work, but Charlotte demonstrated her nifty new harvest tool—the Garden Weasel Nut Gatherer. This ingenious invention makes the task of picking up nuts almost fun! It is basically a flexible wire basket on a pole, and when rolled on the ground, the wires bow to allow a nut in and then flex back to hold it in. The Epps are still quite new to hazelnut farming and enjoyed being a part of the local Christmas market last year, selling bags of hazelnuts as well as homemade hazelnut butter.

The area has a large Mennonite community that also attracted the Epp family who share the culture. Yarrow has a rich history in agriculture and was founded by Mennonite pioneers and settlers in the late 1920s. Daughter Heidi explains, "Yarrow is full of artisans and is a real lifestyle choice. The community plays a significant part of the culture here." In a nutshell, I guess you could say that the Epp family is nuts about their new home.

FARM The Nut House Farm   LOCATION 4080 Stewart Road, Yarrow, BC

THOMAS HAAS ✺ THE CHOCOLATE MAKER

WE ♥ THOMAS HAAS.

Thomas Haas has become Vancouver's most beloved indulgence since his arrival in 1995. Besides being an extraordinary world-class talent, Thomas radiates a magical energy with a delightful sparkle of mischief in his eyes.

Thomas has an astounding career behind him. He was part of the biggest restaurant opening of all time in New York City (chosen as executive pastry chef, Haas stood alongside French superstar Chef Daniel Boulud at the exciting opening of Daniel).

Regarding his art, he says, "I was born into it. As a fourth-generation pâtissier, I was first introduced to the art of making chocolates and pastries in the kitchen of the Café Konditorei Haas, which was opened by my great-grandfather in the Black Forest region of Aichhalden, Germany in 1918."

Lucky for us, his love of the British Columbia sea and mountainscapes brought him back to us to start his own business in 2000 . . . and the rest is sweet history.

"Although I came into the profession at a young age, I believe passion develops over time by recognizing that when there's something you have a talent for; it's fun to keep striving to master that skill. When others recognize that drive within you, it only makes you want to try harder."

The Haas philosophy includes sourcing cocoa beans from two organic plantations from South America, the Caribbean, and Grenada to "ensure that the chocolates we use are fairly traded." As for sourcing from local farmers, indeed he does.

Did you know *haas* means "rabbit" in German? Hmmm . . . Thomas is from the Black Forest, which is also where the Easter Bunny is from. Coincidence?

Thomas Haas Chocolates & Patisserie LOCATION 998 Harbourside Drive, North Vancouver, BC
TWITTER @thaaschocolates FB thaaschocolates WEB thomashaas.com

MOJA COFFEE ☕ THE COFFEE MAKER

GETTING YOUR COFFEE GROOVE ON.

Once upon a time, in the basement of their home in North Vancouver, Doug Finley and Andrew Wentzel began their journey to roast with the most. After investigation and purchase of various coffee beans, and burning a few batches to start, they got into the groove and began mixing their own blends. These blends, created in the basement with a little air roaster, lead to a fan base of frenzied friends who were already demanding the fresh-roasted coffee. New coffee stars were born.

In 2003, the duo joined forces with Gary Sawyer, the owner of Fidalgo Bay Roasting in Mount Vernon, Washington, and Moja (the Swahili word for "one") was created. It represents a term to describe single-origin coffee. Moja now has two cafés, the HQ on Rupert Street, and another on Commercial Drive, as well as servicing other shops like Thomas Haas.

LOCATION 1412 Rupert Street North Vancouver, BC TWITTER @mojacoffee FB mojacoffeeroasters WEB mojacoffee.com

🐬 **THE GOAT CHEESE MAKER**
David Wood
Salt Spring Island, BC

⚓ **THE CHEF**
Morgan Wilson
Victoria, BC

🍷 **THE WINE MAKER**
Misconduct Wine Co.
Penticton, BC

········ **FEATURED INGREDIENT** ··················
Salt Spring Island goat cheese

CHEESECAKE

3½ cups Salt Spring Island goat cheese

½ cup mascarpone cheese

¾ cup Empress honey (or other local honey)

6 tsp cornstarch

1⅔ cup sour cream

6 large eggs

pinch salt

½ tsp lemon juice

zest from a ½ lemon

½ tsp vanilla extract

CHEESECAKE BASE

1¾ cups graham cracker crumbs
  (for a gluten-free option use
  gluten-free cracker crumbs)

¼ tsp cinnamon powder

2½ Tbsp butter, melted

EMPRESS HONEY & SALT SPRING ISLAND GOAT CHEESECAKE

This gorgeous cake is rich but not too sweet. The goat cheese adds a lovely tang and the beautiful Empress honey lends a sparkle of sweetness. Serve with a sweet wine at a table in a bee pen with a chef, a cheese maker, a beekeeper, and a goat named Bess . . . that's what we did! **YIELD: 1 X 6-INCH ROUND CAKE**

CHEESECAKE In a mixer, combine goat cheese, mascarpone, honey, and starch until it reaches a smooth paste consistency. Add the sour cream and mix further. Gradually add in the eggs, salt, lemon juice, zest, and vanilla extract. Mix until combined.

CHEESECAKE BASE Mix all the ingredients together in a bowl, and then spread the mix on the bottom of a foil wrapped 6" cake ring. Compact the crumbs and bake at 300°F for 10 minutes. Pour the prepared goat cheesecake mix on the baked base. Bake at 250°F for 45–50 minutes, until firm in the centre.

········ **DRINK PAIRING** ··

Misconduct Inverno Icewine
A blend of Muscat/Riesling/Viognier—flavours of kumquat and marmalade with hints of vanilla bean on the nose. Explosive ripe fruit with touches of lemon peel, sweet finish with a crispness that lightens the whole experience.

LEFT TO RIGHT: Morgan, Alexander (Beekeep Helper To Beekeeper Theo), David, and Bess the goat

MISCONDUCT WINE CO ♀ THE WINE MAKER

WINERY DOG'S NAME IS NUTELLA.

As you leave Penticton and enter into the winery-o-rama that is the Naramata Bench, there is a lovely stretch of road called Upper Bench that houses a couple of delightful wineries (one has a cheesery too!). The prohibition theme at Misconduct has been a hit, as are the wines (or should I say giggle juice?). Neat fact: the beautiful turquoise labels were designed after the menus on the Titanic. Isn't that cool?

Owner and wine maker Richard da Silva grew up in the agriculture industry in the Okanagan and is now living his dream. His family moved here from Portugal in the 1950s. As a child, he was surrounded with Old World traditions, including wine making.

WINE MAKER Richard & Twylla da Silva   LOCATION 375 Upper Bench Road, Penticton, BC   FB misconductwineco
TWITTER @MisconductWines   WEB misconductwineco.com

DAVID WOOD ⚓ THE GOAT CHEESE MAKER

SAY CHEESE!

David Wood came to Salt Spring Island following a brilliant career in Toronto with his three celebrated gourmet stores: the David Wood Food Shops (Karen Barnaby was chef there in the '80s!).

The solitude and magic of Salt Spring Island drew David and his family and they bought a farm. An expert in the gourmet food business, cheese making was of great interest to David, so he travelled to Europe to learn the craft. One of the most recognizable goat cheese brands available, Salt Spring Island Cheese's pretty packaging always draws the eye. It is a clear container allowing the feature ingredient (truffle, chili, basil, garlic, lemon, pepper, tapenade, or a beautiful pressed edible flower) to be seen on top of the package. One just has to pop it out of the container onto a serving plate for a gorgeous presentation. David explained how he came upon this unique way of packaging his cheese—he was on a plane fiddling with one of the little juice containers with the peel-back lid. An a-ha moment! David makes several other types of goat cheeses on his farm, including feta cheeses, surface ripened cheeses, and even a hard cheese. "The list of what we put in our cheese is short—100% pure goat milk, sea salt, dairy culture, and rennet."

David is passionate about his cheese making and about local food and artisans. "I love the people in this industry. I love anyone who is following their passion." A part of the fabulous Salt Spring Island Farmers' Market, David enjoys the social aspect of being an artisan. "We try as a food producer to connect directly with our customers, restaurants, chefs . . . it's the most rewarding part of the business, to be a part of the community." On his love of Salt Spring Island and its culture David warmly shares, "Salt Spring has an amazing, eclectic community of people from around the world. It is fascinating. Everyone who lives here appreciates that they are here."

FARM Salt Spring Island Goat Cheese   LOCATION 285 Reynolds Road, Salt Spring Island, BC
FB saltspringcheese   TWITTER @ssicheese   WEB saltspringcheese.com

⚓

MORGAN WILSON ☸ THE CHEF

FEEDING THE EMPRESS.

Chef Morgan Wilson is the executive chef at the kitchen helm of Victoria's beautiful Empress Hotel. It has recently been purchased by the Bosa family and the "Grand Old Lady of Government Street" is getting spruced up again to match her former glory as the jewel of the island. Sitting demurely in Victoria's inner harbour, she is a sight to see when arriving by boat or seaplane. Built in 1908, the rooms whisper of the glamourous days of its youth, when the hotel would be filled with socialites and lit by candles and firelight. The Empress has a glittering history of royalty and movie stars who have visited its hallowed halls, and it still glimmers in the afterglow.

Morgan loves his job here. He oversees the remarkable, world-renowned Afternoon Tea at the hotel, where guests can nibble delectable treats while sipping tea in the beautiful lobby—such a civilized tradition. He also heads up the Bengal Room, a richly decorated nod to Queen Victoria's role as Empress of India. The curry buffet has become a routine for many locals.

The Empress Room is the dining area where Morgan fully integrates his farm and sea-to-table practice; it is an elegant affair. Morgan comments on his guests, "In general, people are much more knowledgeable about food. They want to know where the food comes from and it keeps us on our toes!" He feels lucky being on Vancouver Island and having access to such incredible ingredients. The Empress even has its own beehives on the estate where Morgan can access the hotel's own special honey.

Morgan gives a nod to his pastry chef AJ Thalakkat who is the creator of the beautiful goat cheese and honey cake featured in this book. AJ is originally from Bombay and was forced to take leave from the photo shoot after being stung three times, which is why he is not in the final photo. He has since fully recovered. Sorry, AJ!

RESTAURANT Fairmont Empress Hotel   LOCATION 721 Government Street, Victoria, BC
FB fairmontempress   TWITTER @fairmontempress   WEB fairmont.com/empress-victoria

⛵ **THE QUINCE FARMER**
Andrea Jefferson
Vancouver, BC

✳ **THE CHEF**
Andrea Jefferson
Vancouver, BC

🍷 **THE WINE MAKER**
Mireille Sauvé
Vancouver, BC

······ **FEATURED INGREDIENT** ······
Andrea's quince

1 cup water

¾ cup pitted, chopped dates

½ teaspoon baking soda

½ cup grated fresh quince

½ cup of poached quince-optional

1¾ cups all purpose flour, sifted

1½ teaspoons baking powder

pinch salt

½ cup of unsalted butter, soft

¾ cup brown sugar

2 eggs

½ cup pecans, toasted

BUTTERSCOTCH SAUCE

¾ cup brown sugar

½ cups cream

¼ cup butter unsalted

vanilla bean, small piece

pinch of salt

GARNISH

1 cup whipping cream

2 tsp honey

STICKY PECAN DATE & QUINCE CAKE
WITH BUTTERSCOTCH SAUCE & CREAM

A celebration of Chef Andrea's favourite fruit, and her shop's namesake, this sticky, nutty, yummy cake can be enjoyed any time of the day or night. Quince are funny looking, they are kind of homely with bumps and fuzz, but they make up for that in flavour power and work in both savoury and sweet dishes, as proven in this sweet treat.

YIELD: 10 INCH ROUND

Preheat oven to 350°F. Bring water, dates, and baking soda to a boil in a saucepan and simmer for 3 minutes. Cool and add grated and poached quince. Combine flour, baking powder, and salt. In a mixer, cream butter with sugar and then add in eggs one at a time until combined. Add in dry ingredients, alternating with date mixture.

Sprinkle with pecans. Bake 25–30 minutes and then move to rack to cool.

BUTTERSCOTCH SAUCE Combine ingredients in a saucepan and cook for 5 minutes over low-medium heat.

TO FINISH Whip cream with honey and serve cake with a dollop on top.

···· **DRINK PAIRING** ·································

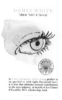

2015 Les Dames White
This is a blend of aromatic white grape varieties from the Okanagan Valley, which is dry on the palate, offering flavours of crisp orchard fruit with floral nuances. It is refreshing on its own as an aperitif or with various salads or appetizers.

ANDREA JEFFERSON ☀ THE CHEF AND QUINCE FARMER

QUINTESSENTIAL QUINCE.

Chef Andrea Jefferson owns and operates Quince, a boutique food shop, cooking school, and café in Vancouver. A chef, sommelier, shopkeeper, teacher—this lady knows her food and wine. Quince offers gourmet, healthy, homemade cuisine available fresh on the lunch menu, as well as frozen takeaway meals in the Quince Express freezer section. Party trays are also available to make home entertaining easier.

Andrea's passion is cooking. "Cooking is almost sacred to me, a kind of practice through which I find out who I am, everyday. The end result of the cooking process also deeply matters to me, seeing the food plated, or even vacuum packed in its finished form; it is validation that I am on the right track and that my business is sustainable," explains Andrea.

The business is named for her mascot quince tree, which provides a bounty of fruit each year for her to process. She says, "I have a garden and I am proud to grow greens and some summer produce for Quince and the quince fruit itself. In principle, buying local is a better choice for the environment as there is less energy spent on shipping. This, to me, is the biggest issue."

Andrea's teaching skills and cooking classes have brought her numerous awards and accolades like "Best Place for Casual Cooking Classes" in the *Georgia Straight*'s Annual Best of Vancouver awards. The classes vary and she also offers team building or private cooking classes as an event.

Andrea's manifesto: "Respect for the ingredients, the craft of cooking, and the customer motivates me to produce food of the highest quality."

SHOP Quince LOCATION 1780 West 3rd Avenue, Vancouver, BC
FB quince.kitsilano TWITTER @quincekitsilano WEB quince.ca

MIREILLE SAUVÉ ♀ THE WINE MAKER

DAME GOOD WINE.

Mireille Sauvé has been operating her successful consulting company, The Wine Umbrella, for ten years in Vancouver. Her business weaves together many aspects of our booming wine industry that include education, sales, promotion, and events. Also a freelance wine writer, she was certified as a wine maker in 1997 and has returned to that craft to make wine for a very special fundraising cause: Les Dames d'Escoffier. Les Dames BC Chapter is an integral part of an international organization of women in the food, wine, and hospitality industries who fundraise to award scholarships to women who want to enter into or further their careers in these fields. It is an extremely well-respected group that has sent many women into various schools and programs, including Mireille nearly twenty years ago. Mireille's scholarship win allowed her to complete her sommelier studies and begin her now very successful career. Says Mireille, "It fills me with inspiration to have this opportunity to give thanks to Les Dames for the support that they gave me, as well as celebrating the many talented women in the wine industry and giving new women a chance to pursue their culinary passions, all at the same time." As an extra perk for all who indulge in a bottle of these wines, this is a most delicious, fresh new way to fundraise for a great cause!

Les Dames Red and Les Dames White are both blends created by women from the thriving vineyards of the Okanagan Valley.

COMPANY The Wine Umbrella   FB thewineumbrella
TWITTER @thewineumbrella   WEB thewineumbrella.com

CHARITIES WE LOVE

LES DAMES D'ESCOFFIER | LESDAMES.CA

Les Dames d'Escoffier is an international philanthropic organization with a thriving BC Chapter. The main goal of the organization is to fundraise for scholarships awarded to women who want to enter or further their careers in the food, wine, and hospitality industry. I am a proud member as well as these other women in this cookbook: Andrea Carlson, Andrea Jefferson, Ann Kirsebom, Barb Finley, Caren McSherry, Dana Reinhardt, Daniela Cubelic, DJ Kearney, Jackie Kai Ellis, Jennifer Peters, Kristen Jordan, Lee Murphy, Mary Mackay, Mireille Sauvé, Stephanie Jaeger. (Karen Barnaby recently stepped down after many years of service.)

PROJECT CHEF | PROJECTCHEF.CA

Teacher and chef Barb Finley created the PROJECT CHEF program. It is a wonderful nonprofit program in 2008 that partners with the Vancouver School Board to teach children about wholesome food. I have had the pleasure of participating in one of Barb's classes and to see her teach is inspiring and the children are so enthusiastic about learning. I took my cookbook into one of the classrooms and left the kids with a project to make their own book. The winner was Savreen Kahlon in Mr. Riddell's grade 4/5 class at Sir William Osler Elementary School for her *Spicy But Yummy Recipes* cookbook featuring a delicious Butter Chicken recipe.

GROWING CHEFS | GROWINGCHEFS.CA

Founded in 2005 by Merri Schwartz (more about Merri on page 39), Growing Chefs! Chefs for Children's Urban Agriculture is a registered charity, based in Vancouver, BC. Its mission is to educate children, families, and community members about healthy eating and healthy food systems. Growing Chefs runs a Classroom Gardening and Cooking Program in elementary schools to get kids excited about growing, cooking, and eating good, healthy food.

Winner Of The Project Chef Cookbook Project: Savreen Kahlon

SLOW FOOD | SLOWFOOD.COM

And as an appropriate partner to the brand of this book, SLOW FISH, is an amazing campaign brought forward by SLOW FOOD. Please read about its very important concept and the work this impressive international organization achieves.

THE FOUNDATION OF HOPE | FOUNDATIONOFHOPE.NET

The Foundation of Hope is a registered charity providing financial assistance to non-governmental organizations (NGOs) actively supporting LGBT+ (lesbian, gay, bisexual, and transgender) refugees and newcomers. Operated by a working board of volunteers, this foundation is the first of its kind in Canada and possibly the world.

SOUP SISTERS AND BROTH BROTHERS | SOUPSISTERS.ORG

In 2009, my friend Sharon Hapton founded Soup Sisters and Broth Brothers in Calgary. Soup Sisters and Broth Brothers, now with chapters across Canada and into the US, organizes groups of people to make soup for their local woman's shelter and/or youth shelter. I am one of the proud founders of the two Kelowna chapters. They also have two cookbooks out! Sign up for one of the most heartwarming experiences you could ever wish for.

SOILMATE | SOILMATE.COM

Created by my brilliant friend Matt Gomez, Soilmate.com is a website that connects consumers with their local food and drink growers, raisers, producers, and supporters. It allows consumers to find specific growers and products, as well as stores and restaurants that support those local growers and carry/use their products. Using My Route, Soil Mate allows consumers to build trips to include farms, markets, stores, restaurants, wineries, craft breweries, and distilleries, including fully customized directions and itineraries. It is the full local food and drink movement in one system, all interlinked. LOVE THIS!!

FOOD WRITERS WE LOVE

STEPHEN WONG
Chef, Food & Wine Writer

Toques off to our region's Chinese chefs! Throughout the centuries, Chinese cuisine has borrowed, adopted, and integrated both methods and ingredients from other cuisines and, in turn, contributed and influenced many others. Here in British Columbia, Chinese chefs and diners deserve much credit for being early pioneers of local cuisine. It is fair to say that some of the best ingredients we see on our regional menus today were discovered or popularized in Chinese restaurants in the '70s and '80s. The list is long: snow pea tops and sprouts, a variety of Asian greens, fresh shiitake mushrooms, specialty chickens, squab, quail, and the list goes one. What they couldn't find they cultivated, some more successfully than others.

But their greatest contribution to the variety of ingredients we now take for granted has to be in the realm of seafood. While French chefs were flying in Dover sole and frog legs from Europe, Chinese chefs were cooking up a storm with local Dungeness crab, rockfish, flounder, lingcod, sablefish, swimming scallops, beach oysters, and spot prawns. They didn't do it because of some high-minded culinary or ecological outlook. Many of these chefs and their customers were Cantonese, who like their seafood fresh (live actually, if possible), and so eating local is simply the shortest path to eating well.

In the 1990s, an influx of immigrants, visitors, and restaurants from Hong Kong elevated Chinese cuisine to a different level, and the world began to take notice. Soon seafood from the cold, pristine waters of British Columbia began to show up on tables across the Pacific. Of course, popularity has its price. BC consumers now have to compete with foreign buyers, and most varieties of seafood have become more expensive. But the upside of this rise in value is that many of the fisheries in BC can afford the research needed to improve the sustainability of the resource.

Geoduck is a shining example of this. I remember first sighting geoducks in Chinatown in the early '80s and they were being sold at 89 cents a pound. Although they were rumoured to be the secret behind the very tasty BC Ferries clam chowder in those days, most of us regarded it more with curiosity than with our appetites. But owing to deft ministrations by some creative Chinese chefs, its sea-sweet flavour and snappy texture, not to mention its suggestively unique physique, geoduck soon became a prized delicacy on moneyed tables across China.

So raise a glass to the Chinese chefs who've help laid the foundation of success in what we now proudly call our very own regional cuisine.

—Stephen Wong

CASSANDRA ANDERTON
Travel, Food, Libations & Lifestyle Writer
www.goodlifevancouver.com

The good news is that our society has become more in tune with our local food systems, and that awareness on sustainability issues has grown immensely. However, we still struggle with the issue of how to feed those who do not have dignified access to nutritious food.

Vancouver Neighbourhood Food Networks (VNFN) is one organization leading the way to a more just and sustainable food system. The VNFN is a group of committed people across the city who are fighting for food justice and resilience. Their mandate includes growing local food in community and school gardens, organizing celebrations involving food to meet physical, spiritual, social, and emotional needs, and increasing community awareness around food security. They are working on amazing initiatives including supplying drop-in meals, bulk buying clubs, mobile produce markets, and emergency food access, They also provide plenty of and educational opportunities such as workshops, lectures and films.

There are many other unique and wonderful initiatives in-progress including the Westside Food Collaborative and the Vancouver Fruit Tree Project Society. From coordinating public fruit-tree picks and intergenerational food processing, to the South Vancouver Food Network's partnership with BC Housing to provide programming for Kid's Club (an after-school care program that works on building food skills such as applesauce making), this is progressive thinking.

Go to vancouverfoodnetworks.com to learn how you can collaborate on, contribute, or benefit from these initiatives.

—Cassandra Anderton

ANYA LEVYKH
Food & Lifestyle Writer

I was born in Odessa, Ukraine, in the former Soviet Union. Living directly by the Black Sea in a fertile region meant that local produce and seafood was abundant, if not necessarily accessible for the average family. Even in a large city like Odessa, however, it was perfectly common to visit an outdoor market every Friday to choose a live chicken from a visiting farmer's stall, and have it killed and dressed in front of you, so you could cook it that day. By the time I was school-aged, my parents had decided to leave the USSR and emigrate to Canada, to Vancouver. We've lived here ever since.

Vancouver is a lot like Odessa; it's a coastal port city with a vast fertile region that produces abundant amounts of food in every form. Of course, back then, words like "organic," "sustainable," "ethical," and "locavore" were not part of the vernacular. Our first shopping trip in a large grocery store was the perfect example. We entered what seemed like a paradise, with food freely available to all, at prices considerably less than your monthly salary and with no need of a Communist Party membership in order to shop. My mother led the way to the meat department in search of chicken. A vast array of pristine plastic trays, filled with pure white meat, and wrapped tightly in plastic, greeted us. After realizing that all of the chicken had penicillin in it (drugs!), we left that store and never came back. It took three months before my mother found a local farmer who raised, as she called it, "happy chickens." Thus began her journey as one of the original "foodies." She just thought of it as looking for "good" food. Proper food, grown and raised the way it was supposed to be.

It wasn't always easy, but in the decades since, Greater Vancouver, from the Fraser Valley up to Whistler and Pemberton, has developed a veritable bevy of high-quality growers, producers, and artisans who create everything from locally smoked salt to artisan sausages that are so good you need to join a waiting list at certain times to get some.

I was lucky to grow up with an appreciation for and exposure to the edible bounty (and the people behind it) that makes this region the culinary destination it has become. This book showcases those ingredients and those people, and the enormous impact they've had on our taste and understanding of what is meant by "good food."

—Anya Levykh

DJ KEARNEY
Vancouver-Based Global Wine Expert

It's an exciting time for BC's young wine lands. Marginal in the extreme, we sit on the outer limits of where grapes can thrive. Our distinctive wines, defined by purity of fruit and natural acidity reflect this northern latitude, unique climate conditions, and complex ancient geology. Although 90 percent of British Columbia's grapes grow in the Okanagan and Similkameen Valleys, there is a dynamic artisan industry closer to the sea, in the mighty Fraser Valley.

In the flat and broad delta formed where the Fraser River cleaves as it heads to the ocean, the climate is benign and far wetter than the desertlike interior. Almost two dozen wineries have sprung up here since 1991 when the first winery opened, supplied by grapes from 81 hectares of vineyards (200.85 acres), forming a scant 1.9% of BC's plantings. Conditions favour earlier ripening grapes like pinot noir, bacchus, pinot gris, siegerrebe, madeleine angevine, and fragrant and fruit-focused wines from this region perfectly suit the pan-Pacific cuisine for which Vancouver is so renowned.

A short and scenic ferry trip across the Georgia Strait reveals the archipelago of Gulf Islands and majestic Vancouver Island. Here we find diverse and sheltered microclimates, varied topography, and fascinating geology for a wider palate of wines from pinot noir, pinot gris, maréchal foch, zweigelt, ortega, and gewürztraminer.

Over the past decade these BC wineries have burgeoned by almost 50 percent, and a network of wine trails from island-to-island offers vinous experiences that are as tasty as they are breathtakingly beautiful. The future is bright for these seaside regions, where maturing vines and sheer human ambition intersect with a growing global appreciation for delicate and articulate wines from the fringe. Best of all is the natural culinary affinity between our fresh and juicy wines and our unique cuisine of sea and coastal lands.

—DJ Kearney

ERIN IRELAND
Food & Restaurant Reporter

Over the past 15 years our dining scene has exploded with quality restaurants, forward-thinking chefs, and there's been a new focus on sustainable sourcing. I think it's safe to say that Vancouver is now officially a city with a very exciting restaurant culture. It's worth travelling here to discover it. Our farm-to-table movement, which is completely taking over in the best way possible, is one of our identifying characteristics, and it sets us apart. Rarely does one find a new restaurant that isn't extremely focused on its sources these days. It truly is a wonderful and delicious time to be living in beautiful Vancouver.

—Erin Ireland

TIM PAWSEY
Food & Wine Writer, Calorific Raconteur

The emergence of a culinary culture usually takes time, often generations, if not millennia. It's no wonder then that only a couple of decades ago, the idea of a truly regional cuisine taking hold in BC seemed improbable at best. We were at a time and place suspended somewhere between Eurocentric continental, homogeneous "Asian" with the faintest whisper of First Nations traditions.

Fast-forward to the present where global influences still shape our tastes, perhaps even more than they once did. But our choice of ingredients is driven by unabashed pride in local producers, from fishers to farmers. Our chefs forage close to home and our wine makers shy away from overwrought oak to make food-friendly wines wrapped in natural acidity. Most of all, as sustainable practitioners, we are learning the baby steps towards understanding that all great cuisines are grounded in uncompromising stewardship of land and sea.

—Tim Pawsey

PHOTO CREDITS

Barnaby, Karen, 127

Blair, Sandy, 137 (bottom right)

Booth, Jay, 46

Born-Tschümperlin, Karolina, 64 (bottom left)

Frye, Amy, 16, 17

Hill, Kate, 172 (second column, second photo down), 184 (top)

Hill, Ronnie Lee, 201

Hill, Terence P., 136 (bottom right)

Kusiewicz, Tracey, 48 (recipe and photo reprinted with the kind
    permission of Arsenal Pulp Press)

Luk, William, 203 (top right)

Murphy, Lee, 186

Shaw, Alexis, 99 (top)

Stamper, Jennifer, 139

Underwater Harvesters Association, 80

Vanthoff, Caroline, x

Watson, Jason, 33 (bottom)

ACKNOWLEDGEMENTS

A heartfelt thank you goes out to the incredible cast of talented people featured in these pages: it gives me such pleasure to shine a spotlight on you. Thank you for all that you do not only for your local community, but also for British Columbia. A deep bow goes to you farmers, fishers, foragers, artisans, drink makers, and chefs who source locally.

Kate Hill: you are a brilliant designer. Thank you so much for helping me hone my vision in creating this beautiful book. It was fun getting to know you on our road trips (especially on our extra-long route to Tofino). Cristi Cooke: thank you for pairing me with Kate for this project. Rebecca Dadson: deep thanks for your creative skill in capturing the magic of these people for the cover of this book. Thanks so much to the amazing volunteer photo crew: Cassandra, Elyse, Melissa, Renske, and Emma. Cassandra Anderton, my old friend: a special thank you for your various contributions throughout this entire creative process. You were an invaluable source of information, and a trusty 911 for me at deadline.

Thanks also to my friend Mireille Sauvé for lending her talented palate to write wine pairings (where noted), and to my friend Karolina Born-Tschümperlin for jumping in with a couple of last-minute winery photo replacements.

For my wonderful mom and dad and my supportive family and friends, thank you for your love during my period of "creative disappearance" and high stress.

Thanks also go to those who gave me shelter while I gallivanted from land to sea and back again interviewing and photographing the stars in the book. To Kevin Perra (Bowen Island), Claire Sear (Vancouver), Brent Beasley (Vancouver), Jay Gildenhuys (Tofino), The Wickaninnish Inn (Tofino), Tofino Vacation Rentals (Tofino), The Fairmont Empress Hotel (Victoria), Hotel Rialto (Victoria), Mary Ann Watson (Cowichan Bay), and to Lise Magee at The Listel Hotel in Vancouver: thank you. Thank you to all of the incredibly efficient, helpful PR women who liased between busy chefs and myself, especially Alana Tees, who fielded more than her share.

Last, but not least, this book would not have been possible without the love, support, and unwavering encouragement of my husband, Mark Pigott. You are my best friend.

INDEX